QuestionTime4

150 Questions and Answers on the Catholic Faith

FR JOHN FLADER

connorcourt
PUBLISHING

Published in 2018 by Connor Court Publishing Pty Ltd.

Copyright © John Flader. 2018

ALL RIGHTS RESERVED. This book contains material protected under International and Federal Copyright Laws and Treaties. Any unauthorised reprint or use of this material is prohibited. No part of this book may be reproduced or transmitted in any form or by any means, electronic or mechanical, including photocopying, recording, or by any information storage and retrieval system without express written permission from the publisher.

Connor Court Publishing Pty Ltd.
PO Box 7257
Redland Bay QLD 4165
sales@connorcourt.com
www.connorcourt.com

Imprimatur
Nihil Obstat: Rev. Peter Joseph STD
Imprimatur: + Most Reverend Anthony Fisher OP, Archbishop of Sydney
Date: 19 December 2017

The *Nihil Obstat* and *Imprimatur* are a declaration that a book or pamphlet is considered to be free from doctrinal or mmoral error. It is not necessarily implied that those who have granted them agree with the contents, opinions or statements expressed,

ISBN: 9781925501827

The Scripture quotations are from the Revised Standard Version, Second Catholic Edition, Ignatius Edition, of the Bible, copyrighted 2006, by the Division of Christian Education of the National Council of Churches in the United States of America, and are used by permission. All rights reserved.

Cover design by Ian James

Printed in Australia

*In memory of St Josemaría Escrivá,
who taught me love for the Church*

CONTENTS

Foreword xiii
Introduction xvi
Abbreviations xvii

I. CATHOLIC DOCTRINE 1

God and creation 3

451. Does God suffer with us? 3
452. God and the universe 5
453. God and the origin of life 7
454. God and the human person 9
455. Scientists and God 12
456. Guardian Angels 14
457. Are Guardian Angels real? 16
458. Why did God create Satan? 18

Jesus Christ 21

459. The genealogy of Christ 21
460. The hour of Jesus 23
461. Jesus after the Resurrection 25

The Church and Salvation 28

462. Canonisations and infallibility 28
463. Is *Laudato si* infallible? 30

CONTENTS

464. Coptic Orthodox and Catholics 32
465. Catholics and Muslims 34
466. The Bible alone? 37
467. Is Scripture alone sufficient? 39
468. Faith alone? 41
469. Salvation by grace alone 44
470. Can non-Catholics be saved? 46
471. Former Catholics and salvation 48
472. Is there any advantage in being a Catholic? 50
473. Why evangelisation? 53
474. Prophecies of Mariana de Jesus Torres 55

Our Lady 58
475. Did Mary suffer pain in giving birth to Jesus 58
476. Is Mary's virginity important? 60
477. Mary, Ark of the Covenant 62

The Last Things 65
478. The Christian meaning of death 65
479. Evidence of life after death 67
480. More evidence of life after death 69
481. Near-death experiences 71
482. Life after death and Pascal's wager... 74
483. Is hell real? 76
484. Is there anyone in hell? 78
485. Ancient views on hell 81

CONTENTS

486. Contemporary views on hell 83
487. Sr Josefa Menendez and hell 85
488. Revelations of Sr Josefa Menendez 87
489. Purgatory in the Bible 89
490. Belief in purgatory in the early Church 92
491. Is purgatory real? 94
492. What is purgatory like? 96
493. Is heaven real? 99
494. Final repentance 101

II. LITURGY AND THE SACRAMENTS 105

The Liturgy 107

495. Latin in the liturgy 107
496. The Tridentine Rite 109
497. Western Liturgical Rites 111
498. Beauty in the liturgy 114
499. Care in the liturgy 116
500. Expressing concerns to pastors 118
501. The history of holy water 121
502. Blessing ourselves with holy water 123
503. What is a Jubilee Year? 125

Baptism and the Eucharist 128

504. Does Baptism guarantee salvation? 128
505. Baptism of children of non-practising parents 130
506. Masses of the Society of St Pius X 132

507. Does Communion forgive sins?.. 134
508. Extraordinary ministers of Communion..................... 137
509. The role of extraordinary ministers............................ 139
510. Extraordinary ministers denying Communion........... 141
511. Communion for the divorced and remarried............... 144

Penance and Holy Orders.. 147
512. Why go to confession?... 147
513. Absolution of abortion... 149
514. Prayer for priests... 151
515. Bishops' insignia... 153
516. The pallium... 156

Matrimony.. 159
517. The Pauline and Petrine privileges.............................. 159
518. Are most marriages null?... 161
519. The validity of marriage.. 163
520. The internal forum and the validity of marriage......... 165
521. Involvement of the divorced in the life of the Church...... 168
522. New procedures for marriage cases............................ 170
523. More on new procedures for marriage cases............... 172
524. Same-sex marriage – why not?................................... 174
525. Consequences of legalised same-sex marriage........... 177
526. Children of same-sex parents...................................... 179
527. Studies on children of same-sex parents..................... 181

III. MORAL LIFE IN CHRIST 185

General moral issues 187
528. Is morality objective?................................. 187
529. Cardinals' "dubia" on moral issues.................... 189
530. Conscience and moral absolutes...................... 191
531. The role of conscience............................... 193
532. Formation of conscience............................. 196
533. Erroneous conscience................................ 198
534. Following our conscience............................ 200
535. Freedom of conscience............................... 203
536. Conscience "at peace with God"..................... 205
537. Sin always hurts the sinner......................... 207
538. Soul and spirit..................................... 209
539. The fruits of the Holy Spirit....................... 211
540. The morality of dreams.............................. 213
541. The enneagram...................................... 216

Relations with God.. 219
542. Loving God above all things........................ 219
543. Respect for the Holy Name of Jesus................. 221
544. Freedom of worship................................. 223
545. The Resurrection and the Lord's Day................ 225
546. Keeping the Lord's Day holy........................ 228
547. Sunday, a day of rest.............................. 230

Relations with our neighbour.. 233
   548. What exactly is mercy?.. 233
   549. Showing mercy... 235
   550. The corporal works of mercy............................... 237
   551. The spiritual works of mercy............................... 239
   552. Vaccination of children....................................... 241
   553. The Church and the death penalty....................... 244
   554. What to do with cremated remains?..................... 246
   555. What is lust?... 249
   556. Sex before marriage.. 251
   557. Is the use of contraception sometimes allowed?... 254
   558. Why is the Church opposed to contraception?...... 255
   559. Can the Church's teaching on contraception change?... 257
   560. Natural family planning....................................... 260
   561. Benefits of natural family planning...................... 262
   562. Is gossip a sin?.. 264

IV. CHRISTIAN PRAYER.. 267

Prayer and devotions... 269
   563. Why doesn't God answer my prayers?................ 269
   564. To whom can we pray?.. 271
   565. Prayer in the early Church 273
   566. The Divine Praises... 275
   567. *Lectio divina*.. 278
   568. Chaplet of Divine Mercy...................................... 280
   569. Perseverance in prayer... 282

CONTENTS

Seasons and feasts 285
   570. Is Advent a season of penance? 285
   571. Ash Wednesday 287
   572. More about Ash Wednesday 289
   573. Veiling statues in Lent 291
   574. Why do we call it Easter? 293
   575. Why Easter eggs? 296
   576. The feast of the Blessed Trinity 298
   577. The feast of Corpus Christi 300
   578. The feast of the Sacred Heart of Jesus 302
   579. The feast of the Immaculate Conception 304
   580. The feast of St Stephen 307
   581. The feast of the Assumption of Our Lady 309
   582. The feast of the Queenship of Mary 311
   583. The feast of the nativity of Mary 314

Our Lady and the Saints 317
   584. Our Lady of Mercy 317
   585. Mary, Undoer of Knots 319
   586. Our Lady of Ransom 321
   587. St Michael, St Gabriel and St Raphael 323
   588. St George 326
   589. St Thomas à Beckett 328
   590. St Dymphna 330
   591. St Catherine of Siena 332
   592. St Francis de Paola 334

593. St Marie-Alphonsine 337
594. Venerable Montserrat Grases 339

Apparitions 342
595. Our Lady of Mt Carmel 342
596. Our Lady of Guadalupe 344
597. Our Lady of Luján 346
598. Our Lady of Fatima 348
599. The legacy of Fatima 350
600. Our Lady of Akita 353

Index 357

Foreword to *Question Time 3*

With the publication of this third volume of his widely popular *Question Time* series in which Fr Flader answers questions on almost every conceivable aspect of the Catholic Faith, a writer who is possibly Australia's most prolific contemporary author on things Catholic has now passed a real milestone: he has answered in book form 450 questions on what the Catholic faith means and teaches and the goals Christians naturally strive for as they seek to be faithful, daily disciples of the Risen Christ rather than merely nominal members of a tribe named "Catholic".

However it would be a mistake to describe Fr Flader as merely prolific. In fact, it would be to risk doing him a disservice because, in the end, while quantity may impress, what really counts is the quality of the thing conveyed or produced. In this sense, what is far more important to note, I think, is that Fr Flader's question and answer format columns have become a ministry which has touched lives everywhere – a textbook model of how meticulously researched, precise, patient, rational and reasonable explanations can enlighten readers and, one suspects, for many, open doors in life that had previously seemed shut tight.

Interestingly, the questions in Fr Flader's book are sifted from the even more numerous questions he has answered for readers in recent years but what most people would not know is that while his weekly column began in Sydney's *The Catholic Weekly* it has grown to be so popular that it now appears regularly in Catholic publications across Australia. This says something important. The weekly *Question Time* columns which first began appearing in *The Catholic Weekly* in 2005 clearly struck a note with readers of the 21st century, much as another Sydney priest's earlier *Radio Replies* did with listeners and readers of the early to mid 20th century. But whereas Dr Rumble often dealt with Protestant objections to Catholicism so characteristic of one era of Australian history, Fr Flader focuses on the questions which naturally arise in the minds of Catholics and other enquirers in an Australian society vastly different from that of three-quarters of a century ago.

It is probably more true now than ever before in the history of this country that the men, women and young people who make up our society are searching for answers to the most important questions of life. Yet while our society, for the time being, appears in many ways to have increasingly cut itself adrift from any deep sense of the presence of God in life, it also decreasingly fails to supply answers to the most basic questions of human existence which the human spirit always seeks.

Father Flader's answers to the questions of faith are therefore invaluable and provide points of reference and certainty which readers know will not suddenly transform or disappear like the constantly changing and dissolving perspectives of postmodern fashionable theories, here today and gone tomorrow. His articles therefore greatly help at least two groups of people I can think of: Catholics who, as a result of their faith, want to know and understand more of the remarkable invitation to life that God offers every one of us and those, not necessarily Catholic, who are searching for truth. And, I hasten to add, they help because they are so interesting. Quite apart from their usefulness for individual reading, Fr Flader's answers would be ideal for use in parish or home-based discussion groups and would also make an excellent gift for a friend or an acquaintance.

As editor of *The Catholic Weekly* I am constantly grateful to be the beneficiary of Fr Flader's scholarship and wisdom which are distilled into his weekly columns and I know our readers are too. I can only commend this latest volume of *Question Time* as an excellent com-

FOREWORD

panion for the home, the daily commute to work or for a holiday, and an excellent aid to all those searching for what the Church teaches and why, as distinct from what so many believe.

Peter Rosengren

Editor, *The Catholic Weekly*

Introduction to *Question Time 1*

Soon after beginning to write the *Question Time* column for *The Catholic Weekly*, I began to receive reports of people who were cutting out the columns and pasting them on paper for future reference, or photocopying them for others. Over the years numerous people have asked if there was any plan to publish the columns as a book.

Now that three years have passed, the time has come to satisfy the desires of these people and to publish the first 150 columns.

The questions and answers are arranged systematically by topic, following the general structure of the *Catechism of the Catholic Church*. Chapter 1 deals with matters of Catholic doctrine, Chapter 2 with questions relating to the sacraments and sacramentals, Chapter 3 with matters of moral life in Christ, and Chapter 4 with questions relating to prayer and Christian devotions.

I am indebted especially to Joanne Lucas, who read most of the columns before they were sent to *The Catholic Weekly* and made helpful comments on their style and content. Also to Fr Peter Joseph and Fr Edward Barry, who made valuable suggestions to improve the final draft.

I am also grateful to Anthony Cappello of *Connor Court*, who graciously offered to publish the book.

I pray that *Question Time* will help those who read it to understand their faith better and to come to a deeper love for Jesus Christ, Our Lady and the Church.

Deo omnis gloria!

Fr John Flader

Abbreviations

AL	Pope Francis, Apostolic Exhortation *Amoris Laetitia* (2015)
AR	Congregation for the Doctrine of the Faith, Instruction *Ad resurgendum* (2016)
CC	Pope Pius XI, Encyclical *Casti connubii* (1930)
CCC	*Catechism of the Catholic Church* (1992)
DD	Pope John Paul II, Apostolic Letter *Dies Domini* (1998)
DH	Second Vatican Council, Declaration on Religious Liberty *Dignitatis humanae* (1965)
Dz	Denzinger-Rahner, *The Sources of Catholic Dogma* (Loreto Publications 2007)
DV	Second Vatican Council, Dogmatic Constitution *Dei verbum* (1965)
FC	Pope John Paul II, Apostolic Exhortation *Famliaris consortio* (1981)
GIRM	Congregation for Divine Worship, *General Instruction of the Roman Missal* (2011)
GS	Second Vatican Council, Pastoral Constitution on the Church in the Modern World *Gaudium et spes* (1965)
HV	Pope Paul VI, Encyclical *Humanae vitae* (1968)
LG	Second Vatican Council, Dogmatic Constitution on the Church *Lumen gentium* (1964)
MV	Pope Francis, Bull proclaiming a Jubilee Year of Mercy *Misericordiae Vultus* (2015)
NA	Second Vatican Council, Declaration *Nostra aetate* on the Relation of the Church to Non-Christian Religions (1965)
OCF	*Order of Christian Funerals* (1988)
RS	Congregation for Divine Worship, Instruction *Redemptionis sacramentum* (2004)
SC	Second Vatican Council, Constitution on the Liturgy *Sacrosanctum Concilium* (1963)
STh	St Thomas Aquinas, *Summa Theologiae*
VD	Pope Benedict XVI, Apostolic Exhortation *Verbum Domini* (2010)
VS	Pope John Paul II, Encyclical *Veritatis splendor* (1993)

I. CATHOLIC DOCTRINE

God and Creation

451 Does God suffer with us?

I have an auntie who is in constant pain from arthritis. I have tried to tell her that God understands her pain and suffers with her, but my parish priest tells me that God is unchangeable and cannot suffer. If this is true, how can I console my auntie?

Let me begin by explaining how your parish priest is right, but then go on to suggest how we can help suffering people by telling them that God indeed understands their suffering, is with them in it and helps them in a way far better than by suffering with them.

We know that God is all perfect in himself and hence unchangeable. God cannot change for the simple reason that to do so would mean to acquire some perfection or modality he does not already possess, but God is infinite and possesses every perfection. St Thomas Aquinas explains it simply in his *Summa Theologiae*: "... everything which is moved acquires something by its movement, and attains to what it had not attained previously. But since God is infinite, comprehending in himself all the plenitude of perfection of all being, he cannot acquire anything new, nor extend himself to anything whereto he was not extended previously" (*STh* I, q. 9, art. 1).

So since God is all perfect he cannot change in any way, and hence he cannot suffer with us, because to suffer would mean to be changed in some way by our suffering. So your parish priest is right. God cannot suffer.

Nor would we want God to be able to suffer with us because then he would be like a creature and unable to help us. What we want, and in fact have, is a God who knows our suffering, who loves us and helps us, who can work a miracle to cure us if he so chooses and in any case gives meaning to our suffering, using it to bring about our salvation.

We know that God knows all things. He knows each one of us and everything about us, for he is not only our creator but also our loving father. He created us through the love of our parents and infused the soul in each one of us at the moment of our conception. Even when mankind sinned and distanced itself from him, he promised a redeemer (cf. *Gen* 3:15) and in the fulness of time, "God so loved the world that he gave his only-begotten Son, that whoever believes in him should not perish but have eternal life" (*Jn* 3:16). So God truly loves us and cares for us.

Pope St John Paul II, in his Apostolic Letter *Salvifici doloris* on the Christian meaning of suffering (1984), explains how Christ, having overcome sin and death by his own suffering and death on the Cross, is present in all human suffering and transforms it into a source of salvation: "Suffering is, in itself, an experience of evil. But Christ has made suffering the firmest basis of the definitive good, namely the good of eternal salvation. By his suffering on the Cross, Christ reached the very roots of evil, of sin and death. He conquered the author of evil, Satan, and his permanent rebellion against the Creator. To the suffering brother or sister Christ *discloses* and gradually reveals *the horizons of the Kingdom of God:* the horizons of a world converted to the Creator, of a world free from sin, a world being built on the saving power of love. And slowly but effectively, Christ leads into this world, into this Kingdom of the Father, suffering man, in a certain sense through the very heart of his suffering. For suffering cannot be *transformed* and changed by a grace from outside, but *from within*. And Christ through his own salvific suffering is very much present in every human suffering, and can act from within that suffering by the powers of his Spirit of truth, his consoling Spirit" (n. 26).

We can understand this by considering that Christ is the head of the Mystical Body, the Church. While he cannot suffer in himself since he is God, he can suffer in the members of his Body and he is, as St John Paul II explains, "very much present in every human suffering". St Augustine explains: "Christ is now exalted above the heavens, but he still suffers on earth all the pain that we, the members of his Body, have to bear. He showed this when he cried out from above, 'Saul, Saul, why do you persecute me?' and when he said: 'I was hungry and you gave me food'" (*Sermon on the Ascension of the Lord*, Mai 98, 1-2).

In summary, God cannot suffer with us but he is present in our suffering and he helps us by transforming our suffering into a means for our salvation. It is up to us to accept our suffering in this light so that it truly unites us with Christ on the cross and brings about our salvation.

452 God and the universe

Whenever I read about explorations of outer space in search of life and see photos of the galaxies, I am amazed by the fact that our planet is so radically different from anything else in the universe and it has just the right conditions to support life. How do we explain this?

This is one of the great mysteries of science. Did the universe just result from chance and somehow manage to throw up a planet in which everything is just right to support life, or was it created by God? Let us examine the question.

For life to exist, there must be an abundant supply of carbon, which is formed under very precise conditions. If the nuclear ground state energy levels necessary for the formation of carbon varied by more than one percent, the universe could not sustain life.

Looking at more obvious facts, the distance of the earth from the sun is just right to support life. Any nearer and it would be too hot, any farther away and everything would freeze. A change of some two percent would mean the end of all life. Likewise, surface gravity and temperature have to be within a few per cent of what they are for the life-sustaining atmosphere to have the right mix of gases necessary for life. And the planet must rotate at just the right speed: too slow and the temperature differences between day and night would be too extreme; too fast and wind speeds would be catastrophic. There are far more examples of the precise conditions needed to support life, but these can suffice for the present.

Scientists and philosophers have come to call this "fine-tuning" of the universe to support life the "Anthropic Principle", from the Greek word for man: *anthropos*. The principle says, simply, that the universe seems to be fine-tuned to support life, human life in particular.

In their efforts to explain away the cause of this fine-tuning, some scientists have proposed the "multiverse" theory, according to which there are many, possibly infinitely many parallel universes, so that it is only natural to expect that in one of them there would be life. But, there is simply no evidence for other universes. Philosopher Richard Swinburne, in his book *Is There A God?* (Oxford University Press 1996, p. 68), sums it up with a touch of humour: "To postulate a trillion-trillion other universes, rather than one God, in order to explain the orderliness of our universe, seems the height of irrationality."

Cosmologist Ed Harrison puts it this way: "Here is the cosmological proof of the existence of God – the design argument of Paley – updated and refurbished. The fine-tuning of the universe provides *prima facie* evidence of deistic design. Take your choice: blind chance that requires multitudes of universes or design that requires only one" (*Masks of the Universe*, New York, Collier Books, Macmillan, 1985, p. 252).

What is more, scientists are finding ever more evidence of the improbability of the universe itself existing at all. Eric Metaxas, in an article in *The Wall Street Journal* reprinted in *The Australian* on 30 December 2014, writes the following: "The fine-tuning necessary for life to exist on a planet is nothing compared with the fine-tuning required for the universe to exist at all. For example, astrophysicists now know that the values of the four fundamental forces – gravity, the electromagnetic force, and the "strong" and "weak" nuclear forces – were determined less than one millionth of a second after the big bang. Alter any one value and the universe could not exist. For instance, if the ratio between the nuclear strong force and the electromagnetic force had been off by the tiniest fraction of the tiniest fraction – by even one part in 100,000,000,000,000,000 – then no stars could have ever formed at all. Feel free to gulp.

"Multiply that single parameter by all the other necessary conditions, and the odds against the universe existing are so heart-stoppingly astronomical that the notion that it all 'just happened' defies common sense. It would be like tossing a coin and having it come up heads 10 quintillion times in a row. Really?"

So, once again, the findings of science lead us back to a supremely intelligent, all-powerful cause of the universe itself and of a planet where life exists. This cause can only be the *Logos*, God, through whom "all things were made" (*Jn* 1:3).

453 God and the origin of life

I was talking recently at work with a very intelligent colleague about how life began in the universe. He maintained that "it just happened" but somehow that didn't satisfy me. Is there any evidence that God must have been involved?

You ask one of the most intriguing questions in the world of science. Scientists themselves are baffled by it. For example, Stuart Kauffman of the Santa Fe Institute says: "Anyone who tells you that he or she knows how life started on the earth some 3.45 billion years ago is a fool or a knave. Nobody knows" (*At Home in the Universe*, London, Viking, 1995, p. 31). Similarly, Francis Collins, director of the Human Genome Project which mapped the genes in the human body, says:

"But how did self-replicating organisms arise in the first place? It is fair to say that at the present time we simply do not know" (*The Language of God*, New York, Free Press, 2006, p. 90).

What we do know is that at the dawn of the universe some 13.8 billion years ago there was no life and now there is life. Some three-quarters of the way from the beginning of the universe until now life suddenly appeared. How did it happen?

By life, of course, we mean organisms capable of replicating themselves, giving rise to other organisms similar to themselves. These organisms are exceedingly complex and highly structured, made up of millions of atoms.

Microbiologist Michael Denton, who was teaching at the University of New South Wales when he wrote his book *Evolution, a Theory in Crisis,* says that the break between the non-living and the living world "represents the most dramatic and fundamental of all the discontinuities in nature. Between a living cell and the most highly ordered non-biological systems, such as a crystal or a snowflake, there is a chasm as vast and absolute as it is possible to conceive." He describes the complexity of even the tiniest of bacterial cells, weighing less than a trillionth of a gram, as "a veritable microminiaturized factory containing thousands of exquisitely designed pieces of intricate molecular machinery, made up altogether of 100 thousand million atoms, far more complicated than any machine built by man and absolutely without parallel in the non-living world" (*Evolution, a Theory in Crisis*, Bethesda Maryland, Adler & Adler, 1986, pp. 249-50). What is more, the "factory" can reproduce its entire structure in a matter of hours.

How could such an organism come about? How could 100 thousand million atoms put themselves together in just the right configuration to be alive and able to reproduce itself? Was it simply a matter of chance, of molecules in the atmosphere colliding with each other over millions of years until suddenly they produced something that was alive? To use a simple example, if you dropped the pieces of a 5000-piece jigsaw puzzle from the ceiling over and over again, would you ever end up with the puzzle perfectly finished? As they say, I don't like your chances.

Denton himself writes: "Is it really credible that random processes could have constructed a reality, the smallest element of which – a functional protein or gene – is complex beyond our own creative capacities, a reality which is the very antithesis of chance, which excels in every sense anything produced by the intelligence of man?" (*ibid.* p. 342)

In the early 1980s, two non-believers, Sir Frederick Hoyle and Chandra Wickramasinghe set out to calculate the probability of the simplest living thing forming itself by chance in the "prehistoric soup". They knew it had to be composed of hundreds of thousands of proteins, each in turn composed of long chains of amino acids in exactly the right configuration to give rise to life. They came up with a probability of one in $10^{40,000}$, that is one in ten with 40,000 zeros after it, an infinitesimal probability. They naturally concluded that life could not possibly have arisen by chance and that it had to be created by a "super-intellect in outer space". Hoyle famously compared the odds against the spontaneous formation of life with the odds of a tornado blowing through a junkyard producing a 747 jet aircraft (cf. *The Intelligent Universe*, London, Michael Joseph, 1983, p. 19).

If life couldn't arise by chance, there is only one alternative. God created it. He is the "super-intellect in outer space".

454 God and the human person

A friend recently tried to convince me that the existence of the human person is a proof for the existence of God. I am not sure I understood everything he said, but it sounded convincing. Can you enlighten me on this?

Your friend makes a very good point, one often overlooked in books and articles which give arguments for the existence of God.

We should begin by explaining what is unique about the human person that makes our very existence an argument for the existence of God. What is unique is precisely our spiritual soul, with its rational intellect and free will. It takes us back to the creation of man in the "image" and "likeness" of God (cf. *Gen* 1:26). This image and likeness are not in our body, for God does not have a body. They are in our soul – our spiritual, immortal soul.

This spiritual soul makes us radically different from all other creatures on earth. The highest apes, while having much in common with us, especially the affective life of nurturing their young and relishing the company of other apes, do not have a spiritual soul. They cannot think, plan what to do the following day, choose freely between alternative courses of action. They simply follow their instincts. A good sign of their lack of rational intelligence is their inability to make progress. Over the centuries animals of all sorts continue to live as their ancestors did for thousands or even millions of years. They are incapable of progress because they cannot think.

We humans, on the contrary, have a rational intellect which allows us to think, to plan, to invent tools and new ways of doing things. The result is that over time we have progressed from making fire, the wheel and weapons with which to hunt, to a state where we have jet aircraft, skyscrapers, computers and rockets capable of sending people to the moon and back. We are clearly radically different from the highest apes. This rational intelligence is, as it were, a spark of the divine intelligence.

Moreover, as a result of our rational intelligence we can weigh up various courses of action, consider the pros and cons of each, and freely decide what to do. We are not bound by our instincts, even though we have them as do higher animals. We have free will, like God, and can make free choices, after deliberating on them.

Where did we get this extraordinary power? Did apes gradually evolve over hundreds of thousands of years to a point where they became human, capable of thinking and choosing? No, there is a radical break between the highest apes and humans. We are not just a little more intelligent than apes, we are radically different from them, as we have just seen.

We have a spiritual element, a spiritual soul which allows us to perform these actions. And no matter for how long bodies evolve they can never become spiritual. Matter and spirit are two different realities. Spirit does not arise out of matter. It is created separately. Angels, who are pure spirits with intelligence and free will, were created directly by God. So were humans.

We accept of course the possibility that the human *body* evolved from some other living thing. Pope Pius XII, in his Encyclical *Humani generis* (1950), said as much: "The teaching authority of the Church does not forbid that, in conformity with the present state of human sciences and sacred theology, research and discussions, on the part of men experienced in both fields, take place with regard to the doctrine of evolution, insofar as it inquires into the origin of the human body as coming from pre-existent and living matter – for the Catholic faith obliges us to hold that souls are immediately created by God" (n. 36). In other words, the Pope accepts the possibility, only the *possibility*, that the human body evolved from some other living thing. But the soul, he says, was created immediately by God.

This has to be the case. Being spiritual, the human soul must come from some other spirit. But from which spirit? It does not come from our parents. They each have their own soul, as each one of us does. We cannot give our soul to another, or share it with another. It is ours for all eternity. Our soul can only come from the infinite spirit who is God. Therefore, if humans exist with a spiritual soul, there must be a spiritual being who gave them that soul. That Being is God.

455 Scientists and God

I am a practising Catholic with six children and my next door neighbour is a scientist who is a good man but is constantly challenging my faith. He says scientists don't believe in God and that I am foolish to believe and go to church. How can I answer him?

In the first place we should know that it is simply not true that scientists don't believe in God. Obviously, there are some scientists, like Richard Dawkins who was in Australia a few years ago, who don't believe. But many of the greatest scientists who have ever lived – among them Kepler, Pascal, Boyle, Newton, Faraday, Mendel, Pasteur and Kelvin – have not only believed in God but have found in their scientific work the evidence for God.

More recently we can mention Albert Einstein, arguably the greatest scientist of the twentieth century. What led him to believe in God was the fact that the universe was not chaotic, as one would expect if it resulted from chance, but rather ordered and intelligible, with universally applicable laws. This moved him to say: "The most incomprehensible thing about the universe is that it is comprehensible." He went on to say that he considered this comprehensibility "a miracle" or "an eternal mystery" and, what is more, this miracle "is being constantly reinforced as our knowledge expands." He summed it up: "My religion consists in a humble admiration of the superior unlimited spirit which is revealed in the minimal details which we are able to perceive with our fragile and weak minds. This conviction, deeply emotional, of the presence of a rational superior power which is revealed in the incomprehensible universe, forms my idea of God" (*Letters to Solovine*, New York, Philosophical Library, 1987, p. 131).

The website www.godandscience.org has numerous statements from eminent scientists testifying to their belief in a God who put order in the universe. Let me cite just a few.

Wernher von Braun (pioneer rocket engineer): "I find it as difficult to understand a scientist who does not acknowledge the presence of a superior rationality behind the existence of the universe as it is to comprehend a theologian who would deny the advances of science."

Paul Davies (British astrophysicist): "There is for me powerful evidence that there is something going on behind it all... It seems as though somebody has fine-tuned nature's numbers to make the Universe... The impression of design is overwhelming".

Alan Sandage (winner of the Crawford prize in astronomy): "I find it quite improbable that such order came out of chaos. There has to be some organising principle. God to me is a mystery but is the explanation for the miracle of existence, why there is something instead of nothing."

George Greenstein (astronomer): "As we survey all the evidence, the thought insistently arises that some supernatural agency – or, rather, Agency – must be involved. Is it possible that suddenly, without intending to, we have stumbled upon scientific proof of the existence of a Supreme Being? Was it God who stepped in and so providentially crafted the cosmos for our benefit?"

Tony Rothman (physicist): "When confronted with the order and beauty of the universe and the strange coincidences of nature, it's very tempting to take the leap of faith from science into religion. I am sure many physicists want to. I only wish they would admit it."

Ed Harrison (cosmologist): "Here is the cosmological proof of the existence of God – the design argument of Paley – updated and refurbished. The fine tuning of the universe provides *prima facie* evidence of deistic design. Take your choice: blind chance that requires multitudes of universes or design that requires only one.... Many scientists, when they admit their views, incline toward the teleological or design argument."

An important book on this topic is *God's Undertaker – Has Science*

Buried God? (Lion Hudson, Oxford 2009), by John Lennox, Oxford Professor of Mathematics. In it Lennox shows the overwhelming evidence for design in the universe and he critiques the arguments of those who challenge it.

So we need not let our faith be undermined by the occasional scientist who challenges it. The evidence for God from science is overwhelming and many eminent scientists admit it.

456 Guardian Angels

I was talking recently with a friend about the importance of teaching our children about guardian angels, and she showed herself extremely sceptical about the very existence of angels. Is this something old-fashioned or is it still important?

We can be absolutely certain about the existence of guardian angels and they are not old-fashioned. We see them mentioned in the Scriptures. In the book of *Exodus* God says to the Israelites: "Behold, I send an angel before you, to guard you on the way and to bring you to the place which I have prepared" (*Ex* 23:20). This passage applies perfectly to each one of us. God has given us an angel to guard us on the way and to lead us to the place God has prepared for us: a room in the Father's house in heaven.

Then too, Jesus himself refers to personal angels of children: "See that you do not despise one of these little ones; for I tell you that in heaven their angels always behold the face of my Father who is in heaven" (*Mt* 18:10-11). The mention of "their angels" implies in some way that the angels are assigned to look after individual children. St Jerome comments on this passage: "How great is the value of the soul that every single person has from birth received an angel for his protection."

A similar passage comes in the *Acts of the Apostles* when an angel comes to St Peter and frees him from prison, after which Peter goes to the house of Mark where a woman named Rhoda hears his voice at the door and tells the people that Peter is there. Not believing that Peter could possibly be there when they knew he was locked up in prison, they say: "It is his angel" (*Acts* 12:15). Again we see here the belief of the early Christians in a personal angel of St Peter.

In view of these passages and the constant tradition of the Church, the *Catechism of the Catholic Church* teaches: "From its beginning until death, human life is surrounded by their watchful care and intercession. 'Beside each believer stands an angel as protector and shepherd leading him to life' (St Basil, *Adv. Eunomium* III, 1). Already here on earth the Christian life shares by faith in the blessed company of angels and men united in God" (*CCC* 336).

So certain is the Church of the existence of guardian angels that she gives us the annual celebration of the feast of the guardian angels on October 2.

The guardian angels assist us in many ways. They may help us avoid a serious accident or get us out of danger, as happened to St Peter. Other times the angel may simply wake us up when the alarm failed to go off, remind us to take something we had forgotten, help us to find something we had lost, find us a parking spot, get us to our destination on time, give us the appropriate words in a conversation, or remind us of what God is asking of us at the time.

Pope Francis, in his homily on the feast of the guardian angels in 2014 said: "According to the tradition of the Church, we all have an angel with us, who protects us, helps us hear things. How often have we heard: 'I should do this, I should not do this, that's not right, be careful'; so often! It is the voice of our traveling companion. Be sure that he will guide us to the end of our lives with advice, and so listen to his voice, don't rebel against it...

"This is not an imaginative doctrine on the angels: no, it is reality. It is what Jesus said, God said: 'I send an angel before you to guard you, to accompany you on your journey, so you will not go wrong.' Ask yourself this question today: How is my relationship with my guardian angel? Do I listen to him? Do I say good morning to him in the morning? Do I ask him: Watch over me when I sleep? Do I speak with him? Do I ask his advice? He is by my side. We can answer this question today, each of us: how is our relationship with this angel that the Lord has sent to watch over me and accompany me on my journey, and who always sees the face of the Father who is in heaven?"

As we can see, guardian angels are a reality and they are not old-fashioned. A simple way to live out what Pope Francis is asking of us is to say each day the well-known prayer to the guardian angel: "Angel of God, my guardian dear, to whom God's love entrusts me here, ever this day [or this night] be at my side, to light and guard, to rule and guide. Amen."

457 Are guardian angels real?

I know the Church's teaching on guardian angels, but since we never see angels can we be sure they actually exist?

I suspect most people who believe in guardian angels can point to some moment in their life when they were convinced that it was their guardian angel who did them some specific service. This may involve saving them from an impending accident, finding a lost object, remembering at the last minute to take something they had forgot, and much more.

Then there are the experiences of others, some of which are very impressive. I was told recently of a woman who was paraplegic and had fallen out of bed when her husband was not at home. She was unable to get back into bed and eventually she fell asleep on the floor. When her husband returned he found her in bed. She had great devotion to her guardian angel.

Guardian angels can sometimes appear in human form. Such is the case with the angel Raphael in the Old Testament. He appeared to the young Tobias and accompanied him on a long journey which ended with remarkable results. Only at the end did Raphael reveal his true identity as an angel (cf. *Tobit* 5:4-5; 12:15).

Many of the saints had vivid experiences of their guardian angel. Among them is St Josemaría Escrivá. In 1931 during a wave of anticlericalism in Spain, he was walking in Madrid when three young men approached. One rushed forward shouting, "I'm going to get him", and raised his fist to hit him. One of the others shouted, "No, don't hit him." This man then said to St Josemaría, "Little donkey, little donkey." It was an expression St Josemaría used to describe himself, but which only he and his confessor knew. He was sure it was the devil who tried to attack him and his guardian angel who came to his rescue.

Some years ago I heard of a girl who had attended an evening of recollection in Manchester, England, in which one of the meditations was on devotion to the guardian angels. The girl commented afterwards that no one believed in guardian angels anymore. On her way home she was walking through a park and saw a man of unsavoury appearance under a street lamp ahead of her. Doubting whether to keep going or to take a different route she decided to continue. As she passed the man he looked at her and she at him, but to her relief he did not approach her. In the following days she read in the newspaper that a girl had been murdered in the park that night and that a suspect had been arrested. She went to the police to report her experience and she was allowed to speak with the suspect. It was the man she had passed in the park. When she asked why he had not attacked her, he answered: "When you had those two men with you?"

Another well known example, broadcast frequently on the radio at the time, concerns an American marine in the Korean war. The truth of the incident was verified by the sergeant in charge of the patrol and the chaplain. The marine, named Michael, had been taught a prayer to St Michael which began "Michael, Michael of the morning". He said the prayer everyday. One day on patrol during the winter in Korea, he suddenly found himself beside a huge marine he had never met who told him his name was Michael. Michael said that was his name too, and the new marine said, "I know" and began to say the prayer to St Michael. He added, "We're going to have some trouble up ahead." Then it began to snow heavily and the new marine said it would stop shortly, as in fact it did. In the meantime they had become separated from the rest of the patrol.

As they came over a rise they were confronted by seven enemy soldiers with their rifles aimed at them. Michael screamed "Down, Michael" and hit the ground as the rifles fired. The big Michael was still standing, even though they were at point blank range. Michael jumped up to pull him down, but he got hit in the chest himself. He saw the big Michael still standing, surrounded by a bright light and with a sword in his hand, and then passed out. He regained consciousness when the rest of the patrol came up to him. He asked where Michael was, but the others said there had been no one with him at any time and in any case he was the only Michael in the unit. They asked him how he had killed the enemy soldiers and he said he hadn't done anything. In fact his rifle had not been fired. The seven soldiers had been killed with a sword. Guardian angels are real.

458 Why did God create Satan?

One thing I have never understood is why God created Satan, knowing that he was going to bring about so much harm and evil in the world. Is there an answer to this?

The first thing to say is that God did not create Satan, or the devil, as such. God does not create anything bad or evil. Everything he creates is good. As we read in the book of *Genesis*, "God saw everything that he had made, and behold it was very good" (*Gen* 1:31).

Where did the devils come from then? God did create angels, who were pure spirits destined to be with him forever in heaven and to serve as his messengers and guardians of human beings on earth. The *Catechism of the Catholic Church* says of them: "As purely *spiritual* creatures angels have intelligence and will: they are personal and immortal creatures, surpassing in perfection all visible creatures, as the splendour of their glory bears witness" (*CCC* 330).

The angels, like us, were given free will and they were able to choose whether to serve God and be with him in heaven, or to serve themselves, to be "like God", as the devil tempted Adam and Eve (cf. *Gen* 3:5). Moved by pride some of the angels rejected God, preferring to serve themselves rather than serve God. The words of the prophet Jeremiah about Israel can be applied to them: "I will not serve" (*Jer* 2:20). In that choice they became separated from God forever and consigned to hell. Jesus himself says of those people who would be forever damned: "Depart from me, you cursed, into the eternal fire prepared for the devil and his angels" (*Mt* 25:41).

So it was not God who created Satan, but Satan himself who as an angel rejected God and became a devil. As the Catechism says, "Satan was at first a good angel, made by God: 'The devil and the other demons were indeed created naturally good by God, but they became evil by their own doing'" (Lateran Council IV (*Dz* 428; *CCC* 391).

Since they are separated forever from God and suffering the indescribable pains of hell, the devils are angry with themselves and God and they look with envy upon human beings who, though inferior to angels in their nature, are blessed by God and the object of his infinite love. So they set about tempting us to sin so that we too will be separated from God. In the words of St Peter, "Your adversary the devil prowls around like a roaring lion, seeking some one to devour" (*1 Pet* 5:8). We know how much harm Satan is doing: in individual souls, in families, in nations.

So then why did God create Satan when he knew how much harm he would do? We could ask the same question about ourselves: why did God create me when he knew I would sometimes sin and cause harm to others? The answer lies in God's love. He wanted there to be creatures – angels and humans – made in his image and likeness, with intelligence and free will, capable of making free choices and of sharing in God's own life here on earth through sanctifying grace and of being with him forever in heaven.

But in so doing, God "ran the risk" that angels and men would misuse their freedom and even reject him. Nonetheless, this would be a better world than if there were no creatures with intellect and free will, capable of knowing and loving God.

What is more, even though Satan, and we ourselves, can cause great harm through the misuse of our freedom, God's power is always greater. Christ, after all, came to cast out devils. The Catechism teaches: "Although Satan may act in the world out of hatred for God and his kingdom in Christ Jesus, and although his action may cause grave injuries – of a spiritual nature and, indirectly, even of a physical nature – to each man and to society, the action is permitted by divine providence which with strength and gentleness guides human and cosmic history. It is a great mystery that providence should permit diabolical activity, but 'we know that in everything God works for good with those who love him'" (*Rom* 8:28; *CCC* 395). Indeed, it was the very work of Satan in seducing our first parents that brought about the great good of the Incarnation of the Son of God and our Redemption.

So we can thank God for having created angels, who serve as our guardians here on earth, even though some of those angels sinned and became devils. God always brings good out of evil.

Jesus Christ

459 The genealogy of Christ

Why is the genealogy of Christ different in the Gospels of Matthew and Luke, particularly from King David down to Jesus? And who was Joseph's father? Matthew says Jacob whilst Luke says Heli. Is there any significance in the fact that Matthew gives Jesus' genealogy starting from Abraham whilst Luke goes all the way back to Adam?

We can begin with the importance of genealogies in Jewish culture. For the Jews, as for other Eastern peoples of nomadic origin, family trees were of great importance since a person's identity was linked to family and tribe, more so than to place of birth. In the case of the Jews there was the added religious significance of the genealogy establishing that one belonged by blood to the chosen people, to the kingly family of David or to the tribe of Levi, from which priests were chosen. Since these rights passed down the male line, usually only men's names appear.

In Matthew's genealogy, four women are mentioned: Tamar, Rahab, Bathsheba and Ruth. All of them were Gentiles, not Jews, and all except Ruth were guilty of sexual immorality, showing that God came to save all peoples, including sinners.

As you note, Matthew traces Jesus' origin starting from Abraham while Luke starts from Jesus and goes all the way back to Adam. Since Matthew was writing primarily for Christians of Jewish origin, he wanted to show that Jesus belonged to the chosen people descended from Abraham and to the house and family of King David, and hence was the promised Messiah. Luke was writing primarily for Christians of Gentile background, and by tracing Jesus' origin back to Adam he shows that Jesus was truly man and had come as priest to save all mankind.

In this sense St Thomas Aquinas writes: "Luke sets forth Christ's genealogy not at the outset but after Christ's baptism, and not in the descending but in the ascending order, as though giving prominence to the priest who expiated our sins at the point where the Baptist bore witness to him, saying, 'Behold him who takes away the sins of the world.' And in the ascending order he passes Abraham and continues up to God, to whom we are reconciled by cleansing and expiating" (*STh* 3, 31, 3 ad 3).

If one compares the two genealogies, from Abraham to David they are the same whereas from David on they are completely different. It should always be remembered that some people in the Bible had more than one name (Abram/Abraham, Jacob/Israel, Solomon/Jedidiah), and that gaps in a family tree were quite common. This alone, however, is not sufficient to explain the great differences between the genealogies. More than a dozen explanations have been given, two of which are more plausible.

The first is that both evangelists are giving Christ's genealogy following the line of St Joseph, but that one follows the law of Levi and the other does not. According to this law, if a man died without having children his brother was to marry the widow and the first-born son of this marriage was the legal son of the deceased man (cf. *Deut* 25:5-6).

The other explanation is that Matthew's genealogy follows St Joseph's line, through King David's son Solomon, while Luke follows Mary's line, through David's son Nathan. In both cases Jesus is descended from King David. If this explanation is correct, Joseph's father was Jacob and Mary's father Heli. But this raises the further question of why Luke says Mary's father was Heli, whereas tradition calls him Joachim.

Another interesting aspect of Matthew's genealogy is the inclusion of King Jeconiah, one of the last kings before the Babylonian captivity. God had pronounced a curse on Jeconiah such that no descendant of his was to sit on the throne of David: "... for none of his offspring shall succeed in sitting on the throne of David, and ruling again in Judah" (*Jer* 22:30). Since St Joseph was a linear descendant of Jeconiah, neither he nor his offspring could sit on the throne of King David. But Jesus was not the son of Joseph. He was the son of Mary, as Matthew points out (cf. *Mt* 1:19), and thus he was able to fulfil the prophecy of the angel to Mary: "the Lord God will give to him the throne of his father David" (*Lk* 1:32).

As is clear, we can answer some questions about the genealogies but others remain.

460 The "hour" of Jesus

At Cana Jesus tells his mother that his hour has not yet come, and nonetheless he works his first miracle at her intercession. What exactly did he mean by his "hour"?

The "hour" of Jesus appears frequently in the Gospel of John, the first time in the passage you cite at the wedding feast of Cana. When Mary tells Jesus that the wine has run out he answers: "My hour has not yet come" (*Jn* 2:4). Clearly his "hour" does not refer to the manifestation of his divinity in general, since he will manifest it moments later when he works his first miracle, changing water into wine.

The Greek word used for hour in most of these passages is *ora*, which is properly translated as *hour*. Another word Jesus uses is *kairos*, meaning more exactly *time*. For example, Jesus tells his disciples "Go to the feast yourselves; I am not going up to this feast, for my time has not yet fully come" (*Jn* 7:8). Even though he uses a different word, it is clear that his meaning is very similar to that when he spoke to his mother at Cana.

Later in that same chapter, St John himself says: "So they sought to arrest him; but no one laid hands on him, because his hour had not yet come" (*Jn* 7:30). The same idea of no one arresting him because his hour had not yet come appears again in the next chapter (cf. *Jn* 8:20).

As his final Passover approaches and after his triumphal entry into Jerusalem on Palm Sunday, Jesus reveals something of the content of his hour when he tells his disciples: "The hour has come for the Son of man to be glorified" (*Jn* 12:23). A few lines later he clarifies it even further: "Now is my soul troubled. And what shall I say? 'Father, save me from this hour'? No, for this purpose I have come to this hour. Father, glorify your name" (*Jn* 12:27-28). So his hour involves his own glorification but at the same time some element of suffering.

Pope John Paul II comments on this passage: "With these words Jesus reveals the inner drama that is oppressing his soul in view of his approaching sacrifice. He has the possibility of asking the Father that this terrible trial might pass. On the other hand, he does not wish to flee from this painful destiny: 'For this purpose I have come'. He has come to offer the sacrifice that will bring salvation to humanity" (Address, 14 Jan. 1998).

The aspect of suffering is further borne out when Jesus compares his own hour to that of a woman in labour: "When a woman is in labour, she has pain, because her hour has come; but when she is delivered of the child, she no longer remembers the anguish, for joy that a child is born into the world" (*Jn* 16:21). The hour of Jesus too involves pain but also new life. In his long priestly prayer in the Last Supper, Jesus repeats the idea of giving life. He says to the Father: "Father, the hour has come; glorify your Son that the Son may glorify you, since you have given him power over all flesh, to give eternal life to all whom you have given him" (*Jn* 17:1).

What do we glean from all this? That Jesus' hour involves his glorification brought about by his painful death on the cross and his Resurrection, through which he gives eternal life to all mankind. It is the culmination, the fulfilment of the whole purpose of his becoming man: to redeem us by his death and Resurrection. "For this purpose I have come to this hour."

But, paradoxically, Jesus' hour is also the hour of his enemies. He says to the chief priests and captains of the temple when they come to arrest him in the Garden of Gethsemane: "This is your hour, and the power of darkness" (*Lk* 22:53). In this hour, which is so crucial for mankind, the forces of darkness, of evil, of Satan rally together to do battle with God and somehow try to thwart his plan. The *Catechism of the Catholic Church* describes it dramatically: "It is precisely in the Passion, when the mercy of Christ is about to vanquish it, that sin most clearly manifests its violence and its many forms: unbelief, murderous hatred, shunning and mockery by the leaders and the people, Pilate's cowardice and the cruelty of the soldiers, Judas' betrayal – so bitter to Jesus, Peter's denial and the disciples' flight. However, at the very hour of darkness, the hour of the prince of this world, the sacrifice of Christ secretly becomes the source from which the forgiveness of our sins will pour forth inexhaustibly" (*CCC* 1851).

We give thanks to Jesus for going through with his hour to free us from our sins.

461 Jesus after the Resurrection

After his Resurrection Jesus didn't seem to be present all the time and he sometimes wasn't recognised by people who knew him well. How do we explain this?

The first thing we should say is that after his Resurrection Jesus did not return to normal life like the three persons he had raised from the dead: Lazarus, the daughter of Jairus and the son of the widow of Naim. All of these had died and returned to normal life to be given back to their families.

What is more, if we suppose that their souls were already in the state of natural happiness we call the Limbo of the Fathers, where the good people of the Old Testament were awaiting Christ's death for their Redemption, they would have had to leave that state of great happiness and return to this "valley of tears" here on earth, as we say in the "Hail, Holy Queen". We say "valley of tears" not because life on earth is meant to be sad, but because in comparison with the happiness of heaven it can seem so. In this respect, while their returning to life would have been a great joy for their loved ones, it would have been a source of disappointment, to say the least, for themselves!

Jesus' Resurrection was not like theirs. He did not return to normal life but rather to a different state outside space and time. As the *Catechism of the Catholic Church* explains it, "Christ's Resurrection was not a return to earthly life, as was the case with the raisings from the dead that he had performed before Easter: Jairus' daughter, the young man of Naim, Lazarus. These actions were miraculous events, but the persons miraculously raised returned by Jesus' power to ordinary earthly life. At some particular moment they would die again. Christ's Resurrection is essentially different. In his risen body he passes from the state of death to another life beyond time and space. At Jesus' Resurrection his body is filled with the power of the Holy Spirit: he shares the divine life in his glorious state, so that St Paul can say that Christ is 'the man from heaven'" (cf. *1 Cor* 15:35-50; *CCC* 646).

What were the characteristics of Christ's body after his Resurrection? First of all, it was the same body he had before he died and it was a physical body, not just an apparition. In the words of the Catechism, "By means of touch and the sharing of a meal, the risen Jesus establishes direct contact with his disciples. He invites them in this way to recognise that he is not a ghost and above all to verify that the risen body in which he appears to them is the same body that had been tortured and crucified, for it still bears the traces of his passion" (cf. *Lk* 24:30-43; *Jn* 20:20-27; 21:9-15; *CCC* 645). In this sense, Jesus is not like the apparitions of Our Lady and saints down the ages, who appear on earth but without a physical body. Jesus, on the contrary, walks beside the disciples on the way to Emmaus and shares a meal with them, and he invites St Thomas to put his finger into the wounds in his hand and his hand into the wound in his side (cf. *Lk* 24:13-31; *Jn* 20: 27).

Christ's body was what we call a glorified body, much like we will have after the resurrection of the body on the last day. The Catechism explains: "Yet at the same time this authentic, real body possesses the new properties of a glorious body: not limited by space and time but able to be present how and when he wills; for Christ's humanity can no longer be confined to earth and belongs henceforth only to the Father's divine realm. For this reason too the risen Jesus enjoys the sovereign freedom of appearing as he wishes: in the guise of a gardener or in forms other than those familiar to his disciples, precisely to awaken their faith" (*CCC* 645).

That is, during the forty days between his Resurrection and his Ascension into heaven, Jesus is not constantly on earth. He appears only occasionally, when and where he wishes. He sometimes appears suddenly, as he did in the Upper Room on Easter Sunday in the evening, and he disappears just as suddenly, as with the disciples of Emmaus (cf. *Lk* 24:31, 36). What is more, he is able to appear in the Upper Room passing through locked doors (cf. *Jn* 20:19), and he is able to appear without being recognised by those who knew him well, as he did to Mary Magdalene and the disciples of Emmaus (*Jn* 20:14-15; *Lk* 24:16). And of course, being God, he is always in heaven in the presence of the Father and Holy Spirit even when his body is on earth.

The Church and Salvation

462 Canonisations and infallibility

While watching the canonisation of Popes John XXIII and John Paul II on television, I noticed that Pope Francis used the expression "we define" in declaring these Popes to be saints. Is this equivalent to the definition of a dogma and therefore an infallible judgment?

It is indeed an infallible judgment. Most of the medieval theologians, among them such notable figures as St Antoninus, Melchior Cano, Francisco Suarez and Cardinal Robert Bellarmine were of the view that the canonisation of a saint is an infallible judgment. St Thomas Aquinas, arguably the greatest theologian of all, writes: "Since the honour we pay the saints is in a certain sense a profession of faith, i.e., a belief in the glory of the saints, we must piously believe that in this matter also the judgment of the Church is not liable to error" (*Quodlib.* IX, a. 16).

The *New Catholic Encyclopedia* explains why such a judgment must be infallible: "The pope cannot by solemn definition induce errors concerning faith and morals into the teaching of the universal Church. Should the Church hold up for universal veneration a man's life and habits that in reality led to [his] damnation, it would lead the faithful into error. It is now theologically certain that the solemn canonisation of a saint is an infallible and irrevocable decision of the supreme pontiff. God speaks infallibly through his Church as it demonstrates and exemplifies its universal teaching in a particular person or judges that person's acts to be in accord with its teaching."

The very rite of canonisation shows the Church's belief that it is indeed an infallible judgment. The Cardinal Prefect of the Congregation of the Causes of the Saints makes three petitions to the Holy Father, beseeching him on behalf of the Church to enrol the Blessed among the saints. In the third petition he says: "Most Holy Father, Holy Church, trusting in the Lord's promise to send upon her the Spirit of Truth, who in every age keeps the supreme Magisterium immune from error, most earnestly beseeches Your Holiness to enrol these, her elect, among the Saints." The reference to trusting in the assistance of the Spirit of Truth, the Holy Spirit, who "keeps the supreme Magisterium immune from error" shows the belief that infallibility is involved.

The Pope then reads the formula of canonisation: "For the honour of the Blessed Trinity, the exaltation of the Catholic faith and the increase of the Christian life, by the authority of our Lord Jesus Christ, and of the Holy Apostles Peter and Paul, and our own, after due deliberation and frequent prayer for divine assistance, and having sought the counsel of many of our brother Bishops, we declare and define Blessed N. and N. [to] be Saints and we enrol them among the Saints, decreeing that they are to be venerated as such by the whole Church. In the name of the Father, and of the Son, and of the Holy Spirit."

Here too, the reference to the authority of Jesus Christ and of the Holy Apostles Peter and Paul, to due deliberation and frequent prayer for divine assistance, and the use of the formal words "declare and define" show that the Pope is exercising his teaching authority at the highest level.

What exactly is the object of the infallible judgment? It is not the holiness of life of the person nor the existence of the miracle which confirms this holiness, but rather the fact that the person is indeed in heaven and hence can be the object of veneration by the whole Church. Before making this judgment the Church undertakes a long and rigorous process of examining the life and virtues of the person, as well as the fact of the miracle attributed to him or her. Only when this process is complete and the Church is certain that the person is now in heaven will she make a judgment of sanctity and proceed to the canonisation.

It should be understood that the declaration of sanctity does not imply that the person did not commit sins, even serious ones. Some of the saints, among them St Augustine, led turbulent lives before they were converted and began a new life in God. As they say, the saints did not all begin well, but they all ended well.

463 Is *Laudato si* infallible?

Everyone is talking about Pope Francis' new Encyclical Laudato si, with many praising it and some harshly criticising it. Some of the critics say we are free to disagree with it since it is not an infallible document anyway. Is this the case?

Laudato si has received considerable attention from the media and politicians, probably more than any other Encyclical since Pope Paul VI's *Humanae vitae* in 1968. As we recall, that Encyclical reaffirmed the Church's perennial rejection of contraception.

An Encyclical, from the Greek word for circle, is a circular letter from the Pope addressed to a large number of people, the whole Church or even the whole world. Pope Francis, in fact, addresses *Laudato si* to "every person living on this planet" (n 3). An Encyclical of itself is not an infallible document but rather an expression of what is called "ordinary Magisterium".

When does the Pope teach infallibly? The Second Vatican Council explained it simply: "The Roman Pontiff, head of the college of bishops, enjoys this infallibility in virtue of his office when, as supreme pastor and teacher of all the faithful – who confirms his brethren in the faith (cf. *Lk* 22:32) – he proclaims in an absolute decision a doctrine pertaining to faith or morals" (*LG* 25). In such cases he is said to be speaking *ex cathedra,* literally *from the chair.*

For a papal statement to be considered *ex cathedra* it must meet three conditions. Firstly, it must be *universal*; i.e. made by the Pope as supreme pastor and teacher of the whole Church, not of only a part of the Church. Secondly, it must be on a matter of *faith or morals*, which is the area within which the Church has authority to teach. And thirdly, it must define a doctrine by an *absolute decision*; that is; teach in a definitive way a truth to be accepted by all the faithful.

Very rarely would a Pope use an Encyclical to define a truth infallibly. The last two definitions of dogmas, of Mary's Immaculate Conception in 1854 and of her Assumption in 1950, were made in documents known as Apostolic Constitutions. But it is still possible for an Encyclical to include infallible statements. For example, it is widely held that Pope Paul VI's *Humanae vitae* was teaching infallibly when it taught the immorality of contraception, since this had been the Church's constant teaching over the years.

Laudato si does not intend to define any new dogma. But that does not mean that it can be disregarded or that we are free to disagree with its core teachings. On the contrary, the Second Vatican Council taught: "This loyal submission of the will and intellect must be given, in a special way, to the authentic teaching authority of the Roman Pontiff, even when he does not speak *ex cathedra* in such wise, indeed, that his supreme teaching authority be acknowledged with respect, and that one sincerely adhere to decisions made by him, conformably with his manifest mind and intention, which is made known principally either by the character of the documents in question, or by the frequency with which a certain doctrine is proposed, or by the manner in which the doctrine is formulated" (*LG* 25).

Laudato si contains different types of statements. Some form part of the perennial moral teaching of the Church, among them the respect we should have for God's creation, the need to care for the environment, the responsibility to look after the poor, etc. These teachings should be given "loyal submission of the will and intellect". We are not free to disagree with them.

Other statements are of a more scientific, factual nature, like the extent of the human contribution to climate change, the human cause of the extinction of some species of living things, the extent of pollution caused by industrial waste, etc. Similarly the Pope makes some suggestions as to how to resolve some of the problems in this area, leaving it up to experts to decide how best to proceed. Since these statements are not matters of faith and morals but rather of science, economics and politics, a person is free to question or even disagree with them, just as scientists, economists and politicians disagree among themselves.

But disagreement over statements of this sort should not distract us from studying and accepting the core teachings, which are of fundamental importance. Let us not throw the baby out with the bath water!

464 Coptic Orthodox and Catholics

A friend who is Coptic Orthodox has tried to convince me that their Church is the true Church and that we Catholics and other Christians separated from the Church after the Council of Chalcedon. How do I answer her?

We can begin by recalling that Our Lord founded a Church with St Peter as its head (cf. *Mt* 16:18-19; *Jn* 21:15-17). This Church was one and it was united under the Pope, whose authority was recognised by all as it spread throughout the Roman Empire in the following centuries. According to tradition, it was St Mark the evangelist who founded the Church in Egypt, in Alexandria, around the year 42 AD and by the end of the first century the Church had spread throughout Egypt. I say this because the Coptic Orthodox Church is based in Egypt.

Because of the popularity of the ideas of the Alexandrian priest Arius, who denied that the Word who became flesh was truly God, the Council of Nicaea was held in 325 to resolve the matter. The Council, following the teaching of St Alexander of Alexandria and especially St Athanasius, also of Alexandria, condemned Arius and declared that the Word was indeed God, "true God from true God, begotten, not made, consubstantial with the Father", as we say in the Nicene Creed on Sundays. The Church in Egypt accepted the teaching of the Council.

The Church in Egypt also accepted the teachings of the next two Councils, the Council of Constantinople in 381, which declared the divinity of the Holy Spirit, and the Council of Ephesus in 431, which declared that Christ was one divine Person with both a divine and a human nature and that Mary was truly the Mother of God. The teachings of St Cyril of Alexandria were very influential in the declarations of the Council of Ephesus.

But then came the Council of Chalcedon. The teaching of St Cyril on the one person in Christ came to be understood by the Patriarch of Alexandria Dioscurus and the monk Eutyches to mean that in Christ there was only one nature, with the divine and human natures so united that they were physically one. The teaching was known as monophysitism. It should be understood that St Cyril himself had died in 444 and thus was not there to explain his teaching. Eutyches was condemned at a synod in Constantinople in 448. He appealed to Rome but Pope Leo I condemned him and explained the true doctrine in his Dogmatic Epistle. Eventually a council was convened which met in Chalcedon in 451 with some 600 bishops present. The Council, following Pope Leo's Dogmatic Epistle, condemned the error of monophysitism and declared that in Christ there were two natures, divine and human.

This time the Church in Egypt did not accept the findings of the Council. They established their own patriarchate of Alexandria, calling their head the Pope, and no longer recognised the authority of the Bishop of Rome. Thus was born what is now known as the Coptic Orthodox Church. Since the Church in Egypt had accepted the teachings of the previous Councils, and Eutyches himself had recognised the authority of the Pope when he appealed to him, they should have accepted the teaching of Pope Leo and the Council of Chalcedon. Thus it is clear that it was they who separated from the one true Church of Christ, not vice versa.

At the Council of Florence in 1442 a Coptic Orthodox delegation signed a document accepting reunion with the Catholic Church, but there was little support for it in Egypt and it had no effect. Then in 1713 the Coptic Patriarch of Alexandria again agreed to union with Rome but this too was not to last. Finally in 1824 the Pope established a Coptic Catholic Patriarchate of Alexandria for the small number of Coptic Catholics. Their number has since grown considerably.

We should acknowledge that relations between the Coptic Orthodox Popes and the Catholic Pope have been very cordial in recent times. Less than a year after becoming Pope of the Church of Alexandria, in October 1972 Pope Shenouda III visited Pope Paul VI, the first Alexandrian Pope to do so since the schism of 451. In May 1973, he drafted a declaration on the nature of Christ that was agreed upon by the Roman Catholic Church and the Oriental and Eastern Orthodox Churches, an important step towards re-establishing Christian unity. And in May 2013, Pope Shenouda's successor Pope Tawadros II had a cordial meeting with Pope Francis in Rome. This was followed by another very cordial meeting between Pope Francis and Pope Tawadros during Pope Francis' visit to Egypt in May 2017. We should pray that the union of these important Churches may soon come about so that we can once again be one in Christ.

465 Catholics and Muslims

With the news of violence against Christians by Muslims in different countries, I have some Catholic friends who are very hostile towards Muslims. I am of two minds myself. Does the Church have anything to say about this?

The Second Vatican Council's Dogmatic Constitution on the Church *Lumen gentium* spoke about the relations of the Church with other religions. With regard to Muslims it said: "But the plan of salvation also includes those who acknowledge the Creator, in the first place amongst whom are the Muslims: these profess to hold the faith of Abraham, and together with us they adore the one, merciful God, mankind's judge on the last day" (*LG* 16).

In *Nostra aetate,* the Declaration on the Relation of the Church to Non-Christian Religions, the Council said: "The Church has also a high regard for the Muslims. They worship God, who is one, living and subsistent, merciful and almighty, the Creator of heaven and earth, who has also spoken to men. They strive to submit themselves without reserve to the hidden decrees of God, just as Abraham submitted himself to God's plan, to whose faith Muslims eagerly link their own. Although not acknowledging him as God, they worship Jesus as a prophet, his virgin Mother they also honour, and even at times devoutly invoke. Further, they await the day of judgment and the reward of God following the resurrection of the dead. For this reason they highly esteem an upright life and worship God, especially by way of prayer, alms-deeds and fasting" (*NA* 3).

As is clear from these passages, Muslims believe in the one God, the same God that Jews and Catholics worship, they honour Jesus as a prophet and they have great devotion to Our Lady. They are included in God's plan of salvation.

At the same time we must acknowledge that with the advance of Islam into the West from the seventh century on, there were battles between Christians and Muslims that left hostility on both sides. The Declaration *Nostra aetate* dealt with this: "Over the centuries many quarrels and dissensions have arisen between Christians and Muslims. The sacred Council now pleads with all to forget the past, and urges that a sincere effort be made to achieve mutual understanding; for the benefit of all men, let them together preserve and promote peace, liberty, social justice and moral values" (*NA* 3). These words are very applicable to the present situation.

In recent decades there has been ongoing dialogue between the Church and representatives of Islam, and Popes have visited Muslim countries and met with their leaders. In November 2014 Pope Francis visited Turkey, as Pope Benedict XVI had done in 2006. In an address to the President of the "Diyanet", the organisation in charge of religious affairs, he alluded to the ongoing violence against Christians in Iraq and Syria: "Particular concern arises from the fact that, owing mainly to an extremist and fundamentalist group, entire communities, especially – though not exclusively – Christians and Yazidis, have suffered and continue to suffer barbaric violence simply because of their ethnic and religious identity. They have been forcibly evicted from their homes, having to leave behind everything to save their lives and preserve their faith... Human life, a gift of God the Creator, possesses a sacred character. As such, any violence which seeks religious justification warrants the strongest condemnation because the Omnipotent is the God of life and peace... We, Muslims and Christians, are the bearers of spiritual treasures of inestimable worth. Among these we recognise some shared elements, though lived according to the traditions of each, such as the adoration of the All-Merciful God, reference to the Patriarch Abraham, prayer, almsgiving, fasting... elements which, when lived sincerely, can transform life and provide a sure foundation for dignity and fraternity. Recognising and developing our common spiritual heritage – through interreligious dialogue – helps us to promote and to uphold moral values, peace and freedom in society."

In sum, the violence against Christians, as the Pope said, comes from extremist fundamentalist elements, not from Muslims as a whole. We should pray for peace and harmony, so that Christians and Muslims can live together as brothers and sisters, children of the one God.

466 The Bible alone?

I have a born-again Christian workmate who is trying to convince me that the Bible alone is sufficient to ground our faith and that we don't need tradition or the Church. How do I answer him?

This view is one of the fundamental pillars of Protestant thought and it goes by the Latin name of *sola scriptura*: Scripture alone. Those who hold to it, like your workmate, say we don't need the Church or tradition to teach us – the Bible is sufficient. There are several problems with this.

The first is that without tradition and the Church we would not even have the Bible. For the first twenty years of the Church, as far as we know, there were no written texts that today make up the New Testament. The apostles went out and preached the faith, the people heard their preaching and came to believe it and in turn pass it on to others, and this preaching gradually became concretised in such practices as the Mass, Baptism, Confirmation, the ordination of sacred ministers, funeral rites, prayer for the dead, etc. This handing on of the faith by word of mouth and the customs that grew out of it are what we know as tradition. Indeed, the word tradition comes from the Latin *traditio*, meaning *handing on.* For those first years there simply was no Bible and, in a sense, the Church did not need one. The Church functioned perfectly well without it.

Then, mainly in the 50s and 60s of the first century the apostles and others began to write down some of their preaching in the Gospels, as well as the history of the early Church in the *Acts of the Apostles*, and letters addressed to different communities and individuals. So gradually there appeared a number of early Christian writings which were faithfully copied and passed around among the various communities, and which were read in the Mass. But at the same time there were numerous other writings which were also highly revered, copied and passed around, writings such as the *Didache, The Shepherd of Hermas*, the letter of Barnabas, the letters of Pope Clement I, etc.

Who decided which writings were to be regarded as divinely inspired and hence part of the Bible and to be read in Mass, and which were not? The *Catechism of the Catholic Church* answers: "It was by the Apostolic Tradition that the Church discerned which writings are to be included in the list of the sacred books" (*CCC* 120). That is, the Holy Spirit guided the bishops of the early Christian communities to discern which writings were to be considered inspired by God and which were not. So it was the tradition of the Church that gave us the Bible. Thus it is foolish to say that the Bible alone is sufficient, when without the tradition we wouldn't even have the Bible.

But the tradition of the Church is needed for a second reason: to interpret the Bible authentically. For example, some Christians today say that Jesus was not the only child of Mary because the Bible says he had brothers and sisters (cf. *Mt* 13:55, *Mk* 3:31-35; 6:3). If we take the Bible on its own we could conclude that Jesus indeed had brothers and sisters and therefore Mary was not a virgin after his birth. But the early Christian communities knew Mary, Joseph and Jesus and they knew Jesus was the only child. This tradition was handed on down the ages and so the Church has always professed that Mary was "ever Virgin".

Thirdly, the tradition of the Church has given us a number of beliefs which are not found explicitly in the Bible at all, beliefs such as the existence of purgatory, the assumption of Mary into heaven, Mary's Immaculate Conception, etc. Because the tradition of the Church was so firm and constant in affirming these beliefs, the Church has defined them as dogmas of faith. So it is simply not true that the Bible alone is sufficient to ground our faith.

Finally, people who believe that Scripture alone is the sole source of our knowledge about the faith should be able to point to a passage in the Bible which says this. But no such passage exists. On the contrary, St Paul makes explicit mention of the importance of oral tradition: "So then, brethren, stand firm and hold to the traditions which you were taught by us, either by word of mouth or by letter" (*2 Thess* 2:15). And St John writes: "But there are many other things which Jesus did; were every one of them to be written, I suppose that the world itself could not contain the books that would be written" (*Jn* 21:25). Many of these things that Jesus said and did which are not recorded in the Bible have been handed on by word of mouth in the tradition, and these too are a source of knowledge of our faith. So no, the Bible alone is not sufficient to ground our faith.

467 Is Scripture alone sufficient?

When I talk with my Protestant friends about matters of faith, they won't accept any belief unless they can find it in the Bible. Some of these beliefs, like purgatory, are not so clear in the Bible. How do I answer them?

Your friends, like most Protestants, subscribe to the belief that the source of all religious truth is the Bible, and that if something is not in the Bible, it is simply not true and not to be believed. They believe that God left in the Bible all he wanted us to believe. This is known as the principle of *sola Scriptura,* scripture alone, as the source of religious truth. Protestants believe we do not need the tradition of the Church, or the teaching authority of the Church, to know what is true.

How do we answer them? There are many ways to show that the principle is simply not defensible, although as always we must discuss these matters politely, calmly and with reason, not emotionally. After all, our Protestant friends are good people and they are as convinced of what they have learned as we are.

Starting from the Bible itself, which Protestants do accept, we can point to two passages which undermine the principle of Scripture alone. The first is at the end of the Gospel of St John, where we read:

"But there are also many other things which Jesus did; were every one of them to be written, I suppose that the world itself could not contain the books that would be written" (*Jn* 21:25; cf. *Jn* 20:30). It is clear from this passage that Jesus said and did many other things besides those recorded in the New Testament. Not everything he taught is in the Bible.

For example, the teaching on purgatory, as you say, is not so clear in the Bible, although numerous passages allude to it. Nonetheless, it is probable that Jesus spoke with the apostles about the importance of praying and offering the Mass for the souls of the faithful departed, since this was a custom that the Jews of the time were living (cf. *2 Mac* 12:42-45). So ancient and widespread was the custom of praying for the faithful departed that St Isidore of Seville, who died in 636 could say: "To offer the sacrifice [of the Mass] for the repose of the faithful departed is a custom observed all over the world. For this reason we believe that it is a custom taught by the very apostles" (*On ecclesiastical offices*, 1). If the apostles taught it, they learned it from Christ.

The second passage, from St Paul, also undermines the *sola Scriptura* principle. In it St Paul says that the foundation of truth is the Church, not Scripture: "I am writing these instructions to you so that, if I am delayed, you may know how one ought to behave in the house of God, which is the Church of the living God, the pillar and bulwark of the truth" (*1 Tim* 3:14-15). For a Protestant the pillar and bulwark of the truth would have to be the Bible, yet St Paul clearly says it is the Church.

What is more, it has always been the Church, basing itself on the writings of the great Fathers such as St Augustine, St Jerome, St John Chrysostom, etc., that has given us the authentic interpretation of the Scriptures. The Scriptures can only be safely understood and interpreted within the living tradition of the Church. For example, this living tradition has always understood Jesus' words about anyone putting away his wife and marrying another as prohibiting divorce and remarriage. Most Protestant denominations allow divorce and remarriage. Who is right on this matter – a Church founded by Jesus Christ which has followed this teaching for two thousand years, or a series of communities founded in the sixteenth century which teach the contrary? One could say the same about belief in the Real Presence of Christ in the Eucharist, so clearly stated by Jesus in the synagogue of Capernaum and repeated by St Paul (cf. *Jn* 6: 51-58; *1 Cor* 11:27-29).

Clearly, Scripture alone is not sufficient. We need the living tradition of the Church to give us the books of the Bible and to safeguard and interpret them according to the mind of Christ.

468 Faith alone?

My husband is a practising Protestant and we often discuss our theological differences. He is very respectful but keeps on insisting that we are saved by faith and not by works. It seems clear to me that good works are also important. How do I convince him?

The idea of *sola fide*, salvation by *faith alone*, stands alongside that of *sola scriptura*, *Scripture alone* as the source of Revelation, as one of the pillars of Protestant thought developed by Martin Luther. Catholics often misunderstand what Protestants are saying on this point, and vice versa, so it is important to understand the issues.

It is helpful in the first place to know what led Martin Luther to believe that we are saved by faith alone. Luther was an Augustinian Catholic monk and so he was well versed in Catholic theology. But he was deeply troubled as a human person. He struggled to live chastity and other virtues and in spite of his penances, prayers, good works, Masses and confessions he could not find inner peace. He hated the very word "righteousness", or holiness, feeling himself a sinner through and through no matter how hard he tried to improve.

Then he came upon a text in St Paul's letter to the Romans which resolved all his difficulties: "The righteous shall live by faith" (*Rom* 1:17). He saw in this text that in spite of his inner sinfulness he was saved by his faith in Jesus Christ and that God overlooked his sins, which were covered over by the merits of Christ. That is, we are saved, or declared righteous, by faith in Christ's work on Calvary, not by our own works. We can still do good works, especially to our neighbour, but we are not saved by them but rather by our faith in the merits of Christ.

What are we to make of this view? When Luther taught that we are saved by faith alone, he meant by "saved" what can also be called "justified". When we Catholics speak of being saved we normally think of going to heaven, to eternal salvation. But Luther had in mind not the eternal salvation of the soul, but rather the initial step of passing from the state of sin to the state of righteousness before God, what we call justification. The *Catechism of the Catholic Church* says of it: "The grace of the Holy Spirit has the power to justify us, that is, to cleanse us from our sins and to communicate to us 'the righteousness of God through faith in Jesus Christ' and through Baptism" (*CCC* 1987; *Rom* 3:22). Notice that justification comes about not only through faith in Jesus Christ, as Protestants believe, but also through Baptism.

Luther was right in saying that this process of justification cannot be merited or deserved, no matter how many good works we do. It is always a grace freely conferred by God on the person. This is seen most clearly in the Baptism of infants, who can bring no good works, and in the conversion of someone like St Paul, who had been persecuting the Church. His conversion, his justification, was an unmerited gift from God.

Also, since justification is the passing of the soul from the state of original sin or mortal sin to the state of grace, and we cannot merit anything before God when we are in the state of sin, it is obvious that it is not our works that justify us but the grace of God. Only when we are in the state of grace can our good works be meritorious, that is deserving of an increase of grace and of storing up treasure in heaven. When we are in the state of original sin before Baptism, or in the state of mortal sin after Baptism, our works have no merit. It is the undeserved grace of God, won for us by Christ's death and resurrection, that lifts us out of the state of sin. For this reason the Catechism says: "Our justification comes from the grace of God. Grace is *favour, the free and undeserved help* that God gives us to respond to his call... (*CCC* 1996). So in this sense, we can agree with Protestants.

Nonetheless, if good works are not necessary for our initial justification, they are necessary for our subsequent sanctification and eternal salvation. It is in this sense that St James writes: "What does it profit, my brethren, if a man says he has faith but has not works? Can his faith save him? ... So faith by itself, if it has no works, is dead" (*Jas* 2:14, 17). He goes on to say: "But some one will say, 'You have faith and I have works.' Show me your faith apart from your works, and I by my works will show you my faith. You believe that God is one; you do well. Even the demons believe – and shudder" (*Jas* 2:18-19). Yes, even the devil believes in God, but he has no good works to show for it and so he cannot go to heaven.

Jesus often teaches the importance of good works for eternal salvation. In answer to the question, "Teacher, what good deed must I do, to have eternal life?", he answers, "If you would enter life, keep the commandments" (*Mt* 19:16-17). And in his account of the last judgment he makes eternal salvation dependent on good works: "Come, O blessed of my Father, inherit the kingdom prepared for you from the foundation of the world; for I was hungry and you gave me food..." (*Mt* 25:34-35). So faith is necessary for salvation, but so are good works.

469 Salvation by grace alone

I have always believed that by Baptism we are made holy and pleasing to God but a Protestant friend says I am wrong, that we remain sinners and are only declared righteous by God in virtue of the merits of Jesus Christ. Are we Catholics wrong on this point?

As we know, we Catholics have the fullness of the faith taught by Jesus Christ and we belong to his Church, which teaches under the guidance of the Holy Spirit. The Church has been in existence since Jesus founded it on the apostles and it is not going to be wrong on any matter of doctrine. The Protestants came in the sixteenth century and, while they pretend to have understood certain matters that somehow evaded the minds of brilliant thinkers and saints like St Augustine and St Thomas Aquinas, some of their interpretations of Scripture are only partially correct or simply wrong. The question you raise is one of them.

The question is related to one of the pillars of Protestant thought often referred to as the principle of *sola gratia*, justification *by grace alone*. It stands alongside the principles of *sola scriptura*, Scripture alone without the need for tradition and the Church, and *sola fide*, justification by faith alone.

According to traditional Protestant teaching, man can do nothing to merit justification or salvation, which is solely the work of God through the grace he gives us, hence justification by grace alone. In one sense we can agree with this, since all our good works are preceded, accompanied and followed by God's grace. Without God, we can do nothing. This was declared by the Church against the errors of Pelagius at the time of St Augustine. Pelagius, a British monk, affirmed that we do not need grace to perform good works, but that we can save ourselves without the help of God. This error was condemned by the Council of Orange in the year 529 in Canons 5 and 6 (cf. *Dz*

178-179). So it is clear that we need grace, as the Protestants say, in order to be justified.

Nonetheless, although we need grace in order to be justified, grace alone is not sufficient. We can and we must cooperate with that grace through our free actions. The belief of the Protestant reformers is that as a result of original sin, human nature is essentially corrupted and man is incapable of good actions which are pleasing to God. This error was condemned in the Council of Trent in Session 6: "If anyone shall say that man's free will moved and aroused by God does not cooperate by assenting to God who rouses and calls, whereby it disposes and prepares itself to obtain the grace of justification ... let him be anathema" (Can. 4, *Dz* 814).

This brings us to the specific error you mentioned in your question. It was the Protestant belief that in justification God simply covers over our sinfulness with the merits of Christ, leaving us inherently sinful and incapable of good acts. Thus we would only be declared righteous by God, not made righteous in ourselves. Against this error the Council of Trent declared in that same Session 6: "If anyone shall say that men are justified either by the sole imputation of the justice of Christ, or by the sole remission of sins, to the exclusion of grace and charity, which is poured forth in their hearts by the Holy Spirit and remains in them, or even that the grace by which we are justified is only the favour of God: let him be anathema (Can. 11, *Dz* 821).

Thus the Catholic teaching is that with justification through Baptism or the sacrament of Penance not only are our sins forgiven but the grace of God is poured into our soul, making it holy and pleasing to God. We are truly made righteous, holy, with our soul lit up by the divine life within us. This new state of grace and holiness is symbolised by the candle lit from the Easter candle and given to the newly baptised person. We are a new creation, holy and pleasing to God.

It is interesting to note that as the fruit of ongoing dialogue between the Vatican's Pontifical Council for Promoting Christian Unity and the

Lutheran World Federation, a *Joint Declaration on the Doctrine of Justification* was agreed to in 1999, resolving most of these differences. In 2006 the World Methodist Conference too voted unanimously to accept the declaration. We pray that over time the remaining serious doctrinal differences can be resolved and we can have unity with at least some of the Protestant denominations.

470 Can non-Catholics be saved?

I have a knowledgeable friend who quotes Popes and saints to try to convince me that there are no Muslims, Jews or even Protestants in heaven, because the Church teaches that outside the Church there is no salvation. Is he right?

The statement that outside the Church there is no salvation goes back to the early Church and it has been taught and clarified down the ages. But it must be properly understood, lest it lead to the radical conclusion of your friend that there are only Catholics in heaven.

Among the early Fathers who taught that outside the Church there is no salvation, St Fulgentius of Ruspe, around the year 500, is one of the strongest: "Not only all pagans, but also all Jews and all heretics and schismatics, who finish their lives outside the Catholic Church, will go into eternal fire..." (*On Faith, to Peter* 38.81).

As for Popes, Pope Eugene IV in the Bull *Cantate Domino* (1441), using the same terms as St Fulgentius, taught in an infallible definition: "The Most Holy Roman Church firmly believes, professes and preaches that none of those existing outside the Catholic Church, not only pagans, but also Jews, heretics, and schismatics can ever be partakers of eternal life, but that they are to go into the eternal fire 'which was prepared for the devil and his angels' (*Mt* 25:41) unless before death they are joined with her."

Anyone reading these texts might well be inclined to believe that there are no Muslims, Jews or Protestants in heaven, only Catholics. But this would mean that the immense majority of all mankind would go to hell. Did Jesus become man and die on the cross for only a few, or does he truly want all to be saved and to come to the knowledge of the truth? (cf. *1 Tim* 2:4) It is clearly the latter.

But then how are we to understand the clear teachings of the Church just cited? We must understand them in light of the tradition that one can belong to the Church not only through Baptism with water but also through Baptism of desire. This desire can be either explicit, in the case of catechumens who are preparing to enter the Church, or implicit, in the case of non-Catholics of good will who strive to lead a good life and who follow the will of God as they understand it.

Already in the second century St Justin spoke of the latter: "Those who acted in accordance with what is universally, naturally and eternally good were pleasing to God and will be saved by Christ ... just like the righteous who preceded them" (*Dialogue with Trypho*, 45).

This teaching was stated officially by the Holy See in answer to the errors of Fr Leonard Feeney, S.J., who had been professor of theology at Boston College and chaplain of the St Benedict Center at Harvard from 1945 on. Fr Feeney taught literally that outside the Catholic Church there is no salvation and only Catholics can go to heaven.

To clarify the Church's teaching, the Holy Office, with the approval of Pope Pius XII, sent a letter to the Archbishop of Boston, Cardinal Richard Cushing, on 8 August 1949. It stated, among other things, that in order for someone to be saved, "it is not always required that he be incorporated into the Church actually as a member, but it is necessary that at least he be united to her by desire and longing. However, this desire need not always be explicit, as it is in catechumens; but when a person is involved in invincible ignorance God accepts also an implicit desire, so called because it is included in that good disposition of soul whereby a person wishes his will to be conformed to the will of God."

This teaching was solemnly declared in the Second Vatican Council in the following terms: "Those who, through no fault of their own, do not know the Gospel of Christ or his Church, but who nevertheless seek God with a sincere heart, and, moved by grace, try in their actions to do his will as they know it through the dictates of their conscience – those too may achieve eternal salvation" (*LG* 16).

So when we get to heaven – and let us pray that we will – we will find there not only our fellow Catholics but also people of all beliefs who lived and died well, helped by grace and saved by Christ, who sought to fulfil the will of God as they knew it. Thank God for that.

471 Former Catholics and salvation

Many years ago my brother, who was brought up Catholic albeit without much formation, married a Protestant and ever since has worshipped in a Protestant Church, where he is very active and convinced of his new beliefs. Can he still be saved?

At the outset we should remember that salvation is always a matter between an individual soul and God. Whatever judgments we may make about a soul's state and worthiness for salvation as a result of their decisions here on earth, in the end it is God who judges that soul and we should not presume to play God.

The Church has something to say about the matter in the Second Vatican Council's Dogmatic Constitution on the Church *Lumen gentium*: "This holy Council first of all turns its attention to the Catholic faithful. Basing itself on scripture and tradition, it teaches that the Church, a pilgrim now on earth, is necessary for salvation:

the one Christ is mediator and the way of salvation; he is present to us in his body which is the Church. He himself explicitly asserted the necessity of faith and baptism (cf. *Mk* 16:16; *Jn* 3:5), and thereby affirmed at the same time the necessity of the Church, which men enter through baptism as through a door. Hence they could not be saved who, knowing that the Catholic Church was founded as necessary by God through Christ, would refuse either to enter it, or to remain in it" (*LG* 14).

The final words can sound harsh. They seem to say that someone who knows that the Catholic Church was founded as necessary for salvation and does not enter it or leaves it voluntarily cannot be saved. Naturally these words do not apply to the many Catholics who no longer attend Mass, or who do so only irregularly, but still regard themselves as Catholics. They have remained in the Church and form part of the family of the Church. Naturally, in order to be saved they must repent of their serious sins and be reconciled with God before they die.

Someone, on the contrary, who leaves the Church in order to embrace some other faith, be it Christian or non-Christian, has in fact refused to remain in the Church, so it would seem that in principle they cannot be saved. Nonetheless, we would have to ask, and God would ask in the judgment, whether they really understood the importance of being Catholic, whether they knew that the Church was necessary for salvation. As you say in your question, your brother did not have solid formation in the Catholic faith, so he could very well be in ignorance on this matter. It is likely that most Catholics who leave the Church and embrace some other faith do not fully understand the importance of being Catholic.

When, like your brother, they embrace some other Christian faith, it may very well be that they think it really doesn't matter to which denomination one belongs, as long as it is Christian. Most Christians do believe that salvation comes only through Christ, so these people are convinced that they are on the way to heaven, having taken Jesus as their Lord and Saviour.

The Second Vatican Council goes on to explain how the Catholic Church is related to these other Christians: "The Church knows that she is joined in many ways to the baptised who are honoured by the name of Christian, but who do not however profess the Catholic faith in its entirety or have not preserved unity or communion under the successor of Peter. For there are many who hold sacred scripture in honour as a rule of faith and of life, who have a sincere religious zeal, who lovingly believe in God the Father Almighty and in Christ, the Son of God and the Saviour, who are sealed by baptism which unites them to Christ, and who indeed recognise and receive other sacraments in their own Churches or ecclesiastical communities...; these Christians are indeed in some real way joined to us in the Holy Spirit..." (*LG* 15).

So in summary, we cannot judge whether any individual Catholic who leaves the Church and enters some other faith is saved. It is up to God to do that. What we can do is pray very much for them that they may find the truth and live in accordance with it. We can also speak with them about their situation and give them good reading matter. Their salvation is certain if they return to the Catholic Church and persevere in the faith.

472 Is there any advantage in being a Catholic?

In view of the teaching that anyone, of any religion, can be saved, is there any advantage in being a Catholic? Wouldn't it be easier to be a Buddhist, a Hindu or a Protestant since our faith makes more demands on us than do other religions?

It is not a matter of finding a religion that makes few demands on its members. Such religions abound. It is a matter of finding a religion that comes from God himself and that teaches with divine authority the way to heaven. There is one such religion and it is the one Jesus himself gave us: the Catholic Church.

And yes, the Church does make demands on us, but at the same time it gives us all the help we need to live up to those demands. We are expected to attend Mass on Sundays and Holy Days, to observe certain days and seasons of penance, to love our neighbour as ourselves, to respect the life of the unborn child by not having an abortion, to be faithful to our spouse until death, etc. Of course this makes life harder for us. But it is the way, the truth and the life that leads to happiness here and hereafter.

What is more, the Church's teachings on issues like abortion, euthanasia and the permanence of the marriage bond are not something dreamed up by medieval popes or councils and then imposed on us forever after. They are teachings based on the natural law, on the very nature of the human person, and as such they are applicable to all, whether Catholic or not. Since they are so fundamental to human flourishing, they help us live as decent human beings who respect one another, and a society which lives them is all the better for it.

For this reason we are grateful to Jesus Christ for leaving us a Church which has the assistance of the Holy Spirit to teach us faithfully down the ages the way to happiness in this life and the next. It is true that other religions are not as clear and demanding in their teaching but this only makes it harder for their followers to live the kind of life that will lead to their true good.

What is more, the Church not only teaches us the way to happiness, it gives us in the sacraments the fulness of the means we need to live up to that teaching. Baptism gives us a share in God's own life, with the indwelling of the Blessed Trinity in the soul and the sanctifying grace to make us holy and pleasing to God. Confirmation confirms the grace of Baptism and strengthens us to live up to our commitments as Christians. The Eucharist, which we can receive everyday if we want, unites us fully to Christ and makes it easier to be Christlike in our behaviour. Penance forgives our sins and sends us on our way cleansed and strengthened to begin the spiritual struggle again. The Anointing of the Sick strengthens us when we are in danger of death. Matrimony gives us the grace to be faithful to our commitments in marriage, and Holy Orders gives us sacred ministers to administer the sacraments, say Mass and guide us on our way.

Where would we be without these helps? We should remember that all people in the world, whether Catholic or not, have to struggle to avoid sinning. No one is immune to temptation or sin. But how much easier it is to win out when we have clear teachings of the Church about right and wrong and we have the sacraments to strengthen us and cleanse us when we have fallen. All will be judged on how they lived the basic precepts of morality and it is so much easier when we have the helps the Church gives us.

What is more, attendance at Mass on Sundays is not a burden but a big help to live a good life. In Mass we are surrounded by our fellow Catholics, who pray with us and for us in our struggles. We hear the Word of God, which reminds us of the basic truths about God, life after death, and life here on earth. We have a homily, which suggests practical ways to put into practice what we have heard in the readings and helps us struggle for holiness. We pray together with the priest and the congregation, bringing us closer to God, whom we worship and thank for all his blessings. And above all we receive Communion, which makes us one with Christ.

In short, there is every advantage in being Catholic. Not for nothing do hundreds of thousands of people enter the Church at the Easter Vigil each year, many of them coming from faiths that make far fewer demands on their members. Thank God for the Church.

473 Why evangelisation?

One thing I have never completely understood is this: if all people, even non-Christians, can be saved, why all this emphasis on evangelisation? Shouldn't we just leave non-Catholics and non-Christians in peace since they can be saved without us?

It is interesting that you ask this question since it is one that was asked by many people after the Second Vatican Council. As we know, Christ sent the apostles out to all nations to baptise and teach the faith (cf. *Mt* 28:19-20). Since then, missionaries have gone all over the world to carry out that mandate, often risking and even losing their lives to do so. The missionary spirit has always characterised the Church. Indeed, many Australians are overseas living it out today.

When the Second Vatican Council taught in its Dogmatic Constitution on the Church *Lumen gentium* that "Those who, through no fault of their own, do not know the Gospel of Christ or his Church, but who nevertheless seek God with a sincere heart, and, moved by grace, try in their actions to do his will as they know it through the dictates of their conscience, those too may achieve eternal salvation" (*LG* 16), many began to question the whole purpose of missionary activity. Since all can be saved, even without knowing Christ and his Church, why go to all the trouble of preaching the Gospel to them?

The first thing to remember is that while in theory all can be saved, it is much easier to be saved in the Catholic Church. As I wrote in my last column, in the Church we have the fulness of the truth taught by Jesus Christ about God, man, life after death, morality, etc., and we have the fulness of the means of salvation and sanctification in the Mass and the sacraments.

To say that all can be saved is a little like saying that it is possible by many different ways to get across many kilometres of ocean to the shore. One can swim, but there is the danger of sharks, waves, tiredness or getting hit by a boat. One could also float on a log, but the same dangers would obtain. It would be easier and safer to paddle in a kayak or canoe but it is still not certain the person would arrive. The easiest way is in a large boat, and the Catholic Church is that boat. If we saw people trying to reach the shore by those other means we would do everything possible to invite them into the boat.

We should remember that everyone is looking for truth and happiness, not only in the next life but in this one. In the Church we have the fulness of truth and it is by living in accordance with it that we find the happiness we are seeking. We have found the way and we would like others to find it too.

Pope St John Paul II in 1990 addressed the reason for the Church's missionary activity in his Encyclical *Redemptoris missio*, The Mission of the Redeemer. There he wrote: *"Why mission?* Because to us, as to St Paul, 'this grace was given, to preach to the Gentiles the unsearchable riches of Christ' (*Eph* 3:8). Newness of life in him is the 'Good News' for men and women of every age: all are called to it and destined for it. Indeed, all people are searching for it, albeit at times in a confused way, and have a right to know the value of this gift and to approach it freely. The Church, and every individual Christian within her, may not keep hidden or monopolise this newness and richness which has been received from God's bounty in order to be communicated to all mankind" (n. 11).

Pope Francis too took up the call to mission in his Apostolic Exhortation *Evangelii gaudium* in 2013. He wrote that "evangelisation is first and foremost about preaching the Gospel to those who do not know Jesus Christ or who have always rejected him. Many of these are quietly seeking God, led by a yearning to see his face, even in countries of ancient Christian tradition. All of them have a right to receive the Gospel. Christians have the duty to proclaim the Gospel without excluding anyone" (n. 14).

So if we truly love our fellow man, including many in our own country who do not know Jesus Christ and the Church, we will show this love by doing everything we can to announce the faith to them. They are free to accept it or reject it, but at least they will have heard it.

474 Prophecies of Mariana de Jesus Torres

I understand that an Ecuadorian nun in the seventeenth century made some remarkable predictions about our own time. Can you tell me about them?

The nun in question is Venerable Mother Mariana de Jesus Torres, who was born in Spain and in 1577 went with five nuns of the Conceptionist order to establish a convent in Quito, Ecuador. From time to time she had revelations from Our Lord and Our Lady which are the source of the prophecies you mention. They are detailed in the eighteenth century manuscript *The Admirable Life of Mother Mariana of Jesus Torres*, written by the Franciscan Provincial in Quito who was the director of the Conceptionist convent. A commission of historians and theologians appointed by Cardinal Carlos Maria de la Torre, who died in 1968, found the manuscript "authentic, untampered with, and worthy of belief".

One of the most remarkable prophecies came on 8 December 1634, when Our Lady appeared to Mother Mariana and told her that the Pope's "pontifical infallibility will be declared a dogma of the faith by the same Pope chosen to proclaim the dogma of the mystery of my Immaculate Conception. He will be persecuted and imprisoned in the Vatican by the unjust usurpation of the Pontifical States through the iniquity, envy and avarice of an earthly monarch." All this came to pass two centuries later. Blessed Pope Pius IX declared the dogma of the Immaculate Conception on 8 December 1854, the First Vatican Council under his leadership declared the infallibility of the Pope in 1870, and the Italian state took over the Papal States in 1860, after which the Pope retired to the Vatican where he considered himself a prisoner.

Our Lady told Mother Mariana that at the end of the nineteenth century and especially in the twentieth, Satan would reign almost completely. Prophesying the savage attack on the sacrament of marriage and on Christian spirit in general, Our Lady said: "As for the sacrament of Matrimony, which symbolises the union of Christ with his Church, it will be attacked and profaned in the fullest sense of the word. Masonry, which will then be in power, will enact iniquitous laws with the objective of doing away with this sacrament, making it easy for everyone to live in sin, encouraging the procreation of illegitimate children born without the blessing of the Church. The Christian spirit will rapidly decay, extinguishing the precious light of faith until it reaches the point that there will be an almost total and general corruption of customs. The effects of secular education will increase, which will be one reason for the lack of priestly and religious vocations..."

As regards the priesthood, Our Lady said: "The sacred sacrament of Holy Orders will be ridiculed, oppressed and despised. ...The demon will try to persecute the ministers of the Lord in every possible way and he will labour with cruel and subtle astuteness to deviate them from the spirit of their vocation, corrupting many of them. These corrupted priests, who will scandalise the Christian people, will incite the hatred of the bad Christians and the enemies of the Roman, Catholic and Apostolic Church to fall upon all priests. This apparent triumph of Satan will bring enormous sufferings to the good pastors of the Church...."

Likewise the collapse of customs in the area of sexual morality was predicted: "Moreover, in these unhappy times, there will be unbridled impurity which, acting thus to snare the rest into sin, will conquer innumerable frivolous souls who will be lost. Innocence will almost no longer be found in children, nor modesty in women. In this supreme moment of need of the Church, those who should speak will fall silent."

Let us pray that through the grace of God and the powerful intercession of Our Lady we can turn around some of these lamentable situations in the twenty-first century.

Our Lady

475 Did Mary suffer pain in giving birth to Jesus?

I remember hearing once that Our Lady didn't suffer pain in giving birth to Jesus. Is this true and has the Church said anything about it?

The Church has indeed said something about it and it is solidly grounded in Scripture and tradition.

We can begin by going back to the book of *Genesis*, where after the original sin God said to Eve: "I will greatly multiply your pain in childbearing; in pain you shall bring forth children" (*Gen* 3:16). This would apply to Eve and seemingly to all women after her.

But there is a text in the prophecy of Isaiah that speaks of a woman giving birth without pain and which numerous Fathers of the Church have applied to Our Lady: "Listen, an uproar from the city! A voice from the temple! The voice of the Lord, rendering recompense to his enemies! Before she was in labour she gave birth; before her pain came upon her she was delivered of a son. Who has heard such a thing? Who has seen such things?" (*Is* 66:6-8) The text can obviously apply to Our Lady, who also gave birth to a son, and it is difficult to find anyone else to whom it applies.

Also, Luke tells us that Mary "gave birth to her first-born son and wrapped him in swaddling cloths, and laid him in a manger" (*Lk* 2:7). St Thomas Aquinas, who quotes St Jerome, sees in the fact that it was Our Lady who wrapped Jesus in swaddling cloths evidence that she suffered no pain in giving birth and so was able to do this by herself (cf. *STh* III, q. 35, art. 6). Normally a midwife would have performed this task but in Mary's case none was needed.

Among the earliest Christian writings to attest to Our Lady's giving birth without pain are the *Odes of Solomon*, Coptic Christian hymns dating to the end of the first century or beginning of the second. There we read: "The Virgin became a mother of great mercy; she laboured, but not in pain, and bore a son. No midwife came" (*Ode* 19).

At the end of the second century St Irenaeus applied two texts of Isaiah, including the one we have just mentioned, to Jesus' birth. "For behold, [the prophet Isaiah] says, the virgin shall conceive and bring forth a son: and he, being God, is to be with us (cf. *Is* 7:14) ... And yet, concerning his birth the prophet says in another place: Before the pains of travail came on, she escaped and was delivered of a man-child" (cf. *Is* 66:7; *Demonstration of the Apostolic Preaching*, 54).

St Gregory of Nyssa, around the year 380, wrote similarly of Our Lord's birth: "His conception did not result from the union of two humans; his birth was not polluted in any way: there were no labour pangs", and he went on to quote the text of Isaiah 66:7 (*On the Song of Songs*, 13).

Finally, we can cite St John Damascene, who wrote around the year 730: "His birth was in accordance with the laws of parturition, while in that it was painless it was above the laws of generation. For, as pleasure did not precede it, pain did not follow it, according to the prophet who says, 'Before she travailed, she brought forth, and again, before her pain came she was delivered of a man-child'" (*Is* 66:7; *An Exposition of the Orthodox Faith*, IV, 14).

Although there has never been a dogmatic definition of this truth, there are statements in the ordinary magisterium of the Church which proclaim it. For example, Pope Alexander III wrote a letter in 1169 explaining the basics of the Catholic faith in which he said: "[Mary] indeed conceived without shame, gave birth without pain, and went hence without corruption..." (*Ex Litteris Tuis*).

Later, the sixteenth century *Roman Catechism* issued after the Council of Trent taught: "To Eve it was said: *In sorrow shalt thou bring forth children.* Mary was exempt from this law, for preserving her virginal integrity inviolate she brought forth Jesus ... without experiencing, as we have already said, any sense of pain" (1, Art. III, 45-46).

This belief later passed into the celebration of the liturgy, where the Church is always very careful not to allow anything contrary to the faith. The Mass of "Mary at the Foot of the Cross II", celebrated in the Latin rite before the 1969 reform of the liturgy, says that Our Lady, "who had given him [Christ] birth without the pains of childbirth was to endure the greatest of pains in bringing forth to new life the family of your Church".

So the belief that Mary gave birth without pain in Bethlehem is solidly grounded indeed. At Christmas we can give thanks to God for allowing Our Lady to give birth in this way.

476 Is Mary's virginity important?

I was talking recently with a Catholic friend who said she didn't believe in Mary's virginity and that anyway it wasn't an important truth of our faith. Is it important?

Our Lady's virginity is one of the most fundamental teachings of our faith. Without it some of the most important pillars of our faith fall. It makes all the difference in the world whether Mary was a virgin or not. Why is it so important?

We can begin by recalling that after the original sin of our first parents, Adam and Eve were banished from the garden of paradise and angels were posted at the entrance with flaming swords to prevent anyone going back (cf. *Gen* 3:24). This was symbolic of the fact that as a result of their sin heaven was now closed and no one could enter until God in some way reconciled mankind with him.

We recall too that after the fall God promised to send one of the offspring of Eve, who would crush the head of the serpent, indicating that he would triumph over Satan and re-establish the damaged relationship of mankind with God. (cf. *Gen* 3:15). This was the promise of a redeemer. But how was God going to bring it about?

In the fullness of time God sent the angel Gabriel to announce to Mary that she was to give birth to a son, telling her that "you shall call his name Jesus" (*Lk* 1:31). Later an angel announced to Joseph in a dream that the child Mary was carrying should be called Jesus, "for he will save his people from their sins" (*Mt* 1:21). That is, this son of Mary would have the mission of making up for original sin and for all the personal sins of mankind. He was to be the promised redeemer, the saviour.

The angel also told Mary that her son "will be called the Son of the Most High; and the Lord God will give to him the throne of his father David, and he will reign over the house of Jacob for ever; and of his kingdom there will be no end" (*Lk* 1:32-33). It is clear from these words that the son of Mary would also be the Son of God, the "Son of the Most High". He would be God. After all, only God can forgive our sins. Only God can be our redeemer.

But how could Mary give birth to God if her child was the son of Joseph and herself? The child would be man, like any other child born of two parents, but he would not be God. This is why it is so important for Mary to be a virgin. Only if she conceived Jesus without the intervention of Joseph, through some sort of divine intervention, could her child be God and able to redeem us.

We know how God brought this about. When Our Lady asked the angel how she could conceive a son when she was a virgin, he answered: "The Holy Spirit will come upon you, and the power of the Most High will overshadow you; therefore the child to be born will be called holy, the Son of God" (*Lk* 1:35).

That is, God himself would be the Father of Jesus by sending the

Holy Spirit to bring about Jesus' conception in the womb of Mary. Thus Jesus was fully man as the son of Mary, who conceived him and bore him in her womb for nine months, and also fully God, since he had no human father and was conceived by the Holy Spirit.

In this way Mary fulfilled the prophecy of Isaiah, "Behold, a virgin shall conceive and bear a son, and shall call his name Immanuel" (*Is* 7:14). Mary was the virgin who conceived and her son was Immanuel, which means God with us (cf. *Mt* 1:23). In short, only if Mary was a virgin and conceived Jesus by the Holy Spirit and not by Joseph, would Jesus be both the Son of God and the Son of Man and hence able to redeem us. Naturally, as God he could have redeemed us without taking on our human nature, but by taking it on he redeemed our nature through his divinity.

The *Catechism of the Catholic Church* deals with this question in paragraphs 502-507 and says: "The eyes of faith can discover in the context of the whole of Revelation the mysterious reasons why God in his saving plan wanted his Son to be born of a virgin. These reasons touch both on the person of Christ and his redemptive mission, and on the welcome Mary gave that mission on behalf of all men" (*CCC* 502).

So yes, the virginity of Mary is important. Very important. Without it Jesus would not be God and we would not be redeemed.

477 Mary, Ark of the Covenant

Why do we call Our Lady the Ark of the Covenant in the litany of Loreto? I have always been intrigued by this title.

To answer your question we must go back to the Old Testament and remind ourselves what the original ark was. In so doing we will find many parallels between the ark and Our Lady.

After giving the Israelites the Ten Commandments on tablets of stone, God commanded Moses to make an ark of acacia wood in which to place them. It was to be overlayed with pure gold inside and out, with cherubs on top, "and in the ark you shall put the covenant that I shall give you. There I will meet with you..." (*Ex* 25:21-22). Also to be placed in the ark were Aaron's rod that had budded and a golden urn containing the manna (cf. *Heb* 9:4).

We see here many figures of Mary. She was all pure and holy, like the gold of the ark. Instead of the tablets of the old covenant, the "ten words" or Decalogue, she had in her womb Jesus himself, the one Word of God, the new covenant. Aaron's rod was the symbol of his priesthood and Jesus was the true high priest. The manna was the figure of the Eucharist, of Jesus the living bread come down from heaven. And Mary fulfils the words "There I will meet with you" since in her, God becomes present and meets with mankind. Mary is truly the ark of the new and eternal covenant.

Later the Old Testament ark was placed in the tent of meeting and "the cloud covered the tent of meeting, and the glory of the Lord filled the tabernacle" (*Ex* 40:34). The cloud, or glory cloud, is a symbol of God's presence, as the *Catechism of the Catholic Church* explains: "In the theophanies of the Old Testament, the cloud, now obscure, now luminous, reveals the living and saving God, while veiling the transcendence of his glory—with Moses on Mount Sinai, at the tent of meeting... The Spirit comes upon the Virgin Mary and 'overshadows' her, so that she might conceive and give birth to Jesus" (*CCC* 697). Thus the cloud that overshadowed the tent and the ark is a symbol of the "power of the Most High" which overshadowed Mary in the Annunciation (cf. *Lk* 1:35).

We see more parallels between the ark of the covenant and Mary in the visitation of Our Lady to Elizabeth. In the Old Testament, when the ark is brought to King David he exclaims: "How can the ark of the Lord come to me?" (*2 Sam* 6:9). These are the same words Elizabeth uses when Mary comes to her: "Why is this granted me, that the mother of my Lord should come to me? (*Lk* 1:43). The ark then remains in the house of O'bed-e'dom for three months, just as Mary remained with Elizabeth for three months. As a result, "The Lord blessed O'bed-e'dom and all his household" (*2 Sam* 6:11). Elizabeth uses the word "Blessed" three times, referring to Mary and Jesus in her womb. So too, the ark was carried to Jerusalem "with rejoicing", with David "leaping and dancing before the Lord" (*2 Sam* 6:12, 16). When Mary brought Jesus in her womb to Elizabeth, Elizabeth exclaims that "the child in my womb leaped for joy" (*Lk* 1:44).

Although the ark had been lost in Old Testament times, it reappears in the book of Revelation: "Then God's temple in heaven was opened, and the ark of his covenant was seen within his temple… And a great sign appeared in heaven, a woman clothed with the sun… she was with child…" (*Rev* 11:19-12:2). The ark here is clearly Mary, the woman about to give birth.

So the idea that Mary is the Ark of the Covenant has deep scriptural roots and early Fathers of the Church recognised it. In the third century Gregory the Wonder Worker wrote: "Let us chant the melody that has been taught us by the inspired harp of David, and say, 'Arise, O Lord, into your rest; you, and the ark of your sanctuary.' For the Holy Virgin is in truth an ark, wrought with gold both within and without, that has received the whole treasury of the sanctuary" (*Homily on the Annunciation to the Holy Virgin Mary*).

A century later St Athanasius wrote: "O noble Virgin, truly you are greater than any other greatness. For who is your equal in greatness, O dwelling place of God the Word? To whom among all creatures shall I compare you, O Virgin? You are greater than them all, O Covenant, clothed with purity instead of gold! You are the ark in which is found the golden vessel containing the true manna, that is, the flesh in which divinity resides" (*Homily of the Papyrus of Turin*).

What a beautiful title for Mary: Ark of the Covenant!

The Last Things

478 The Christian meaning of death

I was talking recently with a group of friends at work about a funeral I had just attended and one of my colleagues said she didn't want to talk about death because it makes her sad. What can I tell her to show the beauty of our Catholic understanding of death?

I suspect there are quite a few people who don't want to think about death, let alone talk about it. Why is this? For most it is probably that they focus on the suffering that may accompany dying and then on death as the end, without raising their thoughts to what lies beyond.

How can we help them? To begin with, we should remember that death is a "fact of life" for everyone, absolutely everyone. It is a consequence of original sin and it will come sooner or later to everyone, whether they believe in life after death and in God or not. Not thinking about death is not going to delay or take away its inevitability. In view of that, it makes no sense to avoid considering it and it makes every sense to prepare for it.

For us Christians death and what follows it have a very positive meaning. Death is not the end of our existence, but only the gateway to eternal life with God. Even Jesus died, to redeem us, and in dying, so to speak, he redeemed death itself. He rose again on the third day and our soul will rise again to eternal life – or of course to eternal damnation if we do not repent of our serious sins before we die. As the *Catechism of the Catholic Church* puts it, "For those who die in Christ's grace it is a participation in the death of the Lord, so that they can also share his Resurrection" (*CCC* 1006).

We should never forget this. After death we can rise up to the indescribable happiness of heaven. "Life is changed, not ended", we say in the first Preface in Masses for the faithful departed. But not only is it changed, it is changed for the better, for the very much better. The Catechism expresses it like this: "Because of Christ, Christian death has a positive meaning: 'For to me to live is Christ, and to die is gain" (*Phil* 1:21). 'The saying is sure: if we have died with him, we will also live with him' (*2 Tim* 2:11)" (*CCC* 1010).

In the same passage in which St Paul says "to die is gain" he goes on to say: "My desire is to depart and be with Christ, for that is far better" (*Phil* 1:23). So too the psalmist speaks of his desire to be with God: "As a deer longs for flowing streams, so longs my soul for you, O God. My soul thirsts for God, for the living God. When shall I come and behold the face of God?" (*Ps* 42:1-2)

This desire for God directs our attention beyond death to what lies ahead for the soul. It does not focus on death but on what comes after it. It takes death for granted and looks forward to the eternal life that follows it. This is how we too should look upon death: not as some sad and unfortunate end, but as the gateway to eternal happiness.

St Cyprian describes death in a beautiful way: "What an honour, what happiness to depart joyfully from this world, to go forth in glory from the anguish and pain, in one moment to close the eyes that looked on the world of men and in the next to open them at once to look on God and Christ! You are suddenly withdrawn from earth to find yourself in the kingdom of heaven" (*Tract. ad Fortunatum*, ch. 13).

And St Ignatius of Antioch, on his way to Rome to be martyred, wrote to the Church in that city: "All the ends of the earth, all the kingdoms of the world would be of no profit to me; so far as I am concerned, to die in Jesus Christ is better than to be monarch of earth's widest bounds. He who died for us is all that I seek; he who rose again for us is my whole desire… Here and now, as I write in the fullness of life, I am yearning for death with all the passion of a lover. Earthly longings have been crucified; in me there is left no spark of desire for mundane things, but only a murmur of living water that whispers within me, 'Come to the Father' (*Lett. to Romans,* 6, 1-9; 3).

Likewise, St Teresa of Avila writes: "I want to see God and, in order to see him, I must die" (*Life*, ch. 1). And St Thérèse of Lisieux: "I am not dying; I am entering life" (*The Last Conversations*).

What could be more positive and encouraging than this? We are truly blessed to be able to look on death in such a hope-filled way.

479 Evidence of life after death

A colleague of work has recently been diagnosed with terminal cancer and we were discussing what happens after death. One friend says that after death there is nothing, that life is finished. How do I convince him that there is indeed life after death?

Unfortunately there are many people who think like your colleague – that with death all is ended and there is nothing afterwards. They sometimes say that no one has ever come back from the dead to tell us about it, and this confirms them in their belief. How do we answer them? It is not enough to say that Jesus spoke about eternal life, or that we believe in it. They want hard evidence, even if, as Jesus said, "neither will they be convinced if some one should rise from the dead" (*Lk* 16:31). We will consider here three different arguments and in my next column I will consider two more.

The first is the fact that people have in fact come back from the dead and appeared on earth, among them Our Lady. Her apparitions at Fatima to three small children aged 10, 9 and 7 each month from May through October 1917 are perhaps the most convincing because Our Lady made a prophecy there that came true several months later. In the July apparition she told the children that in October she would work a miracle that all would see. On October 13 some 70,000 people trudged through the rain and mud in the hope of seeing the miracle. Although it had been raining steadily, suddenly the clouds parted and the sun appeared. It began to revolve, sending out rays of light of different colours that lit up the surroundings and then it seemed to fall from the sky towards the people, who fell on their knees and begged God for mercy. To their great relief the sun returned to its place. All those present and some in the surrounding villages saw the miracle. Even sceptics reported seeing it and anti-clerical newspapers in Lisbon wrote articles on it. The fulfilment of the prophecy in such a dramatic way can only be explained if Mary did in fact come back to earth to prophesy the miracle and then bring it about. Naturally, it is God himself who worked the miracle.

A second argument for life after death comes from the many cases of near-death experiences in which people died clinically while their spirit or soul left the body and went into another world where they encountered other people. A particularly well known and convincing case is that of a three year-old boy named Colton Burpo from Nebraska, U.S.A., popularised in the book and later the film *Heaven is for Real.* While undergoing surgery in 2003, Colton appeared to have died but meanwhile his soul went to heaven and he was later able to describe events he could not possibly have known about in life. He spoke of meeting his unborn sister, who had been miscarried by his mother and who told him her name, and also his great-grandfather, who had died thirty years before Colton was born. This could not be attributed to his imagination, since he did not know he had an unborn sister and the description he gave of his great-grandfather, whom he had never known, was accurate and could only come from having seen him in the next life.

The third argument comes from the very nature of the human person, composed of a material body and a spiritual soul. Our soul is clearly spiritual because through it we can think and we can know immaterial objects and ideas like God, love, honesty, etc., and we can love, desire and freely choose to do this or that. Through it we make progress, from making tools and planting crops to building skyscrapers, airplanes and computers. Animals have no spiritual soul and cannot do these things.

The soul is clearly distinct from the body even though it is intimately united to it as long as we live. When we die the body decays but the soul, being spiritual, cannot decay or be destroyed. It lives on necessarily. While by reason alone we cannot know what happens to the soul after we die, we can know that it must necessarily continue in existence. The well documented near-death experiences of thousands of people confirm the independent existence of the soul. Through revelation we know what does happen to the soul after death: it goes to heaven or hell, or to purgatory as the antechamber of heaven.

So as Christians we live in the hope of eternal life and when someone is dying we console them with this hope, helping them to prepare for eternity with God. The thought of death does not frighten us. Rather it fills us with the desire to be with God and to enjoy the "supreme, definitive happiness" which is heaven, as the *Catechism of the Catholic Church* explains (*CCC* 1024).

480 More evidence of life after death

You said in a recent column that you were going to offer more evidence for life after death, besides Our Lady's fulfilled prophecy at Fatima, near-death experiences in which someone met people in the next life, and the fact that the soul, being spiritual, must necessarily live on when the body dies. What are these other types of evidence?

They are documented cases of people from purgatory and hell – yes hell! – appearing on earth in ways that can only be explained if these people were really in a state of life after death.

Let us begin with apparitions of souls in purgatory. Even though there are books and books relating them, I will use a recent one, *Hungry Souls* (TAN Books, Charlotte, North Carolina, 2012) by Dutch psychotherapist Gerard van den Aardweg. The author visited the church of the Sacred Heart of Suffrage near the Vatican in Rome, where there are exhibits of ten artifacts related to appearances of souls in purgatory, all of them involving burn marks.

In one there is a clearly visible burn mark of the right hand of a Benedictine choir sister named Clara Schoelers, who had died of the plague in 1637 and appeared to Maria Herendorps, a lay sister in the Benedictine monastery of Vinenberg, near Warendorf, Germany, on 13 October 1696. The burn mark of the hand is on Herendorps' apron and there are imprints of both hands on a piece of linen. Schoelers had been in purgatory for 59 years.

Another burn mark left by a soul in purgatory is in the shrine of the Black Madonna in Czestochowa, Poland. Kept there since the nineteenth century is a corporal, the square linen cloth over which the Body and Blood are consecrated in Mass, with the mark of a hand burned through several layers of the folded cloth. It seems that two priests of the Pauline Fathers, who look after the shrine, had promised each other that the one who died first would give the other some sign of life after death. One of them had been dead for a long time without sending any sign and the other was thinking this very thought at the end of Mass one day as he was folding the corporal into the customary nine layers. Doubt came over him as to whether there really was life after death when suddenly a burning hand appeared and scorched the corporal, leaving burn marks on many layers of the cloth. The hand then disappeared.

There is no way to explain the burn marks of a human hand produced in such a remarkable way except by acknowledging that the person whose hand it was had come from life beyond the grave. And of course that the person was somehow on fire. In virtually all such apparitions the person lets it be known that he or she is in purgatory. These accounts are attested to by reliable witnesses and are authenticated by Church authorities only after careful examination.

Apparitions from souls in hell are far less common but they too exist. Van den Aardweg relates two such apparitions taken from the book *Hell* written by Mgr Louis-Gaston de Ségur of Saint-Denis (Paris) in 1876. The first one involved someone from Mgr de Ségur's own family and it took place in Moscow a short time before the bitter campaign of 1812. Mgr de Ségur's maternal grandfather, Count Rostopchine, Military Governor of Moscow, was a close friend of General Count Orloff, a convinced atheist. One day, after a big meal and many drinks, Count Orloff and one of his friends, General V., also an atheist, began ridiculing religion and especially hell. When Count Orloff suggested the possibility of life after death, General V. proposed that whichever of them died first would come back and give word of it to the other. This was readily accepted by Orloff.

Some weeks later General V. was sent to the front to do battle with Napoleon's army. He had been gone two or three weeks when suddenly early one morning Count Orloff burst into Count Rostopchine's room in his dressing gown visibly disturbed. He explained that a half hour before he was lying in bed when suddenly the curtains of the bed parted and General V. appeared in front of him, standing upright and pale with his hand on his chest. He said: "There is a hell and I am there!" Then he disappeared. Ten or twelve days later word came to Count Rostopchine that General V had been killed by a bullet through the chest. It was at the very hour General V. appeared to Count Orloff.

Is there life after death? One would be very foolish not to believe it. Very foolish indeed.

481 Near-death experiences

We often read of people who have seemingly died and then come back to life, who relate what they saw before they recovered. Can we take these accounts as credible evidence of life after death?

Near-death experiences are very personal and can be considered something akin to private revelations in the sense that they need not be believed by others, and they should be judged carefully on the merits of each one. Some are clearly more credible than others. Some are clearly not consistent with what the Church teaches on life after death while others present no problems.

Since even canonised saints have had visions of heaven, hell and purgatory, and some have had near-death experiences, we certainly cannot reject them out of hand. One example is that of St Josemaría Escrivá. On 27 April 1954, having suffered from a severe case of diabetes for ten years, he suddenly collapsed and appeared to have died. After ten minutes he regained consciousness and was thereafter completely cured of the diabetes, something which is medically inexplicable. While he lay there he saw his whole life pass by very quickly, as if in a film, and he was able to ask God to forgive his failings.

There are literally thousands of people who have reported similar experiences, and there are dozens of books currently available which record them. Two of the most well-known are those of Dr Eben Alexander and Dr Gloria Polo.

Dr Alexander, a neurosurgeon who has taught at various universities including Harvard Medical School, is the author of the best-selling *Proof of Heaven: A Neurosurgeon's Journey into the Afterlife*, published in 2012. In it he relates how in 2008, while in an induced coma after suffering meningitis, he was taken into a state where he experienced what we would call heaven and he encountered God. Before that experience he could not reconcile his knowledge of neuroscience with belief in God, heaven or even the soul as something different from the brain. His experience completely transformed him, and today he believes that true health can only be achieved when we acknowledge that God and the soul are real and that death is not the end of our existence but only the passage into a different form of life.

Dr Gloria Polo is a Colombian orthodontist whose life was transformed radically when she was struck by lightning in May 1995 while walking on the campus of the National University of Bogotá with her 23-year old nephew, who was killed instantly. She went into cardiac arrest and her body was badly burned, both inside and out. Although she had been attending Sunday Mass, she had not been to confession since she was thirteen, she was using an intrauterine device for contraception, she had had an abortion and had paid for others to have them, and she lived a very materialistic, self-centered and ungodly life. What is more, she had told others that devils do not exist and even that God did not exist.

While her body lay on the operating table, she began to see devils coming after her and she found herself falling down a tunnel into hell, with people young and old screaming in pain and grinding their teeth. She saw that the sins that condemned her most included aiding and participating in abortion, receiving holy communion in a state of mortal sin, fortune-telling, and speaking evil of priests.

In that state, she also saw the great suffering of the souls in purgatory. Then she passed through a beautiful tunnel of light to a place of great joy and peace where she was able to embrace her deceased relatives. She also experienced her own judgment, seeing her whole life played out as in a movie with all her actions, good and bad, and the consequences of them. She understood how God regards sexual immorality, abortion and methods of contraception that cause abortions, as well as how he looked on her materialism, her excessive concern for what she wore and how she looked, and her lack of faith.

She was given a second chance in order to amend her ways and to tell others what she had experienced. She has written her account in the book *Struck by Lightning: Death, Judgement and Conversion*. While we are not required by the Church to believe accounts such as these, common sense tells us that we would be very foolish to ignore them.

482 Life after death and Pascal's wager

I remember hearing once about an argument for living as if there were life after death called Pascal's wager. Can you enlighten me as to exactly what this argument is, as I have a friend who doesn't believe in life after death?

The argument, as you say, is called Pascal's wager and it comes from Blaise Pascal (1623-1662), the famous French mathematician, physicist, inventor and philosopher. The wager comes in his posthumously published *Pensées*, or *Thoughts*, in Part III, Section 233. It is intended to show that it is better to wager that there is a God and therefore life after death, and to live one's life in accordance with that belief, than to bet that there is no God and no life after death. A summary of the wager goes like this.

Either there is a God or there is not. Pascal says that reason cannot decide between the two. That is, we cannot know by reason alone whether there is a God. It should be said, contrary to this statement of Pascal, that human reason can show that there is a God, starting with arguments presented by Aristotle and St Thomas Aquinas and, more recently, with arguments from the cosmos. But for those who are not certain, Pascal's argument continues.

We can consider human life then like a game, in which at the end there is a God and life after death or there is not. It is like tossing a coin, which will come up heads or tails. Heads means there is a God and you live happily with him for ever in indescribable bliss. Tails means there is no God and your life comes to an end. You must wager; you must decide how you are going to live. It is not optional.

In fact, we could add, people do wager. Many believe in God and try to live in accordance with his commandments, telling him they are sorry when they fail and starting over. Others, relatively few, bet there is no God and don't worry about God's laws, although they try not to get caught by the laws of men. Some of these, nonetheless, "hedge their bets" and endeavour to live a decent life "just in case".

Let us first consider the consequences if we bet that there is a God and life after death. If we win and there is a God, we gain everything. We bet the finite life we live on earth and we gain the infinite, union with God in heaven for all eternity. If we lose and there is no God, we lose nothing. We simply cease to exist after living a good life here on earth. So betting on God offers the chance to gain everything and lose nothing.

Alternatively, we can bet there is no God and live our life accordingly: in self-indulgence, dishonesty, pride, laziness, etc. If we win and there is no God we gain nothing, we simply cease to exist. But if we lose and there is a God, we miss out on the infinite reward of eternal life with him in heaven. We lose everything. And of course, although Pascal doesn't say it, this implies suffering for all eternity in hell.

It is clear from this argument that it would be foolish indeed to bet that there is no God. There is nothing to gain and everything to lose, whereas betting that there is a God promises everything to gain and nothing to lose.

But there is more to it than what awaits us after death. Pascal does not mention this but it is important to consider that those who live a good life here on earth find great happiness already in this life. They will fail often, as we all do, but the very effort to be kind, generous, honest, hard working, loyal, brings its own reward. The psalm says it all: "Blessed are those whose ways are blameless, who walk in the law of the Lord" (*Ps 119:1*).

Conversely, those who disregard God's law and the good of others may make a lot of money and have many possessions but they do not have the peace of mind, the joy of life that the others do. As C.S.

Lewis says in his book *The Great Divorce,* which is an allegory on heaven and hell, those who go to heaven begin their heaven on earth and those who go to hell begin their hell on earth.

So independently of what awaits us in the next life, already in this life we reap the rewards of betting that there is a God and life after death and living accordingly. And if we bet that there is no God we suffer in this life as well as in the next.

It is clear which is the better wager.

483 Is hell real?

How do I help someone who knows what the Church teaches on hell but who doubts whether there really is such a place?

When someone is sceptical about an aspect of the faith for which there is no immediate evidence it is often difficult to convince them, no matter what arguments or "proofs" we use. We recall Our Lord's parable of the rich man and Lazarus, in which the rich man, now in hell, begs Abraham to send Lazarus to his father's house to speak with his five brothers, lest they go to hell too. Abraham answers: "'They have Moses and the prophets; let them hear them.' And he said, 'No, father Abraham; but if someone goes to them from the dead, they will repent.' He said to him, 'If they do not hear Moses and the prophets, neither will they be convinced if some one should rise from the dead'" (*Lk* 16:19-31). So we cannot expect the sceptics to believe in hell even if we tell them of people who have seen hell. In fact there are such people.

We can begin with Gloria Polo, about whom I wrote in this column some time ago. A Colombian dentist, Gloria was struck by lightning in 1995 and suffered a cardiac arrest. While apparently dead she was shown her judgment in which she was condemned to hell and was taken there to see it. I have also written about Sr Josefa Menendez, a

Spanish nun who died in 1923. She was taken to hell numerous times and describes in her book *The Way of Divine Love* the excruciating pain she suffered and the cries of hatred and despair of the damned souls she saw there. Likewise, the three children at Fatima saw a vision of hell, which they described as a sea of fire with demons and lost souls shrieking and groaning with sorrow and despair.

Dutch psychologist Gerard van den Aardweg relates two vivid accounts of apparitions from hell in his book *Hungry Souls*. They are taken from the little book *Hell* written by Bishop de Ségur of Saint-Denis, Paris, in 1876. Bishop de Ségur's grandfather Count Rostopchine was a close friend of Russian General Count Orloff, a protagonist in the first story, giving it great credibility.

Shortly before 1812, General Orloff and General V. were ridiculing religion, especially hell, at a dinner and they agreed that, if by chance there was life after death, whichever of them died first would come back to tell the other about it. Some weeks later General V. was sent to the front to take up an important command in the war then raging. Early one morning several weeks after that Count Orloff suddenly burst into the room of Count Rostopchine looking pale and greatly disturbed. He explained that he had been lying in bed when suddenly General V. appeared in the room, standing upright and pale with his right hand on his chest and saying, "There is a hell and I am there!" Then he disappeared. Ten or twelve days later an army messenger brought the news that General V. had been shot in the chest and killed at the very hour he appeared to Count Orloff.

When Bishop de Ségur told this story to the Superior of a religious community in 1859, the latter related another story told to him by a relative of the woman protagonist, who was then still alive. This woman, at the time a widow of about twenty-nine years of age, was in London in the winter of 1847 to 1848. She was very worldly, wealthy and attractive, and was sinning with a young man. One night around one in the morning, as she was falling asleep, a glimmer of light appeared at the door of her room and gradually became brighter and larger. Then she saw the door open slowly. It was the young man, who entered and came over to her. He took her by the left wrist and said, "There is a hell." The pain in her wrist was so great that she passed out.

A half hour later she came to and called for her chambermaid, who noticed the smell of burning when she entered the room. She looked at the woman's wrist and saw a burn the size of a man's hand so deep that the bone was laid bare. What is more, the carpet was burned with the imprint of a man's steps from the door to the bed and back again. The next day the woman learned that the man had died at the same time he appeared to her. After that the woman wore a broad gold bracelet to cover the burn mark.

So there is a hell. We can pray for all those we know who are living far from God so that they repent and do not go there. Perhaps our prayers will save them.

484 Is there anyone in hell?

I recently read that some theologians have argued that we can hope no one is in hell and that all will be saved. Is this a reasonable position to hold?

We can start with Jesus' own teaching. We know he spoke numerous times about the existence of hell, warning his listeners to be on guard. For example, in his description of the Last Judgment he speaks of the Son of man coming in his glory for the final judgment and saying to those on his left hand: "Depart from me, you cursed, into the eternal fire prepared for the devil and his angels; for I was hungry and you gave me no food, I was thirsty and you gave me no drink... And they will go away into eternal punishment, but the righteous into eternal life" (*Mt* 25:31-46).

He also spoke about how difficult it is to be saved and how easy to be damned: "Enter by the narrow gate; for the gate is wide and the way is easy, that leads to destruction, and those who enter by it are many. For the gate is narrow and the way is hard, that leads to life, and those who find it are few" (*Mt* 7:13-14). His listeners clearly understood that it is not easy to be saved, to a point where someone once asked him: "Lord, will those who are saved be few?" He answered, "Strive to enter by the narrow door..." (*Lk* 13:23-24)

From the very fact of Jesus' repeated teaching we can be certain that there is a hell. Jesus, who is full of mercy and wants all to be saved (cf. *1 Tim* 2:4) would not warn people about a state after death that did not exist, or to which no one was going to go. Precisely because he loves us so much and wants all to be with him, he warned us about the real possibility of hell so that we would live good lives and not go there.

Common sense and experience confirm the real possibility of going to hell. Given the effects of original sin such as pride, self-centredness, laziness, self-indulgence, etc., we know well that unless we struggle to resist temptations and to do good, it is very easy to lapse into a way of life that is grievously sinful and offensive to God. We know people who have wandered off the path and now lead lives of grave sin, saying they don't believe in God or life after death and consequently do not pray. It is true that anyone can repent on their deathbed, but we cannot be sure such people will do it. Hell is thus a very real possibility for many.

As if this weren't enough, the Church has always taught the existence of hell. In 1547 the Council of Trent, in its Decree on Justification, solemnly taught that some are damned: "Although it is true that 'He died for all' (*2 Cor* 5:15), not all, however, receive the benefit of his death, but only those to whom the merit of his Passion is communicated" (*Dz* 795). And in 1549, Pope Pius II condemned the proposition that "all Christians must be saved" (*Dz* 717b).

More recently the *Catechism of the Catholic Church* states: "The teaching of the Church affirms the existence of hell and its eternity" (*CCC* 1035). What is more, the numerous people down the ages – St Teresa of Avila, Sr Josefa Menendez, the three children of Fatima – who have had visions of hell, all speak of the horrible shrieks and groans of the people who are there along with the devils.

Who, then, holds the view that God's mercy is so great that we can reasonably hope that all are saved? In the early Church a few writers, among them Origen, St Gregory of Nyssa and St Maximus the Confessor, held some form of belief that in the end all will be saved. The idea was revived in the twentieth century especially by theologians Karl Rahner and Hans Urs von Balthasar. Rahner held that all people are "anonymous Christians" and so can go to heaven. Von Balthasar, in his book *Dare We Hope That All Men Be Saved?*, bases himself mainly on the Church's liturgy to argue that indeed we may hope that all are saved. Even so reputable a figure as Bishop Robert Barron says in his book *Catholicism* that "we may, as Hans Urs von Balthasar insisted, *reasonably* hope that all will find salvation..." (p. 258).

On the other hand, Ralph Martin, a consultor to the Pontifical Council for the New Evangelisation, in his book *Will Many be Saved?*, argues strongly against the idea of universal salvation, as do Fathers Jean Galot, Michael Hull, Regis Scanlon and James T. O'Connor.

In summary, especially in view of the Church's official teaching, it would seem that the hope that there is no one in hell is unacceptable. As for me, while I too hope and pray that all will be saved, I firmly believe that, in spite of God's infinite mercy and because of his respect for our freedom, there are many people who will not be saved. Perhaps very many. And so I will continue to believe, and to teach others, that there is a hell but that, if we strive to love God with our whole heart and to do his will, repenting of our sins, praying and receiving the sacraments, there is very little likelihood that we will go there.

485 Ancient views on hell

Some time ago you mentioned that there are contemporary writers who argue that we can hope that no one goes to hell, arguments that quite frankly don't satisfy me. Did the Fathers of the Church and other early writers have anything to say about this?

Cardinal Avery Dulles, in an excellent article entitled "The Population of Hell" in the May 2003 issue of *First Things*, examined the question at length, speaking not only about early writers but also about contemporary ones. In this column I will write about the early views and in the next about contemporary ones.

Beginning with the Scriptures, Jesus spoke often about hell, using expressions like "everlasting fire", "outer darkness" and "weeping and gnashing of teeth". Such was the strength of his teaching that someone once asked him if those to be saved would be only few. He replied, "Strive to enter by the narrow door; for many, I tell you, will seek to enter and not be able (*Lk* 13:23-24). On another occasion he said, "Many are called, but few are chosen" (*Mt* 22:14).

Other texts of the New Testament too speak clearly of the reality of hell. St Peter writes: "If the righteous man is scarcely to be saved, where will the impious and sinner appear?" (*1 Pet* 4:18). And the book of *Revelation* teaches that there is a fiery pit where Satan and those who follow him will be tormented forever: "As for the cowardly, the faithless, the polluted, as for murderers, fornicators, sorcerers, idolaters, and all liars, their lot shall be the lake that burns with fire and brimstone, which is the second death" (*Rev* 21:8).

As regards particular individuals who may be in hell, Cardinal Dulles argues that Jesus' words suggest strongly that the apostle Judas must have been damned. Jesus says that he has kept all those whom the Father has given him except the son of perdition (cf. *Jn* 17:12), and he even calls Judas a devil (cf. *Jn* 6:70). On another occasion he says of him: "It would be better for that man if he had never been born" (*Mt* 26:24; *Mk* 14:21). If Judas were among the saved, Dulles argues, these statements could hardly be true. Many saints and Doctors of the Church, among them St Augustine and St Thomas Aquinas, regard it as a revealed truth that Judas went to hell.

What is more, the constant teaching of the Church supports the idea that there are two classes of people after death: the saved and the damned. The Ecumenical Councils of Lyons I (1245), Lyons II (1274) and Florence (1439) all teach this, as do the Bull *Benedictus Deus* of Pope Benedict XII (1336) and the *Catechism of the Catholic Church* (cf. *CCC* 1022 and 1035).

The Church has never defined the question of the relative numbers of those saved and damned. The majority of the eastern Fathers, among them Saints Irenaeus, Basil and Cyril of Jerusalem, taught that the majority were damned. St John Chrysostom went so far as to say: "Among thousands of people there are not a hundred who will arrive at their salvation, and I am not even certain of that number, so much perversity is there among the young and so much negligence among the old."

St Augustine, who may be taken as representative of the western Fathers, argues too that more are lost than saved. In Book 21 of his *City of God* he denies first that all human beings are saved, then that all the baptised are saved, then that all baptised Catholics are saved, and finally that all baptised Catholics who persevere in the faith are saved. He seems to limit salvation to baptised believers who refrain from serious sin or who, after sinning, repent and are reconciled with God.

At the same time a few eastern writers, among them St Clement of Alexandria, St Gregory Nazianzen, St Gregory of Nyssa and Origen sometimes speak as though in the end all are saved. Nonetheless, Origen's views on this question were condemned in a local Council in Constantinople convened by the Emperor Justinian in the year 563.

The great Scholastics of the Middle Ages, among them St Thomas Aquinas, are of the view that relatively few are saved, as are the theologians of the later centuries, among them Francisco Suarez, St Peter Canisius and St Robert Bellarmine in the sixteenth century. So it is clear that the consensus of early writers is that not all are saved, and even that more are lost than saved.

486 Contemporary views on hell

Apart from ancient and medieval writers, are there any people at the present time who have addressed the question of whether we can hope that no one is in hell?

As I mentioned in my last column, Cardinal Avery Dulles, in his excellent article "The Population of Hell" in the May 2003 issue of *First Things*, spoke not only about early writers but also about contemporary ones. As we recall from that column, the majority of writers up to the sixteenth century taught that not only are all not saved but even that more people go to hell than to heaven. There were a few, however, who did believe that everyone might be saved.

It is in the middle of the twentieth century that the view that possibly no one is in hell once again appears. Among its principal exponents is the Jesuit Karl Rahner. He says that Jesus' words on hell appear to be rather warnings than predictions. While allowing for the real possibility of eternal damnation, Rahner says that we must at the same time maintain "the truth of the omnipotence of the universal salvific will of God, the redemption of all by Christ, the duty of men to hope for salvation." Rahner therefore believes that universal salvation is a possibility.

Another proponent of that possibility is the theologian Hans Urs von Balthasar. In his book *Dare We Hope That All Men Be Saved?* he says that we have a right and even a duty to *hope* for the salvation of all, because it is not impossible that even the worst sinners may be moved by God's grace to repent before they die. At the same time he concedes that since we are able to reject God's grace we cannot be sure of salvation and we should think of the danger in which we stand. Although Cardinal Dulles regards von Balthasar's position as at least not contrary to Catholic teaching, he mentions that a number of theologians have been very critical of it. Among them are Fathers Jean Galot, Michael Hull and Regis Scanlon.

Interestingly, von Balthasar quotes a passage from Edith Stein, St Teresa Benedicta of the Cross. She says that since God's all-merciful love descends upon everyone, it is probable that this love produces transforming effects in their lives. To the extent that people open themselves to that love, they enter into the realm of redemption. On this ground St Teresa Benedicta finds it possible to hope that God's omnipotent love finds ways, so to speak, of outwitting human resistance.

Pope St John Paul II in his book *Crossing the Threshold of Hope* mentions the theory of von Balthasar. After posing the question of whether a loving God can allow any human being to be condemned to eternal torment, the Pope replies: "And yet the words of Christ are unequivocal. In Matthew's Gospel he speaks clearly of those who will go to eternal punishment (cf. *Mt* 25:46)." As justification for this assessment the Pope asks whether God, who is ultimate justice, can tolerate terrible crimes and let them go unpunished. Final punishment, he says, would seem to be necessary to reestablish the moral equilibrium in the complex history of humanity. Indeed, in view of the terrible atrocities committed at the time of the Second World War and since then, these words of Pope John Paul make much sense.

Although not cited by Cardinal Dulles, Cardinal Joseph Ratzinger, before becoming Pope, explained why God's fatherhood allows some to go to hell: "God never, in any case, forces anyone to be saved. God accepts man's freedom. He is no magician, who will in the end wipe out everything that has happened and wheel out his happy ending. He is a true father; a creator who assents to freedom, even when it is used to reject him. That is why God's all-embracing desire to save people does not involve the actual salvation of all men. He allows us the power to refuse. God loves us; we need only to summon up the humility to allow ourselves to be loved" (*God is Near Us,* Ignatius 2003, pp. 36-37).

In summary, down the ages there have been different views on the question of whether there is anyone in hell. The majority, from the Fathers of the Church to the present, have taught that in view of human freedom there will be some, perhaps many, who are not saved. And even those who argue for universal salvation tend to be cautious and limit themselves to holding out only hope that all are saved. As for us, if we struggle to do God's will and repent when we fall, we need have no fear of hell and rather we can look forward to eternal life in heaven.

487 Sr Josefa Menendez and hell

A friend recently lent me a book by a Spanish nun named Sr Josefa Menendez, who had special revelations from God, including seeing the devil and visiting hell. I am finding the book very inspirational and would like to know whether Sr Josefa's writings have been approved by the Church.

Sr Josefa and her writings have been approved by the Church and, what is more, her cause of beatification has been opened. I will say something about her life here and about her messages later

Sister Josefa was born in Madrid on 4 February 1890. She felt called by God to the religious life and, after many trials, in 1920 she entered the French convent of Les Feuillants in Poitiers as a Coadjutrix Sister of the Society of the Sacred Heart at the age of 29. She died there less than four years later.

Sr Josefa carried out her tasks in the convent with great grace and humility. When over the course of the next four years she received many revelations from God, she retired all the more into a deep sense of littleness and unworthiness. Her superiors had rarely seen anyone more obedient and docile, ever ready to submit to their authority and to sacrifice herself.

Sr Josefa was mentally sound and strong, very simple in her life of piety. The special graces and gifts she received from God, whose weight was often crushing, purified her. Some of the extraordinary visions and revelations shook her to the core and at times required an almost superhuman endurance, convincing her superiors that they were truly from God.

Among her trials were temptations from the devil to doubt God's voice and her own religious vocation, but she remained strong and resisted the temptations. At times the devil tried to deceive her by appearing as Our Lord or Our Lady and, when that failed, he attacked her with grievous bodily pains. These included beating her with an invisible fist, especially during her prayer, and violently dragging her away from the chapel or preventing her from entering it. Even in the presence of other nuns her clothes were set on fire and she suffered burns that took a long time to heal. At times the devil appeared to her in the form of a savage dog, a snake, or a human being.

Among her other sufferings were being taken to hell numerous times, where she spent long hours in unspeakable agony, suffering bodily pains and hearing the cries of hatred, despair and pain of the damned. After those experiences she looked on suffering, no matter how severe, as very little to bear if by it she could save a soul from hell. As if this weren't enough, she also had visions of the passion and death of Our Lord, suffering in her body the same pains that Christ did. In spite of all this she humbly went about her normal daily routine in the convent.

Because of her simplicity Our Lord once told her: "I will reveal to you the burning secrets of my Heart and many souls will profit by them. I want you to write down and keep all I tell you. It will be read when you are in heaven. Do not think that I make use of you because of your merits, but I want souls to realise how my power makes use of poor and miserable instruments." On 7 June 1923, Our Lord added: "If I could have found a more wretched creature, I should have chosen her for my special love, and through her revealed the longings of my Heart. But I have not found one, and so I have chosen you."

Under obedience Sr Josefa wrote down her revelations day by day. They were published in 1938 in Toulouse under the title *Un Appel à l'Amour* by the Apostleship of Prayer. Cardinal Eugenio Pacelli, later to become Pope Pius XII, wrote a foreword for the book. A second, more complete edition was published in French in 1944 with the *Imprimatur* of Archbishop Saliège of Toulouse. It was translated into English as *The Way of Divine Love*. The authenticity of her account is attested to by her superior and her spiritual director, Father Boyer, O.P.

Sr Josefa died on 29 December 1923 at the age of thirty-three. *The Way of Divine Love*, published in Milwaukee in 1972, bears the *Nihil Obstat* and *Imprimatur* of that Archdiocese. There are recent editions of the book published by TAN and Baronius.

488 Revelations of Sr Josefa Menendez

I have heard that a nun named Sr Josefa Menendez received many revelations from God during her short life. What were some of them?

Sr Josefa, as I wrote in my previous column, was a Spanish nun who spent just four years in a convent in Poitiers, France, before her death in 1923 at the age of thirty-three. She was a privileged soul, on whom Our Lord poured out many graces at the same time as he gave her an extraordinary share in his sufferings. It was during those years in the convent that Sr Josefa received numerous revelations from Our Lord and Our Lady. She wrote them down, as Our Lord asked her to do, so that they could benefit many people after her death.

One of the most frequent themes of the messages was Jesus' overwhelming love for mankind through his Sacred Heart. It was as if he were repeating in the twentieth century what he had made so clear to St Margaret Mary Alacoque in the seventeenth. At the same time it was a preparation for the revelation of the Divine Mercy that Christ would give to St Faustina a few years later, beginning in 1931 (cf. J. Flader, *Question Time 2*, q. 293). On the night of 24 February 1921 Our Lord called Sr Josefa to spread this devotion: "The world does not know the mercy of my Heart. I intend to enlighten them through you.... I want you to be the apostle of my love and mercy."

Our Lord revealed his great compassion and love for sinners, telling Sr Josefa: "Do you not know that the more wretched a soul is, the more I love her? ... The fact that I have chosen a soul does not mean that her faults and miseries are wiped out. But if in all humility that soul acknowledges her failings and atones by little acts of generosity and love, above all, if she trusts me, if she throws herself into my Heart, she gives me more glory and does more good to souls than if she had not fallen. What does her wretchedness matter to me, if she gives me the love that I want?" (20 October 1922) And on the feast of the Sacred Heart, 8 June 1923, Jesus told her: "I will love you, and by the love I have for you souls will realise how much I love them. Since I forgive you so often, they will recognise my mercy."

On one occasion Our Lord told Sr Josefa what he was thinking when he washed the feet of the apostles in the Last Supper: "In the first place I would teach souls how pure they must be to receive me in Holy Communion. I also wished to remind those who would have the misfortune to sin that they can always recover their innocence through the Sacrament of Penance. And I washed the feet of my apostles with my own hands, so that those who have consecrated themselves to apostolic work may follow my example, and treat sinners with humility and gentleness, as also all others that are entrusted to their care. I girded myself with a white linen cloth to remind them that apostles need to be girded with abnegation and mortification, if they hope to exert any real influence on souls. I wished also to teach them mutual charity, which is ever ready to excuse the faults of others, to conceal them and extenuate them, and never to reveal them. Lastly, the water poured on the feet of my apostles denotes the zeal that burned in my Heart for the salvation of the world" (25 February 1923).

Some of the most striking revelations of the importance of love come in Sr Josefa's numerous visions of hell. She writes: "One of these damned souls cried out: 'This is my torture... that I want to love and cannot; there is nothing left me but hatred and despair. If one of us could so much as make a single act of love... This would no longer be hell... but we cannot, we live on hatred and malevolence.'" Another soul cried out: "The greatest of our torments here is that we are not able to love him. While we hunger for love, we are consumed with desire of it, but it is too late" (23 March 1922). This is combined with Our Lord's burning desire to save souls from going to hell. On one occasion he told Sr Josefa: "Help me; help me to make my love for men known, for I come to tell them that in vain will they seek happiness apart from me, for they will not find it. Suffer, Josefa, and love, for we two must win these souls" (13 June 1923).

We do well to have these same thoughts in our hearts and especially in our actions.

489 Purgatory in the Bible

I have many Protestant friends and when we discuss my belief in purgatory they always tell me there is nothing about it in the Bible and therefore we shouldn't believe in it. Are there any scriptural texts I can use to show them that purgatory is a reality?

Before looking at the biblical texts, there is abundant evidence in the first centuries of the Church's belief in a state of purification after death, or purgatory. One of the Fathers of the Church goes so far as to say that the custom was so widespread that it was believed to have been taught by the very apostles. This evidence from tradition, even if there were nothing in the Bible, should be enough to convince a well-meaning person of the advisability of praying for those who have died, and therefore of the reality of purgatory.

As regards scriptural texts, there are a number which are frequently used to back up the Church's teaching on purgatory, even if by themselves they do not "prove" its existence.

Perhaps the most convincing one is from the *Second Book of the Maccabees* in the Old Testament. After a battle in which a number of Jewish soldiers have been killed it is discovered that under the tunic of each of the fallen is a token of the idols of Jamnia. To wear such a token is of course sinful. The account tells us that "they turned to prayer, begging that the sin which had been committed might be wholly blotted out" (*2 Mac* 12:42). Judas, their leader, then took up a collection to be sent to Jerusalem for a sin offering on behalf of the fallen. "In doing this he acted very well and honourably, taking account of the resurrection. For if he were not expecting that those who had fallen would rise again, it would have been superfluous and foolish to pray for the dead. But if he was looking to the splendid reward that is laid up for those who fall asleep in godliness, it was a holy and pious thought. Therefore he made atonement for the dead, that they might be delivered from their sin" (*2 Mac* 12:43-45). This passage clearly shows the belief of the Jews in the second century before Christ that sins could be atoned for after death, implying the belief in purgatory.

This belief carried over to the first Christians, who continued the practice of praying for the dead. Because the belief and custom were so deeply ingrained and generally accepted, there was no need to mention them explicitly in the New Testament. Nonetheless, there are some passages which can be understood as referring to purification of sins after death.

An important one comes from Jesus himself, who says: "... but whoever speaks against the Holy Spirit will not be forgiven, either in this age or in the age to come" (*Mt* 12:32). Here Jesus clearly implies the possibility of sins being forgiven after death, that is in purgatory.

Then too, Jesus says in the Sermon on the Mount, with regard to someone in debt to another: "Make friends quickly with your accuser, while you are going with him to court, lest your accuser hand you over to the judge, and the judge to the guard, and you be put in prison; truly, I say to you, you will never get out till you have paid the last penny" (*Mt* 5:25-26). While in itself this text cannot prove anything regarding purgatory, it has been used to speak about a debt before God owing for sin, which must be paid in full before the soul is free. In the second century Tertullian, for example, understands by prison the realm of the dead, and by the last penny the sins that must expiated there before the person is free to go to heaven (cf. *De anima* 58).

Another text which is often used comes in the *First Letter to the Corinthians*. Here St Paul is speaking of how each person builds his life on the foundation of Jesus Christ, and in the judgment the quality of his work will be "revealed with fire, and the fire will test what sort of work each one has done. If the work which any man has built on the foundation survives, he will receive a reward. If any man's work is burned up, he will suffer loss, though he himself will be saved, but only as through fire" (*1 Cor* 3:13-15). The Latin Fathers of the Church understood this passage as referring to a transient purifying punishment by fire in the next life, and hence to purgatory (cf. St Augustine, *Enarr. in Ps.* 37, 3; Caesarius of Arles, *Sermo* 179).

While none of these passages can be taken to "prove" the existence of purgatory to the satisfaction of a non-believer, they do make a powerful case for it in light of the Church's constant practice of praying for the dead.

490 Belief in purgatory in the early Church

I was talking recently with a Protestant friend about praying for a mutual acquaintance who had passed away and she denied there was any need for it since there is no purgatory. Is there any evidence in the early Church of prayer for the faithful departed?

I answered a similar question many years ago, which appears as question 25 in my book *Question Time 1*). There I mentioned the text of the *Second Book of the Maccabees* in which Judas the Maccabean orders a collection to be taken up and sent to Jerusalem for a sacrifice to be offered for the souls of his fallen comrades killed in battle: "Therefore he made atonement for the dead, that they might be delivered from their sin" (*2 Mac* 12:45). From this text it is clear that the Jews in the centuries before Christ believed in prayer for the faithful departed, and therefore in the possibility of a state of purification after death which we call purgatory.

This belief carried over to the apostles who, undoubtedly following the teaching of Christ, continued the custom of praying and offering Mass for the faithful departed. The custom is set in stone on the tombs of Christians of the first centuries, where we find inscriptions like: "Eternal light shine upon thee, Timothea, in Christ"; "Let [the reader] pray to God to take to himself her spirit holy and pure" and "Thee, O heavenly Father, we implore to have mercy."

Around the year 216 Tertullian describes how the Church prayed for the dead and offered Mass for them on the anniversary of their death: "A woman, after the death of her husband ... prays for his soul and asks that he may, while waiting, find rest; and that he may share in the first resurrection. And each year, on the anniversary of his death, she offers the sacrifice" (*Monogamy* 10:1–2).

In the middle of the fourth century, St Cyril of Jerusalem writes of the Mass: "Then we make mention ... of all among us who have already fallen asleep, for we believe that it will be of very great benefit to the souls of those for whom the petition is carried up, while this holy and most solemn sacrifice is laid out" (*Catechetical Lectures* 23:5:9).

Around the year 392 St John Chrysostom writes of the holy souls: "Let us help and commemorate them. If Job's sons were purified by their father's sacrifice (*Job* 1:5), why would we doubt that our offerings for the dead bring them some consolation? Let us not hesitate to help those who have died and to offer our prayers for them" (*Homilies on First Corinthians* 41:5).

Also, we recall St Monica's request to her son Augustine just before her death: "Lay this body anywhere…This only I ask of you, that you remember me at the altar of the Lord, wherever you may be" (St Augustine, *Confessions* 9, 10-11).

St Augustine himself around the year 421 wrote: "That there should be some fire even after this life is not incredible, and it can be inquired into and either be discovered or left hidden whether some of the faithful may be saved, some more slowly and some more quickly in the greater or lesser degree in which they loved the good things that perish, through a certain purgatorial fire" (*Handbook on Faith, Hope, and Charity* 18:69).

So widespread was the custom of praying and offering Masses for the faithful departed that St Isidore of Seville could write in the seventh century: "To offer the sacrifice for the repose of the faithful departed is a custom observed all over the world. For this reason we believe that it is a custom taught by the very apostles" (*On ecclesiastical offices*, 1).

These texts are just a handful of the many that could be cited from the early Church. It is clear from them that the custom of praying and offering Masses for the dead, based on the corresponding belief in purgatory, was universally accepted and practised in the early centuries. Not only Catholics but Eastern Orthodox and Jews live the custom to this day. The practice was not challenged until the sixteenth century, when Protestants denied it.

So belief in purgatory rests on a very solid foundation indeed. It would be foolish and dangerous to deny it. Frankly, I pity those who deny the existence of purgatory and who will one day end up there with no one to pray for them because they fostered the belief that it doesn't exist.

491 Is purgatory real?

I was talking recently with an Orthodox friend who said that when we die we go either to Paradise or Hades which, by the way, are not the final heaven and hell, and there is no separate purgatory. Can we be sure that there really is a purgatory?

In my last two columns I explained the scriptural evidence for belief in a state of purification after death and the evidence from the practice in the early Church of praying and offering Masses for those who have died. Along with the Church's formal teaching on the existence of purgatory, this should be more than enough to convince us that purgatory is real. By the way, the Eastern Orthodox, who separated from the Catholic Church after 1054, do pray for the faithful departed but they believe they are in the general state they call Hades, the realm of the dead which includes both hell and what we call purgatory.

If someone still remains sceptical, and of course many do, perhaps the apparitions of souls from purgatory can help them. There are whole books with accounts of these apparitions and, frankly, they are very convincing. Let me relate just a few, some of them taken from the recent book *Hungry Souls* by Dutch psychologist Gerard van den Aardweg.

We can begin in the modest museum in the church of the Sacred Heart of Suffrage very near the Vatican in Rome. The museum was started in 1893 by Fr Victor Jouët, founder of the Archconfraternity of the Sacred Heart of Jesus for Aid to the Holy Souls. At present the museum contains ten items, most of them consisting of burn marks of hands and fingers left by souls from purgatory on books or clothing.

One of the most impressive is the nightshirt of Joseph Leleux. On eleven consecutive nights in 1789 Leleux heard frightening noises in his house in Wodecq, Belgium. Then on 21 June his mother, who had died twenty-seven years before, appeared to him and reminded him that he had an obligation to have Masses celebrated for her soul. She reproached him for his wayward life and begged him to change his ways and work for the Church. Then she laid her hand on the sleeve of his nightshirt, burning into it a clearly marked imprint of her hand. Leleux converted and founded a congregation of pious lay people. He died in the fame of sanctity in 1825.

Another item is from Father Panzini, a former abbot from Mantua, Italy, who appeared to the Venerable Isabella Fornari, abbess of the Poor Clares in Todi on the eve of All Souls Day in 1731. He left an imprint of his left hand and a cross burned deeply into the wood of Mother Isabella's worktable, another of his hand on a sheet of paper and a third on the sleeve of her tunic. The latter burn passed through the tunic and burned her shirt, leaving a blood stain on it.

Another impressive burn mark from a soul in purgatory is kept at the shrine of Our Lady of Czestochowa in Poland, in the care of the Order of St Paul the First Hermit. According to an account written around 1890, two of the priests at the shrine had promised one another that the one who died first would give the other a sign from the next life. When considerable time had passed after the death of one of them, the other was wondering what had happened. Then when he was folding the corporal at the end of Mass a hand suddenly appeared, laid itself on the corporal and disappeared. It left a clearly-defined burn that passed through many layers of the folded corporal.

The reason for souls from purgatory leaving burn marks is that they are frequently seen in their apparitions as if on fire. St Margaret Mary Alacoque, who did much to promote devotion to the Sacred Heart, relates the following experience: "When I was praying before the Blessed Sacrament on the feast of Corpus Christi, a person enveloped in fire suddenly stood before me. From the pitiable state the soul was in, I knew it was in purgatory and I wept bitterly. This soul told me it was that of a Benedictine, who had once heard my confession and ordered me to go to Holy Communion. As a reward for this, God permitted him to ask me to help him in his sufferings. He asked me to apply to him all I should do or suffer for a period of three months... It would be difficult for me to describe what I had to endure during those three months. He never left me and seeing him, as it were on fire and in such terrible pain, I could do nothing but groan and weep almost incessantly..." After three months of her hard penances, the soul went to heaven.

In modern times both St Padre Pio and St Faustina had visits from souls in purgatory. In short, purgatory is real. And it is for all, not just Catholics. Believe it.

492 What is purgatory like?

I have lots of questions on purgatory. Do the souls there know we pray for them? Can they pray for us? Do their sufferings increase or decrease over time? For how long are they there?

Gerard van den Aardweg, the Dutch psychologist I have quoted before in this column, has an Epilogue in his book *Hungry Souls* relating the repeated apparitions of a man to his daughter that answers your questions and many more.

The man died in 1870 and appeared numerous times to his daughter Sister Mary Seraphine, a nun in Malines, Belgium. The account of the apparitions was first published in 1872, and then in 1895 it was included by J.A. Nageleisen in his book *Charity for the Suffering Souls: An Explanation of the Catholic Doctrine of Purgatory* (reprinted by TAN Books, Rockford 1982).

On 27 July 1870 Sr Mary received a letter from France informing her that her father had died on July 17. From that time on she often heard sounds of moaning like those of her father in his illness, and a voice crying out, "Dear daughter, have mercy on me, have mercy on me, have mercy on me!" On October 14, when she was about to fall asleep she saw her father standing near her bed, looking very sorrowful and enveloped in flames. She felt as if the flames were scorching her too. From then on she saw her father every evening, except for a few days at the end, until he finally went to heaven.

When she asked if he was relieved by the many Masses being offered for him he answered yes, but that he also wanted the Stations of the Cross. He explained that the rest of his children thought he was already in heaven and weren't praying for him. This is confirmed by a letter they wrote to their sister: "Father died like a saint, and is now in heaven." Only Sr Mary and an old servant named Joanna were praying for him. So the souls in purgatory clearly know who is praying for them – and who is not.

Her father explained on one occasion that it was not necessary for the sisters to pray continually for him: "Every work, even the least, performed in the state of grace and offered to God, is meritorious and of atoning value, and serves to lessen our punishment." He went on: "Oh, if people would know what purgatory is! They would suffer everything in order to escape it and to release the poor souls confined in it."

He explained that at first he was sentenced to many years in purgatory but that through the intercession of Our Lady, to whom he had great devotion, his time was reduced to a few months. Nonetheless, his suffering was so intense that he said in October, "If I shall have to remain in purgatory three months more it will seem an eternity."

On October 30 he said: "Alas, the world does not believe that the fire of purgatory is similar to that of hell. If a person could but once visit purgatory, he would never more commit the least sin, so rigorously are the souls punished."

In answer to Sr Mary Seraphine's explicit questions as to whether the souls in purgatory know who prays for them and whether they are permitted to pray for the faithful on earth, he answered yes to both.

He explained that, having seen the infinite majesty of God, the sacred humanity of Christ and the Blessed Virgin Mary in his particular judgment, he felt a continuously increasing and ardent longing to see them again. On November 30 he said: "It seems an eternity to me since I arrived in purgatory. At present my greatest torment is the intense longing to behold God and to enjoy his possession." He said that St Joseph, Our Lady and his guardian angel often visited purgatory to comfort him.

Many souls in purgatory relate that their greatest pain is the intense longing to see God, the pain of loss, and that this pain increases over time as their love for God grows. At the same time many say that the pain of fire, the pain of sense, correspondingly decreases. But there is general agreement that the greatest pain is not the fire but the pain of loss.

The man also appeared to another sister in the monastery and told her that her father, who had neglected his religious duties for a long time and had died without the sacraments, had been saved but he would be in purgatory for twenty years. He also said that her sister, who had died sixteen years before at the age of eight, had been released from purgatory a short time before and was now in heaven.

This answers your question about the length of time for which souls are in purgatory. It varies, depending on the state of the soul at the moment of death. The more temporal punishment for sin remaining and the more bad habits and attachments caused by sin, the longer the time in purgatory, which can be many years.

Finally, during Midnight Mass on Christmas Eve the man appeared to Sr Mary in great radiance and said: "My punishment is ended. I come to thank you and your community for all the prayers said for me. From now on I shall pray for you all." Let us pray very much for all those who have died. In that way, not only do we help them but, by the mercy of God, we can be sure that if we go to purgatory ourselves there will be many people to pray for us.

493 Is heaven real?

I have a friend who is very sceptical about life after death and would like some sort of proof that heaven is real. He says no one has ever been in heaven and come back to earth to tell us about it. What can I tell him?

When it comes to "proof" we have to be very careful. What we can give is strong arguments for the existence of life after death, but these may or may not convince the other person. It is the same with the existence of God, where in one sense his existence is staring us in the face in his wonderful work of creation, but this may not convince a sceptic or an atheist. The most convincing "proof" for the existence of life after death is arriving there and seeing that it is a reality. But then it may be too late!

Coming back to your question, the following considerations may prove helpful. The first is that there *are* people who have been in heaven and have come to earth to tell us about it. The most important is Jesus Christ himself, who spoke often of life after death, of judgment, heaven and hell. But why should a sceptic believe that Jesus is God who has come to earth? After all, he was the son of a carpenter from Nazareth and he died crucified in Jerusalem.

Well, we have multiple testimonies about Jesus in some very ancient writings, written only some twenty or thirty years after his death. They are, of course, the Gospels. They tell us that Jesus not only claimed to be God but showed it by such remarkable feats as raising three people from the dead, curing a man born blind and prophesying his own death and resurrection, which came to pass.

St Paul too had a vision of heaven (cf. *2 Cor* 12:2-4) and came back to tell us about it. He found heaven indescribably beautiful and could only write: "What no eye has seen, nor ear heard, nor the heart of man conceived, what God has prepared for those who love him" (*1 Cor* 2:9).

If the sceptic wants more recent "proof" of heaven from someone who has been there, we can tell him about Our Lady, who died in the first century and has appeared on earth numerous times, bringing about miracles that admit of no human explanation. One thinks of the image she left at Guadalupe in Mexico in 1531 imprinted miraculously on a cactus fibre cloak, which has baffled scientists as to its origin and preservation, not to mention some of the details on it. Or Mary's apparitions in Fatima in 1917, where she told the three children several months beforehand that on October 13 she would work a great miracle. In fact on that day the miracle of the sun was seen by some 70,000 people. If there is no life after death or heaven, how is it that someone who died two thousand years before can appear on earth and bring about such prodigious works?

One can also speak about the numerous miracles approved by the Church, which came about in answer to prayers to deceased people. Every beatification and canonisation, unless the Pope waives this requirement, requires two authenticated miracles and some of these are truly remarkable. If there is no life after death, how is it that prayers to a person who no longer exists can have any effect?

And then there are the numerous testimonies of people who have died, or almost died, who have experienced the judgment and have seen heaven and hell. One of the most remarkable and well-known is that of Gloria Polo, a Colombian dentist who in May, 1995, was struck by lightning, suffered a cardiac arrest and was badly burned inside and out. She saw her lifeless body on a stretcher in the operating room. She had died in mortal sin and was taken by demons to hell to see what she deserved for her sins. Then she saw the terrible suffering of the souls in purgatory, the joy of souls in heaven, and finally her own judgment, in which she was condemned to hell. The sins that condemned her most included aiding and participating in abortion, receiving holy communion in a state of mortal sin, fortune-telling, and speaking evil of priests. She was given a second chance and came back to life on condition that she share her experience with others. She has done this all over the world and on the internet, writing her account in the book *Struck by Lightning: Death, Judgment and Conversion.*

Yes, there is life after death. There is a judgment, hell, purgatory and heaven and we should do everything possible to prepare ourselves for it. Now, before it is too late.

494 Final repentance

Will God forgive sinners if they are sorry and ask for forgiveness at the very end of their life? I read somewhere that he will and that even Judas would have been forgiven if he had asked God for mercy. Can you shed some light on this?

The short answer is that God will always forgive sinners, even if it be at the very last moment of their life, provided they are sorry for their sins. But a longer explanation is needed to understand the implications of this.

We can start with what the *Catechism of the Catholic Church* says about it. Speaking about who goes to hell the Catechism says: "To die in mortal sin without repenting and accepting God's merciful love means remaining separated from him for ever by our own free choice. This state of definitive self-exclusion from communion with

God and the blessed is called 'hell'" (*CCC* 1033). The implication is that as long as someone in mortal sin does repent and accept God's merciful love, they will be saved, no matter when this is, even at the last moment of their life.

As always, their repentance must be genuine, with a true conversion of heart, even when it comes at the very end of life. As the Catechism puts it, "Interior repentance is a radical reorientation of our whole life, a return, a conversion to God with all our heart, an end of sin, a turning away from evil, with repugnance towards the evil actions we have committed. At the same time it entails the desire and resolution to change one's life, with hope in God's mercy and trust in the help of his grace" (*CCC* 1431). Although the person may not experience all of this, it is clear that repentance must be a real conversion of heart, a rejection of sin, not just a passing thought or sentiment.

How would a person who has lived a life of sin repent at the last moment? It can only be by the grace of God, who moves them to repent. The Catechism explains: "Conversion is first of all a work of the grace of God who makes our hearts return to him: 'Restore us to thyself, O LORD, that we may be restored!' God gives us the strength to begin anew" (*Lam* 5:21; *CCC* 1432).

But conversion must also involve the person's free response to that grace: "It is in discovering the greatness of God's love that our heart is shaken by the horror and weight of sin and begins to fear offending God by sin and being separated from him. The human heart is converted by looking upon him whom our sins have pierced" (*CCC* 1432).

Is it easy for someone who has lived far from God, in some cases in repeated grave sin and even denying belief in God, to repent at the last moment? No it is not. Their pride and hard heart may often lead them to reject God, even when it means everlasting punishment in hell. God always offers them sufficient grace to be saved, but he also respects their freedom to refuse it. This is sad, but it is a necessary consequence of human freedom.

Does God actually give a hardened sinner this grace at the very last moment of their life? We can never know for certain but it is most likely that the answer is yes. After all, he "desires all men to be saved and to come to the knowledge of the truth" (*1 Tim* 2:4). He will stop at nothing to rescue sinners from eternal damnation. He is ever rich in mercy. He is the good shepherd who goes in search of the lost sheep (cf. *Lk* 15:3-7) and who lays down his life for his sheep (cf. *Jn* 10:11). He is the Son of man, who came "to give his life as a ransom for many" (*Mt* 20:28). "So it is not the will of my Father who is in heaven that one of these little ones should perish" (*Mt* 18:12-14).

This is confirmed by various reports of souls in purgatory appearing to people on earth and telling them that certain individuals who had seemed to die far from God were in fact saved and were now in purgatory. Naturally, such reports can be believed or not, but they do suggest that God has saved some hardened sinners at the very last moment.

Two final thoughts on the question. First, we should pray very much for those we know who are living far from God so that God will grant them the grace of repentance, and we should do all we can to help them humanly: talking with them, giving them good books and articles to read, inviting them to speak with a priest, etc. Second, after someone like this has died in apparent rejection of God, we should continue praying for them, since they may have been saved at the last moment and are now atoning for their many sins in purgatory. We should never assume that anyone has gone to hell. After all, to pray for the living and the dead is one of the spiritual works of mercy.

II. LITURGY AND THE SACRAMENTS

The Liturgy

495 Latin in the liturgy

I was received into the Church in the early 1960s when Latin was the only language of the Mass. I am still fond of Latin but there are few Masses in that language these days. When and why did the Church change to the vernacular and can a priest still celebrate in Latin?

In answering your question it will be helpful to go back to the beginning of the Church and see how the use of Latin developed. The first language of the Mass was in fact Aramaic, a form of Hebrew spoken by the first Christians in Palestine at the time of Christ. Words like *abba* and *maranatha* are Aramaic. Aramaic is still used in parts of the Mass in some of the Eastern rites, especially for the consecration.

As the faith spread throughout the Mediterranean region the liturgy was celebrated in the language of each people. This included such languages as Syriac, Coptic, Armenian and especially Greek, which was commonly spoken throughout the Mediterranean world, including in Rome. In Rome today one can still see many ancient Greek inscriptions on tombs and monuments. The *Kyrie eleison, Christe eleison* still used in the penitential rite of the Latin Mass is of course Greek. From around the third century Latin became more widely spoken in the Roman Empire and by the fourth it came to replace Greek as the language of the liturgy.

It should be remembered that in the first centuries there were no books with the prescribed prayers to be said in Mass, so the bishop or priest would say the prayers extemporaneously, following a set pattern. It was not until around the sixth century that the present Roman Canon, also known as Eucharistic Prayer I, appeared in Latin, to be used as written. The Leonine and Gelasian Sacramentaries of around that time were written in Latin and were, as it were, the first missals. After that Latin became the sole language of the liturgy in the Latin or Roman rite.

The Second Vatican Council determined that Latin was to be preserved. Its Constitution on the Liturgy *Sacrosanctum Concilium* established: "The use of the Latin language, with due respect to particular law, is to be preserved in the Latin rites. But since the use of the vernacular, whether in the Mass, the administration of the sacraments, or in other parts of the liturgy, may frequently be of great advantage to the people, a wider use may be made of it, especially in readings, directives and in some prayers and chants" (*SC* 36). The Constitution added: "Nevertheless, care must be taken to ensure that the faithful may also be able to say or sing together in Latin those parts of the Ordinary of the Mass which pertain to them" (*SC* 54).

After the Council bishops' conferences all over the world began to ask for permission to celebrate Mass in the vernacular and soon virtually the whole world was doing it. Nonetheless, the official version of the missal published by the Holy See is still in Latin, the latest of which is the third *typical edition,* published in 2000. Public Masses celebrated by the Holy Father at the Vatican are usually in Latin, so that it is clearly seen that the Church has a common, universal language. It unites the faithful from all over the world with each other and with the early Church. Millions of young people from all over the world singing the Credo in Latin in World Youth Days are a testimony to the importance of this universal language.

Can a priest still celebrate Mass in Latin? The Vatican's Instruction *Redemptionis Sacramentum* (2004) says that "priests are always and everywhere permitted to celebrate Mass in Latin" (n. 112). This refers to the *Novus Ordo,* or Ordinary Form of the Mass, the Mass celebrated in the vernacular in our parishes. Many priests do in fact say Mass in Latin privately and some parishes and other groups have occasional public Masses in Latin. Some parishes say or sing at least parts of the Mass in Latin, such as the Gloria, Credo, Sanctus, Pater

Noster, and Agnus Dei, in addition to the Greek *Kyrie eleison*. And of course priests of the Priestly Fraternity of St Peter habitually say the Extraordinary Form of the Mass, the Tridentine Rite, in Latin, as do other priests.

Interestingly, Cardinal Francis Arinze, then Prefect of the Congregation for Divine Worship, said in an address in the U.S. on 11 November 2006: "In big churches where there are many Masses celebrated on a Sunday or feast day, why can one of those Masses not be in Latin?" (*L'Osservatore Romano,* English edition, 23 May 2007, p. 8)

We can pray that more use will be made of this beautiful ancient language, apart from its regular use in the Extraordinary Form or Tridentine Rite in many places.

496 The Tridentine Rite

A friend recently took me to a Tridentine Rite Mass which I found very different from my normal parish Mass. It was celebrated in Latin and the priest had his back to the people. Where does this Mass come from and where does it fit into the Church's liturgy?

Let us go back to the beginning. Ever since the Last Supper in which Christ instituted the Eucharist, telling the apostles to "do this in commemoration of me", the Church has celebrated the Mass. At the beginning there were no printed texts and so bishops and priests said many of the prayers extemporaneously, following a set structure. The Mass began with the Liturgy of the Word, with prayers asking for forgiveness of sins, readings from Sacred Scripture, a homily and prayers of intercession. This was followed by the Liturgy of the Eucharist, with the presentation of the gifts, the Canon or Eucharistic Prayer, the giving of Communion and the dismissal. St Justin Martyr's description of the Mass as it was celebrated in the middle of the second century can be found in the *Catechism of the Catholic Church* in paragraph 1345. The similarity with our present Mass is striking.

The basic elements of the Roman Canon, or Eucharistic Prayer I, were already there at the end of the fourth century in St Ambrose' (c. 340-397) treatise *De Sacramentis*. At the end of the sixth century, Pope St Gregory the Great (590-604) standardised the Mass, giving the Church the Roman Missal, which remained practically unchanged until the Second Vatican Council.

In the sixteenth century the Protestant reformers made drastic changes to the Mass, including to the Roman Canon, removing all elements that contradicted their new theology. To protect the traditional Mass and to ensure that it was celebrated in the same way throughout the Catholic world Pope St Pius V issued a new Roman Missal in 1570. This followed the directives of the Council of Trent, hence the name Tridentine Rite. It should be understood, however, that the Roman Missal promulgated by Pope Pius V was not a new rite since it was essentially the same as that celebrated since the time of St Gregory the Great. A more proper name for it is simply the Roman Rite. In it the priest faces the altar, not the people, leading the people in their worship of God in the sacrifice celebrated on the altar.

Between 1570 and the Second Vatican Council numerous small changes were made to the missal, incorporating new feasts, changing the liturgical rank of some feasts, and adding the name of St Joseph in the Roman Canon in 1962. The last major edition of this missal was issued by Pope St John XXIII in 1962. It incorporated some changes in the liturgy of Holy Week, abolished some vigils and octaves of feasts, removed some feasts for which there had been two celebrations, etc. The whole Church used this missal until 1970, when further changes were made as requested by the Second Vatican Council.

The Council, in its Constitution on the Liturgy, *Sacrosanctum Concilium*, asked for revisions to be made so that "devout and active participation by the faithful may be more easily achieved. For this purpose the rites are to be simplified, due care being taken to preserve their substance. Parts which with the passage of time came to be duplicated, or were added with little advantage, are to be omitted. Other parts which suffered loss through accidents of history are to be restored to the vigour they had in the days of the holy Fathers, as may seem useful or necessary" (n. 50). In particular, the Council asked that more Scriptural passages be read, that the homily be given greater importance, that the prayer of the faithful after the homily be restored, etc. (cf. *ibid.*).

Accordingly a new Roman Missal incorporating these changes was introduced in 1970 and this is the missal we use in our parishes today. It is not a new rite but simply the latest revision of the traditional Roman Rite. It is properly referred to as the Ordinary Form of the Mass, and the Tridentine Rite, which uses the 1962 missal, as the Extraordinary Form.

The latest edition of the *General Instruction of the Roman Missal* (2012) speaks of "the new Missal with which the Church of the Roman Rite will henceforth celebrate the Mass", indicating that this is to be the ordinary form of the Mass everywhere. But Mass can still be celebrated using the 1962 missal as the extraordinary form. It is improperly referred to as the Tridentine Rite. In short there is only one rite, the Roman Rite, with two forms of celebration.

497 Western Liturgical Rites

I was recently on holidays in Milan, Italy, and attended a Mass which was quite different from the one I am used to in Australia. I asked a relative with whom I was staying and he told me it was the Ambrosian rite. I didn't know such rites existed. What is it?

While most people are aware that in addition to the Latin or Roman rite, there are numerous Eastern rites with their own liturgy, among them the Maronite, Melkite, Chaldean, Ukrainian, Syro-Malabar, etc. (cf. J. Flader, *Question Time 1*, q. 23), few are aware that there are also a number of Western liturgical rites, among them the Ambrosian. A big difference between the Eastern and Western rites, however, is that the Eastern rites are used by what are called Eastern Churches, with their own bishops, priests and a body of the faithful, whereas the Western rites are only liturgical rites, with a particular way of celebrating Mass and other ceremonies.

When Pope Pius V standardised the Mass for the Roman rite in 1570 by issuing the Roman Missal, he allowed only those Western rites to continue which had been in existence for at least 200 years. Which are those Western rites?

Let us begin with the Ambrosian, named after St Ambrose, who was bishop of Milan in the fourth century. St Ambrose probably did not write it but he may have contributed to an earlier rite already in use in that city. The earliest manuscripts of the rite date to the eighth century. At various times Popes and others tried to suppress the rite but it has survived and is widely used today in the Archdiocese of Milan as well as in other places, including the diocese of Lugano in Switzerland.

Blessed Pope Paul VI, who had used the rite as Archbishop of Milan, wanted it to be preserved and to be brought into line with the directives of the Second Vatican Council and so a new missal was published in 1976. Apart from the Roman Canon, with some differences, and the other three Eucharistic Prayers of the Roman Missal, the missal contains two early Ambrosian Eucharistic Prayers in which the epiclesis comes after the Consecration, as in the Oriental usage. There are other differences, including the Rite of Peace placed at the beginning of the Offertory and the Lamb of God not being said. The rite has its own readings and a rich variety of Prefaces.

Another ancient rite is the Mozarabic, which was used in Spain and Portugal. It dates back to at least the sixth century but probably goes back to the original evangelisation of the region. Mass in the Mozarabic rite is celebrated daily in the Corpus Christi Chapel, also known as the Mozarabic Chapel, in the Cathedral of Toledo and every Tuesday in Madrid in a monastery of the Poor Clare Sisters. All the churches of Toledo celebrate the rite on the feast of the Incarnation on December 18 and on the feast day of St Ildephonsus on January 23. The rite is also used on certain days each year in the Talavera Chapel of the old cathedral of Salamanca. Pope St John Paul II celebrated Mass with this rite in 1992 and again in 2000.

Also from the Iberian Peninsula is the Bragan Rite, of the Archdiocese of Braga in Portugal. It developed between the eleventh and thirteenth centuries and belongs to the Roman family of rites. A particularity of the rite is the recitation of the *Ave Maria* at the start of Mass and of another Marian prayer, *Sub tuum praesidium*, at the end. After Pope Pius V issued the Roman Missal in 1570 the Rite of Braga fell largely into disuse. Today, although the priests of Braga are authorised to use it, few do so.

In addition to these rites there are also rites used in religious orders. Among them are the rites of the Carthusians, founded by St Bruno in 1084, the Carmelites, founded by hermits around 1200, and the Order of Preachers, or Dominicans, founded by St Dominic in 1215.

To these one should add the Sarum Rite, or the Use of Salisbury, which dates back to St Osmund, bishop of Salisbury, England, in the eleventh century. St Osmund was a Norman and the rite is very similar to that used in Rouen, France. The rite later spread to most of England, Wales, Ireland and Scotland until it was abolished by Queen Elizabeth I in 1559. It was revived to some extent by Anglo-Catholics in the late nineteenth and early twentieth centuries, and it has been used in Catholic churches and some Orthodox ones as well.

498 Beauty in the liturgy

I am an older person and can remember Masses, Eucharistic adoration and hymns that were somehow truly uplifting. I don't find that to the same extent anymore, except in a few parishes. Am I right to lament the loss of beauty in the worship of God?

The liturgy should always be beautiful and I am sorry to say that I agree with you that we have lost much of the beauty we had in years gone by.

Why should the liturgy be beautiful? We should remember that the liturgy is the public worship which the Church, the Mystical Body of Christ, offers to God. It is not merely the action of human beings but especially the action of Jesus Christ, the head of the Mystical Body, along with his members. The liturgy should therefore have a beauty and dignity that reflect its divine actor and object.

Moreover, the liturgy is a participation in the heavenly liturgy where the angels and saints constantly praise God, singing "Holy, holy, holy..." (cf. *Rev* 4:8). As the *Catechism of the Catholic Church* puts it, "It is in this eternal liturgy that the Spirit and the Church enable us to participate whenever we celebrate the mystery of salvation in the sacraments" (*CCC* 1139). In heaven we find the maximum of beauty: the beauty of God himself and of Our Lady, the angels and all the saints, in the splendour of holiness. We read in the *Book of Psalms*: "Honour and majesty are before him; strength and beauty are in his sanctuary" (*Ps* 96:6). It is only right then that the liturgy on earth should reflect as much as possible the beauty of heaven.

In this sense, Pope Benedict XVI writes: "Like the rest of Christian Revelation, the liturgy is inherently linked to beauty: it is *veritatis splendor* [the splendour of truth]. The liturgy is a radiant expression of the paschal mystery, in which Christ draws us to himself and calls us to communion. As Saint Bonaventure would say, in Jesus we

THE LITURGY

contemplate beauty and splendour at their source" (Apost. Exhort. *Sacramentum caritatis*, n. 35; cf. St Bonaventure, *Serm.* 1, 7; 11, 10; 22, 7; 29, 76: *Sermones dominicales ad fidem*).

Pope Benedict goes on to say: "The truest beauty is the love of God, who definitively revealed himself to us in the paschal mystery. The beauty of the liturgy is part of this mystery; it is a sublime expression of God's glory and, in a certain sense, a glimpse of heaven on earth. The memorial of Jesus' redemptive sacrifice contains something of that beauty which Peter, James and John beheld when the Master, making his way to Jerusalem, was transfigured before their eyes (cf. *Mk* 9:2). Beauty, then, is not mere decoration, but rather an essential element of the liturgical action, since it is an attribute of God himself and his revelation. These considerations should make us realise the care which is needed, if the liturgical action is to reflect its innate splendour" (*ibid.*).

In summary, the liturgy should be beautiful because it reflects on earth and praises God's infinite beauty in heaven. Really, it is a matter of love. When we love someone we give them gifts which are truly beautiful: a diamond or gold ring, beautiful flowers, an elegant garment, a well-prepared meal. We should not do any less for God, the source of all beauty.

All aspects of the liturgy should reflect this spirit: the church itself, the altar, the tabernacle, the sacred vessels, the vestments, the way of celebrating by the priest, the music... All should uplift the spirit and lead it to God. Our ancestors left us a great legacy in this regard, with their beautiful Gothic cathedrals, stained glass windows, ornate chalices and monstrances, magnificent vestments and of course spine-tingling, truly uplifting music.

As the *Catechism of the Catholic Church* says, speaking of sacred art in general: "*Sacred art* is true and beautiful when its form corresponds to its particular vocation: evoking and glorifying, in faith and adoration, the transcendent mystery of God – the surpassing invisible beauty of truth and love visible in Christ... Genuine sacred art draws man to adoration, to prayer, and to the love of God, Creator and Saviour, the Holy One and Sanctifier" (*CCC* 2502).

We should do all we can to foster this spirit in a liturgy which is well-prepared and carried out, so that it truly gives glory to God, the source of all beauty, and it unites us with him.

499 Care in the liturgy

In my parish there are certain irregularities in the way Mass is celebrated and frankly I am disturbed by them. Some of my friends tell me not to worry about it. Is this important?

Obviously there will be some "irregularities" which are not particularly important, but in general the priest should be careful to follow what is indicated in the missal. The liturgy is the public and official worship of God which the whole Church, the Mystical Body, offers to God in union with her head Jesus Christ, so it is important that it be celebrated according to the mind of the Church.

For this reason the Church has given us a missal with the texts to be used and with indications known as rubrics which specify when the priest is to bow, make the sign of the cross, genuflect, etc. The word rubrics, by the way, comes from the Latin word for red, because these indications are traditionally printed in red to distinguish them from the rest of the text.

The missal allows the priest to choose from a number of penitential rites, prefaces and Eucharistic prayers, etc. These choices are foreseen and they provide a certain variety in the common celebration of Mass. But apart from them the priest is to follow both the text and the rubrics of the missal. He should not change the wording of any of the prayers, the profession of faith, the Eucharistic Prayer, etc., and he should not leave anything out.

The Church is universal and she has a common worship, so that the faithful can attend Mass anywhere in the world and find it celebrated in basically the same way. Naturally the different rites, especially the Eastern rites (cf. J. Flader, *Question Time 2*, q. 180), have their own way of celebrating Mass which may be quite different in some aspects from the Roman or Latin rite celebrated in most of the world. But even these rites have a common missal used all over the world so that their faithful find themselves at home in the liturgy wherever they may be.

In this way the Catholic Church is seen to be clearly one and universal. It is very different from the protestant denominations, where their worship can be vastly different from one parish to another, let alone from one country to another. The Catholic liturgy is celebrated in the same way not only all over the world, but also in the same way in its basic structure since its institution by Christ. The description of the Mass in the middle of the second century given by St Justin (cf. *CCC* 1345) corresponds remarkably to the Mass we celebrate today.

For this reason the Instruction *Redemptionis Sacramentum* of the Congregation for Divine Worship and the Discipline of the Sacraments together with the Congregation for the Doctrine of the Faith, says: "Finally, the structures and forms of the sacred celebrations according to each of the Rites of both East and West are in harmony with the practice of the universal Church also as regards practices received universally from apostolic and unbroken tradition, which it is the Church's task to transmit faithfully and carefully to future generations. All these things are wisely safeguarded and protected by the liturgical norms" (n. 9).

The Instruction goes on to say: "The Mystery of the Eucharist is too great for anyone to permit himself to treat it according to his own whim, so that its sacredness and its universal ordering would be obscured. On the contrary, anyone who acts thus by giving free rein to his own inclinations, even if he is a priest, injures the substantial unity of the Roman Rite, which ought to be vigorously preserved, and becomes responsible for actions that are in no way consistent with the hunger and thirst for the living God that is experienced by the people today. Nor do such actions serve authentic pastoral care or proper liturgical renewal; instead, they deprive Christ's faithful of their patrimony and their heritage. For arbitrary actions are not conducive to true renewal, but are detrimental to the right of Christ's faithful to a liturgical celebration that is an expression of the Church's life in accordance with her tradition and discipline" (n. 11).

Redemptionis Sacramentum continues: "The reprobated practice by which priests, deacons or the faithful here and there alter or vary at will the texts of the Sacred Liturgy that they are charged to pronounce, must cease. For in doing thus, they render the celebration of the Sacred Liturgy unstable, and not infrequently distort the authentic meaning of the Liturgy" (n. 59; cf. also *General Instruction on Roman Missal*, n. 24).

Let us pray that all priests will have a great love for God, for the Church and for the liturgy, so that they will celebrate Mass with all the dignity and reverence it deserves.

500 Expressing concerns to pastors

Our parish priest makes some changes in the Mass that I know are not proper and that other parishioners too find disturbing. I have spoken with him and he has brushed me off. Is there anything else I can do?

You have done well to speak first with the priest. Out of charity and justice this is always the first thing to do. And of course, pray for him. Many priests will listen graciously and make the necessary changes in the way they say Mass. Others will continue doing what they think best, even though it may not be what the Church intends. What should someone do in this latter case?

The Church is a family, with the Pope as the father – not for nothing do we call him the Holy Father – and she wants what is best for her children. For this reason the *Code of Canon Law* makes ample provision for manifesting concerns to one's pastors: "Christ's faithful are at liberty to make known their needs, especially their spiritual needs, and their wishes to the pastors of the Church" (Can. 212 §2). Moreover, "They have the right, indeed at times the duty, in keeping with their knowledge, competence and position, to manifest to the sacred pastors their views on matters which concern the good of the Church" (Can. 212 §3). Naturally, this refers to all matters, not only the liturgy but any other concerns they may have regarding the teaching of Church doctrine, discipline, the use of money, the fostering of devotions, etc.

When it is a question of irregularities in the celebration of the liturgy, whether in the Mass or in some other ceremony, the Vatican's Instruction *Redemptionis Sacramentum* gives specific indications. In a section at the end of the document entitled "Complaints regarding abuses in liturgical matters" it says: "In an altogether particular manner, let everyone do all that is in their power to ensure that the Most Holy Sacrament of the Eucharist will be protected from any and every irreverence or distortion and that all abuses be thoroughly corrected. This is a most serious duty incumbent upon each and every one, and all are bound to carry it out without any favouritism" (n. 183). Naturally it is especially incumbent on the pastors themselves to ensure that the liturgy is celebrated in accordance with the liturgical books issued by the Holy See.

When those celebrating the liturgy are not faithful to the Church's norms, the other members of the faithful are free to express their concerns. To this end the Instruction goes on to say: "Any Catholic, whether priest or deacon or lay member of Christ's faithful, has the right to lodge a complaint regarding a liturgical abuse to the diocesan bishop or the competent Ordinary equivalent to him in law, or to the Apostolic See on account of the primacy of the Roman Pontiff. It is fitting, however, insofar as possible, that the report or complaint be submitted first to the diocesan bishop. This is naturally to be done in truth and charity" (n. 184).

So when someone has expressed their concern to the priest and he has not changed the way he celebrates the liturgy, the person can then lodge a complaint with the diocesan bishop. The diocesan bishop, by the way, is the bishop at the head of the diocese, not an auxiliary bishop. A polite letter informing the bishop of the abuse in the liturgy and mentioning that the writer has spoken with the priest and nothing has changed is always appreciated by the bishop. He may or may not choose to act on it, but at least he now knows what is going on in his diocese.

The faithful have a right to the liturgy celebrated in accordance with the Church's norms. For this reason, the Instruction adds in the last paragraph: "Let each one of the sacred ministers ask himself, even with severity, whether he has respected the rights of the lay members of Christ's faithful, who confidently entrust themselves and their children to him, relying on him to fulfil for the faithful those sacred functions that the Church intends to carry out in celebrating the sacred Liturgy at Christ's command. For each one should always remember that he is a servant of the Sacred Liturgy" (n. 186).

Bishops have a special responsibility in this regard: "Since he must safeguard the unity of the universal Church, the bishop is bound to promote the discipline common to the entire Church and therefore to insist upon the observance of all ecclesiastical laws. He is to be watchful lest abuses encroach upon ecclesiastical discipline, especially as regards the ministry of the Word, the celebration of the Sacraments and sacramentals, the worship of God and the veneration of the Saints" (n. 177).

Let us pray that all pastors will be faithful to the Church's norms in celebrating the liturgy so that what they celebrate is truly according to the mind of the Church.

501 The history of holy water

Is the use of holy water something recent in the Church or does it go back to the early Church?

There is evidence of using holy water in the Old Testament, where a woman who had been unfaithful to her husband was to drink holy water by way of purification (cf. *Num* 5:17-28). Also before entering the Temple Jews underwent a rite of purification by immersing themselves in a ritual bath called a *mikvah*, as they still do today in some synagogues.

In the Church there is evidence already in the fourth century of the blessing of water and oil in the Pontifical of bishop Serapion of Thumis. In its prayer of blessing we see the healing and purifying purpose of the water: "We bless these creatures in the name of Jesus Christ, your only Son; we invoke upon this water and this oil the name of him who suffered, who was crucified, who rose from the dead, and who sits at the right of the Uncreated. Grant unto these creatures the power to heal; may all fevers, every evil spirit, and all maladies be put to flight by him who either drinks these beverages or is anointed with them, and may they be a remedy in the name of Jesus Christ, your only Son."

Also from the fourth century are other writings which mention the use of water which has been blessed. St Epiphanius, bishop of Salamis in Cyprus, writes that at Tiberias a man named Joseph poured water on a possessed man, after blessing the water with the sign of the cross, saying: "In the name of Jesus Christ of Nazareth, crucified, depart from this unhappy one, you infernal spirit, and let him be healed" (*Contra haeres.*, lib. I, haer. xxx). Joseph, a layman, later used blessed water to overcome witchcraft.

In the fifth century Bishop Theodoret of Cyrus relates that Marcellus, Bishop of Apamea, blessed water with the sign of the cross and that Aphraates cured one of the emperor's horses by having it drink water which had been blessed with the sign of the cross (*Hist. relig.*, c. viii, in P.G., LXXXII, col. 1244, 1375).

In the West St Gregory of Tours writes of a recluse named Eusitius who lived in the sixth century and cured those suffering from a certain fever by having them drink water that he had blessed (cf. *De gloria confess.*, c. 82).

Many of the faithful believed that blessed water possessed the power to cure certain diseases and that this was especially true of baptismal water. For this reason in some places baptismal water was carefully preserved throughout the year. After baptism had been administered the people would come with their vessels to take the water home, some of them sprinkling it on their fields, vineyards and gardens.

As for having holy water in a font at the entrance to churches there is evidence of it in a letter of Bishop Synesius of Ptolemais in North Africa, who died in 414. He writes of "lustral water placed in the vestibule of the temple". The word lustral refers to something that purifies or brightens, that adds lustre. In some places the faithful as they entered the church were sprinkled with blessed water by a clerk who was called a *hydrokometes*, or introducer by water.

Pope St Leo IV (847-855) directed priests to bless water in their churches every Sunday before Mass and sprinkle the people with it. This is the custom of the Asperges, which may still be practised on Sundays, as it is in the Easter Vigil ceremony. Similarly Archbishop Hincmar of Rheims (806-882) directed: "Every Sunday, before the celebration of Mass, the priest shall bless water in his church, and, for this holy purpose, he shall use a clean and suitable vessel. The people, when entering the church, are to be sprinkled with this water, and those who so desire may carry some away in clean vessels so as to sprinkle their houses, fields, vineyards, and cattle, and the provender with which these last are fed, as also to sprinkle on their own food" (*Capitula synodalia*, cap. v, in P.L., CXXV, col, 774).

So the custom of sprinkling ourselves with holy water on entering a church and of using holy water for other purposes goes back a long way. It is part of our Catholic tradition and we do well to use holy water with a sense of its history and meaning. It is especially a reminder of our baptism, by which we were cleansed from sin and filled with the new life of grace.

502 Blessing ourselves with holy water

My little daughter recently asked me why we bless ourselves with holy water on entering a church and I wasn't sure I gave her a complete answer. Can you help me?

Blessing ourselves with holy water has a number of different purposes and meanings. The first goes back to the Old Testament, where those engaging in various functions in the worship of God always washed themselves with water first in order to be purified for their spiritual function.

We see this, for example, as early as the book of Exodus, where God commands Moses to make a bronze laver, or water bowl, for priests to wash themselves: "You shall also make a laver of bronze, with its base of bronze for washing. And you shall put it between the tent of meeting and the altar, and you shall put water in it, with which Aaron and his sons shall wash their hands and their feet. When they go into the tent of meeting, or when they come near the altar to minister, to burn an offering by fire to the Lord, they shall wash with water" (*Ex* 30:18-20). The laver on its base is very much like our holy water font, and its location before the altar is similar to the font's location at the entrance to the church.

This practice was taken up in the early Church, where a fountain was placed in the atrium of basilicas so that the people could wash their hands before entering. One of the most well-known of these was the first-century bronze pine cone, almost four metres high, which stood near the Pantheon in Rome and was later placed in the courtyard of the first basilica of St Peter. It now stands in the Cortile della Pigna, or courtyard of the pine cone, in the Vatican Museum.

When the large atrium gave way to a smaller porch, the fountain was replaced by a smaller holy water font just inside the entrance. The use of the water was meant to be not just an external washing but especially a purification of one's mind and heart. So St John Chrysystom warns of those who "enter church washing their hands but not their hearts" (*Hom. LXXI on St John*). We too should see blessing ourselves with holy water as purifying our mind and heart.

In the ninth century, although the custom already existed before then, Pope Leo IV (847-855) ordered priests to bless and sprinkle the people with holy water every Sunday before Mass, a custom we know as the Asperges, or sprinkling. We see its meaning in one of the formulas of blessing of the water where the priest says: "Almighty ever-living God, who willed that through water, the fountain of life and the source of purification, even souls should be cleansed and receive the gift of eternal life; be pleased, we pray, to bless this water, by which we seek protection on this your day, O Lord. Renew the living spring of your grace within us and grant that by this water we may be defended from all ills of spirit and body, and so approach you with hearts made clean and worthily receive your salvation."

In the sixteenth century St Charles Borromeo, Archbishop of Milan, issued norms for the design of holy water fonts: "The vessel intended for holy water ... shall be of marble or of solid stone, neither porous nor with cracks. It shall rest upon a handsomely wrought column and shall not be placed outside of the church but within it and, insofar as possible, to the right of those who enter."

When we bless ourselves with holy water, apart from purifying our minds and hearts we remind ourselves of our baptism and we can renew our baptismal commitment. In this sense one of the blessings of holy water says: "Blessed are you, Lord, all-powerful God, who in Christ, the living water of salvation, blessed and transformed us. Grant that, when we are sprinkled with this water or make use of it, we will be refreshed inwardly by the power of the Holy Spirit and continue to walk in the new life we received at baptism."

And then of course we make the sign of the cross with the water, reminding ourselves of the cross of Christ by which we were redeemed, as well as the daily crosses we can bear in union with his.

Finally, when we say "In the name of the Father and of the Son and of the Holy Spirit" we remind ourselves of the Blessed Trinity, the central truth of our faith. So the use of holy water is not only ancient in origin but very rich in meaning.

503 What is a Jubilee Year?

Now that the Extraordinary Jubilee Year of Mercy is approaching, can you tell me exactly what a Jubilee Year is and what the difference is between an ordinary Jubilee Year and an extraordinary one?

Jubilee years have their origin in the Old Testament when, at the end of each cycle of seven years times seven, sometimes referred to as a "Sabbath's Sabbath", a special year of rest was proclaimed in which the land would be left fallow without being cultivated, slaves and prisoners would be set free, debts would be forgiven and the mercy of God would be particularly evident.

The jubilee year is described in the book of Leviticus: "And you shall count seven weeks of years, seven times seven years, so that the time of the seven weeks of years shall be to you forty-nine years. Then you shall send abroad the loud trumpet on the tenth day of the seventh month; on the day of atonement you shall send abroad the trumpet throughout all your land. And you shall hallow the fiftieth year, and proclaim liberty through the land to all its inhabitants; it shall be a jubilee for you, when each of you shall return to his property and each of you shall return to his family. A jubilee shall that fiftieth year be to you; in it you shall neither sow, nor reap what grows of itself, nor gather the grapes from the undressed vines. For it is a jubilee; it shall be holy to you; you shall eat what it yields out of the field" (*Lev* 25:8-12).

The very name jubilee in English seems to derive from the Hebrew word *yobel*, which in turn derives from *yobhel*, meaning ram, since the trumpet referred to in the book of Leviticus, the *shofar*, was made from a ram's horn.

In the Church the jubilee year was first observed in the year 1300, when Pope Boniface VIII called for a holy year to mark 1300 years since the birth of Christ. On that occasion the Pope published a Bull in which he granted special indulgences for those who would go to Rome, confess their sins and visit the basilicas of St Peter and St Paul. Residents of Rome were to make the visits each day for thirty days, and visitors to the city for fifteen days.

Interestingly, Pope Boniface did not use the word jubilee in that Bull and he indicated that such a special year was to be celebrated every one hundred years thereafter. Nonetheless, before the middle of the fourteenth century St Bridget of Sweden and the poet Petrarch, among others, urged Pope Clement VI, who was then residing in Avignon, to celebrate a jubilee sooner. The Pope agreed and so the next jubilee year was held in 1350.

Rome and its major basilicas remained the focus of the jubilee, even though the Pope did not return to the city for it. Daily visits to the Basilica of St John the Lateran were added to visits to the basilicas of St Peter and St Paul in order to gain the indulgence. In the next jubilee, held in 1390, the Basilica of St Mary Major was added and since then visits to the four major basilicas have been one of the conditions for gaining the jubilee year indulgence. One of the features of jubilee years is the opening of a special door in the Roman basilicas, through which pilgrims pass by way of symbolising their greater access to God's grace and mercy.

In 1470 Pope Paul II decreed that the jubilee should be celebrated every twenty-five years and this has been the practice ever since, even though in some years the jubilee was not held due to wars or other circumstances. Pope Paul also allowed people from other countries to gain the indulgence by visiting some designated church in their own country, especially the cathedral of each diocese, and this too has remained the custom.

In addition to these ordinary jubilee years there have been several extraordinary ones for special occasions, one of which is the present Jubilee Year of Mercy. Others were held in 1628 and 1629 to pray for peace, 1933 on the occasion of the nineteen hundredth anniversary of Christ's death, 1966 to celebrate the conclusion of the Second Vatican Council, and 1983 as a Holy Year of Redemption.

So the present Extraordinary Jubilee Year of Mercy has a long history. It is a splendid opportunity to receive the mercy of God, especially through the sacrament of mercy, the sacrament of Penance, and to show mercy to others.

Baptism and the Eucharist

504 Does Baptism guarantee salvation?

A friend who has a degree in Theology recently told me that if we are baptised we are assured of heaven. I didn't argue with him because he knows a lot more than I do. Is what he says true?

It is certainly not true, and we know this in a variety of ways.

We can begin with the nature of man as God made us, and as he looks upon us. He made us in his own image and likeness, unlike other animals, and so we have an intellect to know the truth and a free will to choose whether to follow the truth or not. God respects our freedom, our free choices. He doesn't take us to heaven automatically but he does give us all the graces we need to get there, beginning with the grace of Baptism. God treats us as his children, not as toys or robots. He wants us to choose freely to do his will and to repent freely when we have failed to do so. If we have lived well and are in the state of grace when we die, we will go to heaven by our own free choice.

But not everyone lives this way. Common sense and life experience remind us of the many people who have been baptised and then turn away from God and live very immoral lives. If they die in that state they will not be saved. The *Catechism of the Catholic Church* makes this clear: "To die in mortal sin without repenting and accepting God's merciful love means remaining separated from him for ever by our own free choice" (*CCC* 1033).

The Second Vatican Council says as much. In the Dogmatic Constitution on the Church *Lumen gentium* we read: "[Christ] himself explicitly asserted the necessity of faith and Baptism, and thereby affirmed at the same time the necessity of the Church which men enter through Baptism as through a door. Hence they could not be saved who, knowing that the Catholic Church was founded as necessary by God through Christ, would refuse either to enter it, or to remain in it" (*LG* 14). So a baptised person who, with full knowledge of what they were doing and with full consent, refused to remain in the Church would not be saved.

This is born out in the punishment of excommunication which applies for the sins of heresy, apostasy (the total rejection of the faith) and schism of a baptised person. The excommunication, which can be lifted only if the person repents, has effects as regards the person's relations with God: "Whatever you bind on earth shall be bound in heaven, and whatever you loose on earth shall be loosed in heaven" (*Mt* 16:19).

As if this weren't enough, we have the practice of the Church in her funeral rites. We know that Baptism remits original sin and leaves the soul in the state of grace, so that if the person has not committed any personal sins after Baptism they will most certainly go to heaven. Thus when a baptised infant dies before reaching the age of reason, the funeral Mass has white vestments and the prayers indicate the firm belief of the Church that the infant is most certainly in heaven. An example of the Opening Prayer of these Masses is: "… grant that one day we may inherit eternal life with him (her), whom, by the grace of Baptism, you have adopted as your own child and who we believe is dwelling even now in your kingdom."

But when a baptised adult dies, the Church does not presume that the person has gone straight to heaven. Rather, it prays for the repose of their soul with prayers like "… grant, that through this mystery your servant N., who has fallen asleep in Christ, may rejoice to rise again through him." Naturally the soul may be in purgatory and hence on its way to heaven, but one can never be certain of that, as it may have gone to hell.

In this whole matter it is of no use quoting scriptural passages like "He who believes and is baptised will be saved; but he who does not believe will be condemned" (*Mk* 16:16) as if this meant that Jesus is guaranteeing eternal salvation to anyone who is baptised. Not for nothing does Jesus add that in addition to being baptised the person must also believe. If they do not believe they will be condemned.

So we should be under no false illusions. Baptism alone does not guarantee our eternal salvation. We must also live and die well and God, in his mercy, gives us all the graces we need to do that. He wants all to be saved (cf. *1 Tim* 2:4).

505 Baptism of children of non-practising parents

Can you please explain the Church's teaching on the Baptism of children of non-practising parents? I feel that every child has the right to be baptised and to be made a child of God, even if the parents are not practising the faith.

The Church has an official teaching on your question, but the application of this teaching in practice can leave pastors divided. The teaching is found in the *Code of Canon Law*: "For an infant to be baptised lawfully it is required that there be a realistic hope that the child will be brought up in the Catholic religion. If such hope is truly lacking, the Baptism is, in accordance with the provisions of particular law, to be deferred and the parents advised of the reason for this" (Can. 868, §1, 2).

The Latin for "realistic hope" is *spes fundata*, founded hope, for which realistic hope is a faithful translation. This can be distinguished from *spes bene fundata*, well founded hope, which is stronger but this degree of hope is not required. Thus the hope required is not expected to be equivalent to some sort of moral certainty or assurance; a reasonable, realistic, hope is sufficient.

The reason for this is obvious. If there is no hope at all of Catholic upbringing, the child would indeed receive all the benefits of Baptism but would not receive any subsequent formation in the faith or further sacraments. The child would grow up to be a Catholic in name only. Unfortunately, there are a good number of people in this situation around the world today. As baptised Catholics, they are subject to the Church's laws, among them the laws on marriage, so that if they married outside the Church their marriage would not be considered valid in the eyes of the Church.

But what constitutes a "realistic hope" of Catholic upbringing? Here is where pastors can be divided, leading to very different outcomes for the child. One traditional principle to be applied in interpreting any law is that of *favorabilia amplianda, odiosa restringenda*. That is, laws that are favourable to the person, such as those granting rights or privileges, are to be interpreted broadly, so as to maximise the rights or privileges. And laws that are "odious", in the sense of prescribing a penalty or restricting the exercise of rights, are to be interpreted strictly (cf. Can. 18).

Clearly the Baptism of a child is a favour, a benefit of enormous value for the child. Hence in case of doubt as to whether there is sufficient hope of the subsequent Catholic upbringing, the benefit of the doubt is to be given to the child, and the child should be baptised.

If we look at the reality of Catholic life in Australia today, only some twelve percent of Catholics attend Mass regularly on Sundays. So of all the babies born to at least nominally Catholic couples, only some twelve percent would qualify for Baptism if we limited it to couples who are attending Mass regularly and therefore able to give assurance of the Catholic upbringing of their child. This would be disastrous for the Church and for those unbaptised children.

If we tell the non-practising parents that we are unable to baptise their child but must defer it until such time as they can give some assurance of the Catholic upbringing of their child, many will interpret this as a refusal to baptise their child and they will be very angry with the Church, perhaps never setting foot in a church again. On the other hand, if we receive them warmly and discuss their faith situation and hopes for their child, it is very possible that we will discover that they are at least willing to teach their child to pray, to read him or her Bible stories, possibly to send him or her to a Catholic school, all of which gives hope of further faith formation. Added to this, the instructions we give the couple prior to the Baptism on the importance of the sacrament and the duty of the parents and godparents to help the child grow in the faith, plus the homily in the Baptism itself, further strengthen this hope. At least from then on we have a warm relationship with the couple which in itself offers hope for the future.

We should not underestimate either the importance of the grandparents and other family friends who may be fervent Catholics who can give the child some Catholic formation. In view of all of this, I believe we should show the couple the Church's merciful heart by proceeding with the Baptism provided there is at least some small hope of Catholic upbringing.

506 Masses of the Society of St Pius X

I prefer to attend the Extraordinary Form of the Mass but I have recently moved to an area where the only one available is said by priests of the Society of St Pius X. I know these priests are not in good standing with the Holy See but can I still attend their Mass?

In answering your question I will draw on a letter from Mgr Camille Perl, Secretary of the Vatican's Ecclesia Dei Commission, written in 1995 in answer to a question very much like yours.

The Commission was established in 1988 to oversee the granting of permission to priests wishing to celebrate the Extraordinary Form of the Mass, formerly called the Tridentine rite, according to the Missal of 1962. The decree *Ecclesia Dei* of Pope John Paul II which established the Commission encourages bishops to be generous in granting permission for their priests to celebrate this Mass in order to facilitate communion with the Holy See of people who have a particular love for that rite.

Not all bishops have been generous in granting this permission and in one famous case the bishop of Honolulu went so far as to excommunicate Catholics who attended Masses celebrated by priests of the St Pius X Society. The excommunication was unwarranted and was later overturned by the Vatican. This encouraged some traditionalist Catholics to believe that since attending Pius X Society Masses is not an excommunicable offence, it is acceptable to attend them.

A letter asking about attendance at these Masses was written to Cardinal Joseph Ratzinger, at the time Prefect of the Congregation for the Doctrine of the Faith, and it was answered by Mgr Perl of the Ecclesia Dei Commission. It was dated 29 September 1995 and it goes a long way to answering your question:

"We are aware of the lack of authorised celebrations of the Mass according to the 1962 Roman Missal in [certain dioceses] and we can appreciate your desire to assist at the traditional Mass. We also recognise your earnest desire to remain in full communion with the Successor of Peter and the members of the Church subject to him, a desire which obviously prompted you to write this letter. In order to answer your questions we must explain the Church's present evaluation of the situation of the Society of St Pius X.

"1. There is no doubt about the validity of the ordination of the priests of the Society of St Pius X. They are, however, suspended *a divinis*, that is prohibited by the Church from exercising their orders because of their illicit ordination.

"2. The Masses they celebrate are also valid, but it is considered morally illicit for the faithful to participate in these Masses unless they are physically or morally impeded from participating in a Mass celebrated by a Catholic priest in good standing (cf. *Code of Canon Law*, canon 844.2). The fact of not being able to assist at the celebration of the so-called 'Tridentine' Mass is not considered a sufficient motive for attending such Masses.

"3. While it is true that the participation in the Mass and sacraments at the chapels of the Society of St Pius X does not of itself constitute 'formal adherence to the schism', such adherence can come about over a period of time as one slowly imbibes a mentality which separates itself from the magisterium of the Supreme Pontiff. Father Peter R. Scott, District Superior of the Society in the United States, has publicly stated that he deplores the 'liberalism' of 'those who refuse to condemn the New Mass as absolutely offensive to God, or the religious liberty and ecumenism of the post-conciliar church.' With such an attitude the Society of St Pius X is effectively tending to establish its own canons of orthodoxy and hence to separate itself from the magisterium of the Supreme Pontiff. According to canon 751 such 'refusal of submission to the Roman Pontiff or the communion of the members of the Church subject to him' constitute schism. Hence we cannot encourage your participation in the Masses, the sacraments or other services conducted under the aegis of the Society of St Pius X."

As is clear, especially in the last sentence of n. 2, it is illicit to attend a Pius X Society Mass if the person has access to a Mass celebrated by a Catholic priest in good standing, even though this Mass is of the *Novus Ordo*, or Ordinary Form. Therefore, I would certainly advise you to find a parish where you can attend the Ordinary Form and perhaps ask the parish priest or the bishop if an Extraordinary Form Mass can be celebrated there at least from time to time.

507 Does Communion forgive sins?

Pope Francis in Amoris laetitia *says that the Eucharist "is not a prize for the perfect, but a powerful medicine and nourishment for the weak."* Does this mean that Communion actually forgives sins, even mortal sins, and that it can be given as medicine for those in mortal sin?

The text you cite is in footnote 351 of the document and is a quotation from Pope Francis' earlier Apostolic Exhortation *Evangelii gaudium* (2013), n. 47. What he says there is traditional Catholic teaching. Holy Communion is a powerful medicine and it does forgive sins, but not mortal sins.

In the cited paragraph of *Evangelii gaudium* Pope Francis quotes two early Fathers of the Church who teach this. The first is St Ambrose, who writes: "I must receive it always, so that it may always forgive my sins. If I sin continually, I must always have a remedy" (*De Sacramentis*, IV, 6, 28). A second quotation from the same work reads: "Those who ate manna died; those who eat this body will obtain the forgiveness of their sins" (IV, 5, 24).

The other Father of the Church is St Cyril of Alexandria. He writes of those who stay away from Communion because they consider themselves unworthy: "I examined myself and I found myself unworthy. To those who speak thus I say: when will you be worthy? When at last you present yourself before Christ? And if your sins prevent you from drawing nigh, and you never cease to fall – for, as the Psalm says, 'what man knows his faults?' – will you remain without partaking of the sanctification that gives life for eternity?" (*In Joh. Evang.*, IV, 2)

More recently, in 1905 the Vatican repeated this teaching in the Decree *Sacra Tridentina* approved by Pope St Pius X. It came in answer to the errors of Jansenism which taught, among other things, that a person needed to be virtually perfect in order to receive Communion. As a result, people were receiving the sacrament only seldomly. The document recommended daily reception of Communion if possible and taught that Communion is not a reward for virtue but rather a remedy for sin. It said that frequent Communion has as its aim "that the faithful, being united to God by means of the Sacrament, may thence derive strength to resist their sensual passions, to cleanse themselves from the stains of daily faults, and to avoid these graver sins to which human frailty is liable."

Could it be that Communion forgives mortal sins as well as venial sins? No, it does not. For the forgiveness of mortal sins we have the sacraments of Baptism, in the case of adults, and Reconciliation. Communion cannot be given to those in the state of mortal sin. The *Catechism of the Catholic Church* teaches: "The Eucharist is not ordered to the forgiveness of mortal sins – that is proper to the sacrament of Reconciliation. The Eucharist is properly the sacrament of those who are in full communion with the Church" (*CCC* 1395). Even more, "Anyone conscious of a grave sin must receive the sacrament of Reconciliation before coming to Communion" (*CCC* 1385).

But the Catechism, like the Fathers of the Church and earlier Church documents, teaches that Communion does forgive venial sins and it strengthens us to avoid committing mortal sins: "Holy Communion separates us from sin. The body of Christ we receive in Holy Communion is 'given up for us,' and the blood we drink 'shed for the many for the forgiveness of sins.' For this reason the Eucharist cannot unite us to Christ without at the same time cleansing us from past sins and preserving us from future sins" (*CCC* 1393; cf. *1 Cor* 11:26).

How does it do this? "As bodily nourishment restores lost strength, so the Eucharist strengthens our charity, which tends to be weakened in daily life; and this living charity *wipes away venial sins*" (*CCC* 1394). What is more, "By the same charity that it enkindles in us, the Eucharist *preserves us from future mortal sins*. The more we share the life of Christ and progress in his friendship, the more difficult it is to break away from him by mortal sin" (*CCC* 1395).

This teaching is very consoling. We all sin and it is heartening to know that we need not, and indeed should not, stay away from Communion simply because we have committed many venial sins. Holy Communion, like so many other good acts we do, forgives those sins by helping us grow in love for God and our neighbour and it strengthens us to avoid falling into mortal sins. For this reason we should go to Communion as often as we can.

508 Extraordinary ministers of Communion

In my parish there are many lay people helping distribute Communion and I sometimes wonder whether they are truly necessary. Also, the priest sometimes sits down and lets the lay Eucharistic ministers distribute Communion. Is this correct?

First, the term "lay Eucharistic minister" is not correct. The Vatican's instruction *Redemptionis Sacramentum* explains: "As has already been recalled, 'the only minister who can confect the Sacrament of the Eucharist *in persona Christi* is a validly ordained Priest'. Hence the name 'minister of the Eucharist' belongs properly to the priest alone. Moreover, also by reason of their sacred ordination, the ordinary ministers of Holy Communion are the bishop, the priest and the deacon, to whom it belongs therefore to administer Holy Communion to the lay members of Christ's faithful during the celebration of Mass" (*RS*, n. 154).

Even an instituted acolyte is an extraordinary minister: "In addition to the ordinary ministers there is the formally instituted acolyte, who by virtue of his institution is an extraordinary minister of Holy Communion even outside the celebration of Mass" (*RS* 155).

As regards lay people who distribute Communion the Instruction clarifies the terminology: "This function is to be understood strictly according to the name by which it is known, that is to say, that of extraordinary minister of Holy Communion, and not 'special minister of Holy Communion' nor 'extraordinary minister of the Eucharist" nor 'special minister of the Eucharist', by which names the meaning of this function is unnecessarily and improperly broadened" (*RS*, n. 156).

As explained above, only the priest is the minister of the Eucharist, so there are no extraordinary or special ministers of the Eucharist. When the Instruction adds that names like "special minister of Holy Communion" unnecessarily and improperly broaden the meaning of this function, it implies that the use of lay people to distribute Communion should be truly extraordinary, exceptional, not ordinary or special.

When may extraordinary ministers of Communion be asked to exercise their role? The answer is: "only when the priest is prevented by weakness or advanced age or some other genuine reason, or when the number of faithful coming to Communion is so great that the very celebration of Mass would be unduly prolonged. This, however, is to be understood in such a way that a brief prolongation, considering the circumstances and culture of the place, is not at all a sufficient reason" (*RS* 158). Thus if the priest sits down while extraordinary ministers distribute Communion this is justified only if he is ill, elderly or for whatever other reason prevented from doing it himself.

Naturally, terms like "unduly prolonged" or "brief prolongation" are not defined in terms of minutes. If the Mass were to be prolonged by fifteen or twenty minutes on a Sunday, this might perhaps be considered an undue prolongation that would justify the use of extraordinary ministers, especially if the Mass is to be followed shortly thereafter by another one, by a Baptism or wedding, etc.

On a weekday a shorter prolongation would justify their use, since some of the congregation will have to go to work or to another important engagement and if the Mass is unduly prolonged they will not be able to attend it at all. Nonetheless, in many parishes the number of faithful in weekday Masses is not such as to require the use of extraordinary ministers. If Communion is distributed under the species of wine as well as of bread, however, lay people will often be required to present the chalice with the Precious Blood.

What is clearly a disorder is to have several extraordinary ministers in every Mass as a way of giving lay people an important ministry to perform. As the Second Vatican Council explains, the proper role of the lay faithful is to engage in temporal affairs, the affairs of the world, and to order them according to God's law (cf. *Lumen gentium* 31), not to engage in liturgical affairs. It would also be an abuse if there were other priests or deacons in the parish who were available to distribute Communion but who refrained from doing so by way of giving lay people the opportunity. Likewise, if there were numerous priests in a concelebrated Mass sitting down while lay people distributed Communion.

Lay people distributing Communion are a big help in many circumstances, but they should exercise their role only when truly required.

509 The role of extraordinary ministers

My parish priest sometimes asks someone from the congregation to help out with Communion on an ad hoc *basis. Also the lay ministers come up to the sanctuary when the priest is breaking the host, the priest gives the chalice with the Precious Blood to one of the extraordinary ministers who receives from it and then passes the chalice to the next one, and they purify the vessels afterwards. Are these practices acceptable?*

In answer to your first question, the Vatican's Instruction *Redemptionis Sacramentum*, after saying that an instituted acolyte is an extraordinary minister of Holy Communion, adds: "If, moreover, reasons of real necessity prompt it, another lay member of Christ's faithful may also be delegated by the diocesan bishop, in accordance with the norm of law, for one occasion or for a specified time, and an appropriate formula of blessing may be used for the occasion... Finally, in special cases of an unforeseen nature, permission can be given for a single occasion by the priest who presides at the celebration of the Eucharist" (*RS*, n. 155).

Thus the priest who celebrates the Mass can designate someone to assist with Communion for a single occasion "in special cases of an unforeseen nature." This would be the case, for example, when there is a large congregation and there is no other minister of Communion present, whether ordinary or extraordinary. So your priest is justified in asking someone from the congregation to help out on a particular occasion, but this should be truly exceptional. After all, the task of distributing Communion requires specialised training, so asking someone from the congregation who does not have this training to distribute Communion should be a rare occurrence.

As regards when the extraordinary ministers are to come forward the *General Instruction of the Roman Missal* (2012) says: "These ministers should not approach the altar before the priest has received Communion..." (*GIRM* 162). So the extraordinary ministers should not go up to the altar at the breaking of the bread. If they go onto the sanctuary at this time but do not approach the altar itself this would seem to be acceptable. In this way they can go forward to receive Communion as soon as the priest receives it, without delaying the Mass.

The extraordinary ministers should not hand the chalice, or the ciborium for that matter, to one another after they have received from it. The *General Instruction* clarifies that the priest should give the chalice or ciborium directly to each of the extraordinary ministers for distribution to the faithful (cf. *GIRM* 162).

Moreover, the lay faithful should never hand the chalice or ciborium to each other. In a special paragraph for Australia the *General Instruction* says: "It is not permitted for the faithful to take the consecrated Bread or the sacred chalice by themselves and, still less, to hand them on from one to another among themselves" (*GIRM* 160).

Finally, it is for the priest himself, a deacon or an instituted acolyte to purify the vessels after Communion. This is never to be done by extraordinary ministers. The *General Instruction* says: "The sacred vessels are purified by the priest, the deacon, or an instituted acolyte after Communion or after Mass, insofar as possible at the credence table" (*GIRM* 279). As the *General Instruction* makes clear in other paragraphs, if there is a deacon present, he is the one to do the purification rather than the priest; if there is an acolyte, he does it or he assists the deacon or priest; and if neither of these is present, the priest does the purification (cf. *GIRM* 163, 183, 192, 279).

I take advantage of the opportunity to say that if there is any Precious Blood remaining after Communion, it is the priest, the deacon or the instituted acolyte who is to consume it: "Whatever may remain of the Blood of Christ is consumed at the altar by the priest or the deacon or the duly instituted acolyte who ministered the chalice" (*GIRM* 284, b). If there is no deacon or acolyte, "the priest himself immediately and completely consumes at the altar any consecrated wine that happens to remain" (*GIRM* 163). Naturally, if there is a large amount remaining it would be opportune as an exception for the extraordinary ministers to assist him in this. The priest should not consume a large amount on his own for obvious reasons.

510 Extraordinary ministers denying Communion

I have been an extraordinary minister of Communion in a small parish for over thirty years and I see some people coming to Communion who I know should not be coming, given their lifestyle. My parish priest says it is not up to me to judge. What should I do?

This is a dilemma that faces many extraordinary ministers and, of course, many priests. Let me begin with extraordinary ministers. In the long letter expressing your concern you spoke of knowing most of the people in your small parish and you mentioned such lifestyles as unmarried people living together, people who have been divorced and remarried civilly, and people who come to Mass only occasionally and are never seen going to confession.

You mentioned that in your thirty years in this ministry you have never been as confused as you are now. It is easy to understand this, since thirty years ago far more people attended Mass regularly, more went regularly to confession, there were fewer divorces, fewer people lived together without being married, etc. And you rightly said that those who are in the state of mortal sin should not receive Communion without going to sacramental confession beforehand (cf. *Catechism of the Catholic Church*, 1385).

Naturally your parish priest is right that it is not up to you to judge. This is especially the case as regards those who go to Mass seldom in the parish and don't appear to go to confession there. For all you know, they go to Mass somewhere else on the other Sundays and they may go to confession elsewhere without your knowing it. In any case, many people are unaware that it is a serious sin to miss Mass through their own fault (cf. *CCC* 2181).

As regards those who are divorced and remarried civilly or simply living together, it is not up to the extraordinary minister to judge that they are in serious sin and refuse them Communion. They may be living in continence without sexual relations. Or they may be unaware that their lifestyle is objectively contrary to the law of God and to their own true good. In any case, pastoral prudence dictates that one should never refuse Communion and thus embarrass someone publicly, unless it is an obvious and notorious case of unworthiness that is known to all. Therefore, the extraordinary minister can give these people the benefit of the doubt and administer Communion to them.

The parish priest, on the other hand, should be more vigilant. He is responsible for looking after the spiritual welfare of all in his parish, for offering them the means to seek holiness and reach heaven. If he suspects that someone is living a lifestyle that is not in keeping with the law of God, in which they should not receive Communion, he should find the way to speak calmly with them about it privately. What he cannot do is turn a blind eye.

The Catechism is very clear on the divorced and remarried not being able to receive Communion: "If the divorced are remarried civilly, they find themselves in a situation that objectively contravenes God's law. Consequently, they cannot receive Eucharistic communion as long as this situation persists… Reconciliation through the sacrament of Penance can be granted only to those who have repented for having violated the sign of the covenant and of fidelity to Christ, and who are committed to living in complete continence" (*CCC* 1650).

Pope Francis, in his recent Apostolic Exhortation *Amoris laetitia*, speaks about the importance of engaging such couples individually in order to discern their true situation and find the best way to help them (cf. *AL* 300). To leave them in a situation of objective grave sin is to do them a great disservice. Sin always hurts the sinner, even when the sinner is unaware that what he or she is doing is wrong. Moreover, there is the danger of scandal to others who are aware of their situation and see them going to Communion.

Often the priest will be able to persuade a young couple who are living together to separate and perhaps prepare for marriage, and a couple who are divorced and remarried civilly to live as brother and sister and seek a declaration of nullity of their first marriage, or marriages. They will be eternally grateful to the priest for helping them find a way that, deep down, they know is the right one. If for the time being they are not ready or able to follow this advice, they should be told not to receive Communion. Instead, they can come forward to receive a blessing. And always they should be treated with great kindness.

511 Communion for the divorced and remarried

I am confused about some things Pope Francis wrote in Amoris laetitia *concerning circumstances in which divorced and remarried people might be admitted to the sacraments. Can you shed some light on this?*

Much has been written and said about this Apostolic Exhortation of Pope Francis, with numerous critics saying the Pope has departed from traditional Catholic teaching and others defending him. The Pope has always defended the consistency of this document with traditional Catholic teaching – it could not be otherwise – and so it should be read and interpreted in this light.

The teaching of the Church is based on Our Lord's words on divorce and remarriage: "Whoever divorces his wife and marries another, commits adultery against her; and if she divorces her husband and marries another, she commits adultery" (*Mk* 10:11-12). It is clear from this that those who are divorced and remarried civilly are living in an objective situation of grave sin and if they engage in acts of intimacy they are committing adultery. I say "objective" because there may be people who are subjectively not guilty of grave sin due to ignorance or other circumstances which the Pope mentions.

In view of this constant teaching, Pope St John Paul II in his Apostolic Exhortation *Familiaris consortio* (1981), after saying that the divorced and remarried should be welcomed into the life of the Church, went on to say: "However, the Church reaffirms her practice, which is based upon Sacred Scripture, of not admitting to Eucharistic Communion divorced persons who have remarried" (n. 84).

The *Code of Canon Law* (1983) too says that "Those … who obstinately persist in manifest grave sin, are not to be admitted to Holy Communion" (can. 915). The phrase "who obstinately persist in manifest grave sin" includes people who are not validly married in the Church, people in a *de facto* relationship, etc. If there were any doubt about this, on 24 June 2000, the Pontifical Council for Legislative Texts issued a Declaration clarifying that those who are divorced and remarried outside the Church fall under the prohibition of receiving Communion mentioned in Canon 915. The Declaration mentions that the prohibition of receiving Communion when one is in a state of grave sin "is derived from divine law and transcends the domain of positive ecclesiastical laws". That is, the Church is not free to change what is already forbidden by God.

The *Catechism of the Catholic Church* is very clear on the matter: "Today there are numerous Catholics in many countries who have recourse to civil divorce and contract new civil unions. In fidelity to the words of Jesus Christ – 'Whoever divorces his wife and marries another, commits adultery against her; and if she divorces her husband and marries another, she commits adultery' (*Mk* 10:11-12) – the Church maintains that a new union cannot be recognised as valid, if the first marriage was. If the divorced are remarried civilly, they find themselves in a situation that objectively contravenes God's law. Consequently, they cannot receive Eucharistic communion as long as this situation persists... Reconciliation through the sacrament of Penance can be granted only to those who have repented for having violated the sign of the covenant and of fidelity to Christ, and who are committed to living in complete continence" (*CCC* 1650).

What then of Pope Francis' reference to people in this situation who may not be subjectively guilty of grave sin because of particular circumstances? He quotes the Catechism, which says that "imputability and responsibility for an action can be diminished or even nullified by ignorance, inadvertence, duress, fear, habit, inordinate attachments, and other psychological or social factors" (*CCC* 1735; *AL* 302). Later he goes on to say: "Because of forms of conditioning and mitigating factors, it is possible that in an objective situation of sin – which may not be subjectively culpable, or fully such – a person can be living in God's grace, can love and can also grow in the life of grace and charity, while receiving the Church's help to this end" (*AL* 305).

Can these people be admitted to the sacraments? The normal pastoral practice in these cases is to help them realise that, even though they may not be subjectively guilty of sin, their present life is not in keeping with the demands of the Gospel and to show them how they can change, perhaps over time, so that they are once more living as God wants. Only when they are living in conformity with God's law will they find the true wellbeing and happiness they seek. What is not pastoral or merciful is to leave them in that state, just as it would not be merciful to allow someone to go on using heroin simply because they didn't know how much it can harm them.

What this means in practice, if the couple cannot separate – because of the need to care for their children, because of their age, etc. – is to help them live as brother and sister, sleeping in separate bedrooms and abstaining from acts of sexual intimacy. If they agree to do this and are sorry for their sins, they can be absolved in the sacrament of Penance and can be admitted to Holy Communion. If from time to time they fail and have acts of intimacy, they can still be forgiven, as can others who fail in matters of serious sin when they are sincerely trying to avoid falling. To avoid the danger of scandal it is usually recommended that they attend Mass and receive Communion in a parish where they are not known.

Penance and Holy Orders

512 Why go to confession?

My son hasn't been to confession for many years and, along with his wife, I am praying that he will return during this Jubilee Year of Mercy. Can you give me any tips that might help him go and return to the practice of the faith?

You do very well to have this important intention in mind for the Year of Mercy. If every practising Catholic proposed to help at least one person return to confession after a long time away, we would be helping many souls to experience God's mercy. And of course we should all resolve to go regularly ourselves to this great sacrament of mercy.

Pope Francis spoke about some of the reasons for the sacrament in his Wednesday audience in Rome on 19 February 2014: "The Sacrament of Reconciliation is a Sacrament of healing. When I go to confession, it is in order to be healed, to heal my soul, to heal my heart and to be healed of some wrongdoing."

We all commit sins – all of us. Some of these sins, mortal sins, separate us completely from the love of God and cast our soul into darkness, depriving us of the light of Christ we were given at Baptism. We do not find this state a happy one. We want to be healed, to have our burden lifted, to be freed, and for this reason Christ gave us the sacrament of penance on the very evening of his Resurrection (cf. *Jn* 20:21-23). When we finally decide to go to confession, especially after a long time away, we have the joy of hearing the words "I absolve you from your sins" and we know that our Father God embraces us and kisses us as did the father of the prodigal son (cf. *Lk* 15:20). It is an incredibly uplifting and healing experience, a true resurrection.

Pope Francis went on to say that "it reminds us that we can truly be at peace only if we allow ourselves to be reconciled, in the Lord Jesus, with the Father and with the brethren. And we have all felt this in our hearts, when we have gone to confession with a soul weighed down and with a little sadness; and when we receive Jesus' forgiveness we feel at peace, with that peace of soul which is so beautiful, and which only Jesus can give."

Some people will say they don't need to go to confession because they can confess their sins directly to God. The Pope answers: "Yes, you can say to God 'forgive me' and say your sins, but our sins are also committed against the brethren, and against the Church. That is why it is necessary to ask pardon of the Church, and of the brethren in the person of the priest."

Naturally, confessing to a priest requires that we be sincere and say all the things we have done, and this can fill us with a certain shame. Pope Francis comments: "Shame is also good, it is healthy to feel a little shame, because being ashamed is salutary. In my country when a person feels no shame, we say that he is 'shameless'; a *sin verguenza*. But shame too does us good, because it makes us more humble, and the priest receives this confession with love and tenderness and forgives us on God's behalf. Also from a human point of view, in order to unburden oneself, it is good to talk with a brother and tell the priest these things which are weighing so much on my heart. And one feels that one is unburdening oneself before God, with the Church, with his brother. Do not be afraid of confession! When one is in line to go to confession, one feels all these things, even shame, but then when one finishes confession one leaves free, grand, beautiful, forgiven, candid, happy. This is the beauty of confession!"

For those who have been away from confession for a long time the Pope says: "And if much time has passed, do not lose another day. Go, the priest will be good. Jesus is there, and Jesus is more benevolent than priests, Jesus receives you, he receives you with so much love. Be courageous and go to confession!" For those who think their sins are so many or so bad that they can't be forgiven, Pope Francis said in a homily on 23 January 2015: "There is no sin which [God] won't pardon... If you go to confession repentant, he will forgive everything."

The Pope practises what he preaches, going to confession every fifteen or twenty days with a Franciscan priest in the Vatican. Let us follow his lead, and help others to do so too. It will give us all a great joy.

513 Absolution of abortion

The media have recently reported that the Pope has allowed priests all over the world to absolve the sin of abortion, but not the sin of the abortionist who brings it about. I thought priests could always absolve any sin. What is new about this decision?

This news item has raised questions like yours in the minds of many people, so it is good to be able to clarify what the Pope actually said.

The source of the media reports was the letter of Pope Francis to Archbishop Rino Fisichella, President of the Pontifical Council for the Promotion of the New Evangelisation, giving directives for the forthcoming Jubilee Year of Mercy, which is to begin on 8 December 2015. The Pope's letter is dated 1 September 2015.

What did the Pope actually say? With respect to the absolution of the sin of abortion, he wrote: "The forgiveness of God cannot be denied to one who has repented, especially when that person approaches the Sacrament of Confession with a sincere heart in order to obtain reconciliation with the Father. For this reason too, I have decided, notwithstanding anything to the contrary, to concede to all priests for the Jubilee Year the discretion to absolve of the sin of abortion those who have procured it and who, with contrite heart, seek forgiveness for it. May priests fulfil this great task by expressing words of genuine welcome combined with a reflection that explains the gravity of the sin committed, besides indicating a path of authentic conversion by which to obtain the true and generous forgiveness of the Father who renews all with his presence."

As is clear, the Pope makes no distinction between the woman who has undergone the abortion and the abortionist and others who assist in bringing it about. The Church has always intended by the word "procure" to refer to all those involved, both the woman herself and the abortionists. Thus all who are involved in procuring the abortion who "with contrite heart, seek forgiveness for it" may be absolved.

But the question still remains: what is new about this directive? Priests have always been able to forgive the sins of those who seek forgiveness with a contrite heart. This means all sins, no matter how grave. There is no sin that cannot be forgiven, as long as the person is truly sorry for it.

What is special about the sin of abortion is that, in order to emphasise its gravity, the Church attaches the penalty of excommunication to it. Canon 1398 of the *Code of Canon Law* says: "A person who actually procures an abortion incurs a *latae sententiae* excommunication." The words *latae sententiae* mean that the person procuring the abortion *by that very fact* is excommunicated. Before a priest can absolve the sin of abortion, the excommunication must first be lifted and ordinarily this can be done only by the diocesan bishop or his vicars (cf. Can. 1355, §2). In Australia for a long time priests have had the faculty to lift the excommunication themselves and absolve the sin at the same time.

It seems that with the Pope's new directive, all priests will now be able to lift the excommunication themselves and then forgive the sin, thus simplifying the process and opening wide the gate of God's mercy. When the Pope says "notwithstanding anything to the contrary" he is no doubt referring to the above-mentioned provision of the *Code of Canon Law*, which does not allow priests to absolve the sin without first having had recourse to the bishop.

It should always be understood, in any case, that a person having an abortion would not incur the excommunication if they were under the age of sixteen, were ignorant of the law forbidding abortion or acted under the compulsion of grave fear (cf. Can. 1323). In view of this, many people who in fact have had abortions may not have incurred the excommunication.

So we give thanks to the Holy Father for granting this special grace for the Jubilee Year at the same time as we pray for those who have had abortions, that they seek forgiveness of their sin in this Year of Mercy. And we pray for women who are considering having an abortion, that they give the baby in their womb the gift of life.

514 Prayer for priests

My parish priest often asks me to pray for him and I find this strange. After all, he is a priest and a very faithful one. I am the one who needs prayers, not him. Do priests need prayers too? Don't they automatically go to heaven?

We should pray very much for priests, for all priests, no matter how faithful they may seem. After all, they are Christians like the rest of us and they too have to save their soul. They too commit sins and none of us can be sure of our salvation until the day we die. The sacrament of Holy Orders does not confer automatic entry into heaven!

Even more, priests – and all the more, bishops – need more prayers than others because they have to render an account for how they have used the special graces and responsibilities they have received through their priesthood: "Everyone to whom much is given, of him will much be required" (*Lk* 12:48).

Indeed, priests need to render an account not only for their own soul but for how they have helped the many people entrusted to their pastoral care. The role of shepherd of souls carries with it a great responsibility and God will ask an account of how the priest has carried out this mission: "So you, son of man, I have made a watchman for the house of Israel; whenever you hear a word from my mouth, you shall give them warning from me. If I say to the wicked, O wicked man, you shall surely die, and you do not speak to warn the wicked to turn from his way, that wicked man shall die in his iniquity, but his blood I will require at your hand" (*Ezek* 33:7-8).

The Church in her liturgy reflects the need to pray for priests by the various Masses in the missal for priests, for the bishop and for the Pope. And in the Eucharistic Prayers, after praying for the Pope and the bishop, we pray for the clergy.

One stark reminder of the need to pray for priests is the experience of Fr Steven Scheier from the United States. He was ordained a priest in 1973 but, as he admits, was more concerned about what other priests and his people thought of him than about being a good priest for Jesus Christ. In order to be popular he preached about peace, love and joy, but not about morality and dogma. On 18 October 1985 while driving from Wichita, Kansas, to his parish in Fredonia 86 miles away, he was involved in a head-on collision with a truck and was thrown onto the road. He suffered a broken neck and the entire scalp on the right side of his head was torn off, partially sheering off the right side of his brain and crushing many brain cells. Although unconscious, he repeated the Hail Mary over and over again in the ambulance on the way to the hospital.

The doctor, seeing there was not much he could do, sewed his scalp back on and called for a helicopter to transport him to Wichita. He was given a fifteen percent chance of survival. The Protestant parishes and his own Catholic parish in Fredonia prayed all night for his survival and he credits this with saving his life. He returned to his parish in May of the following year.

One day, while reading in Mass the Gospel of the barren fig tree (*Lk* 13:1-9), Fr Steven saw the page illuminated, enlarged and coming off the lectionary toward him. Back in his house he suddenly remembered something that had happened shortly after the accident. He found himself before the judgment seat of God, where Jesus took him through his entire life, showing him how he had failed in so many ways. He had to acknowledge that everything he saw was true and that there was no room for excuses.

At the end of the judgment he was told that he was going to hell and he realised this was what he deserved. Implied in this was that he had committed mortal sins for which he was not sorry. But then he heard a woman say, "Son, will you please spare his life and his eternal soul?" Jesus replied, "Mother, he's been a priest for twelve years for himself and not for me; let him reap the punishment he deserves." "But Son," she said, "if we give him special graces and strengths then let's see if he bears fruit; if not, your will be done." There was a short pause, after which Jesus said, "Mother, he's yours." Even though he didn't have a personal relationship with Our Lady before the accident, ever since he has had great devotion to her.

So priests cannot be assured of going to heaven. They have to make their way in by the narrow gate, like everyone else. And prayer for priests is important – very important.

515 Bishops' insignia

I recently attended the ordination of two bishops and was intrigued by several items they received in the ceremony. Can you tell me the meaning of such things as the mitre and crosier? Also, since this was called an ordination, did the bishops receive a new sacrament?

I will tell you about all the main items of bishops' insignia, starting with the skull cap, or zucchetto. This small round cap, worn towards the back of the head, dates to the thirteenth century and was developed to cover the tonsure, the part of the back of the head that was shaved when a man entered the clerical state. It varies in colour according to the rank of the bishop, with the Pope wearing white, cardinals red and bishops violet. Priests may also wear the skull cap and theirs is black. It can be used at any time but is removed in Mass during the Eucharistic Prayer.

Another item which the bishop can use at any time is the pectoral cross. The name "pectoral" comes from the Latin word for chest since the cross is worn on a chain hanging down over the bishop's chest. The cross of Christ was the instrument of our redemption and it reminds the bishop of his duty to be generous in sacrificing himself for the flock entrusted to his care.

In the ordination ceremony the new bishop is given a ring, which symbolises his spiritual marriage to the Church and his duty to be faithful in imitation of Christ, the bridegroom of the Church. The ring as an official part of the bishop's insignia was first mentioned early in the seventh century and it came to be of general use in the ninth and tenth centuries. The prayer said in conferring the ring reads: "Receive this ring, the seal of fidelity: adorned with undefiled faith, preserve unblemished the bride of God, the holy Church." The ring is worn on the fourth finger of the right hand.

Next the bishop is given the mitre, a large pointed head covering, with two short lappets or flaps hanging down over the back. Its name comes from a Greek word meaning turban. It is worn only in more solemn ceremonies like the Mass, processions, etc., and is removed for the prayers. It is usually white in colour. It has its origin in the Byzantine Empire where officials of the court wore a head covering known as a *camelaucum*. This later developed into a crown and is the origin of the papal crown known as the tiara, which comes to a point at the top. In the Church the mitre dates back to the eleventh century, when it was worn only by the Pope. In the twelfth century it came to be used also by bishops. The prayer said on conferring the mitre makes reference to the crown: "Receive the mitre, and may the splendour of holiness shine forth in you, so that when the chief shepherd appears you may deserve to receive from him an unfading crown of glory."

After the mitre the new bishop is given the crosier, or shepherd's crook, which symbolises his duty to be diligent in watching over the flock entrusted to him. The prayer says: "Receive the crosier, the sign of your pastoral office: and keep watch over the whole flock in which the Holy Spirit has placed you as bishop to govern the Church of God." The crosier is first mentioned as part of the bishop's insignia in the seventh century.

Your question about whether the ordination of a bishop constitutes the conferring of a new sacrament is an interesting one. As we know, there are three degrees of Holy Orders: the diaconate, presbyterate and episcopate. The man is first ordained a deacon, then a priest and finally a bishop. While it might appear to anyone attending these ceremonies that there are three separate sacraments, the reality is that the sacrament of Holy Orders is only one, with three degrees. This has been the case since the beginning of the Church.

The degrees of bishop and priest are a participation in the priesthood of Christ, the head of the Church, and that of deacon is intended to help and serve the bishops and priests. All three degrees are received through the one sacrament of Holy Orders. What is happening is that in each successive ordination ceremony the person is receiving the one sacrament in a progressively fuller way, enabling him to carry out more functions and conferring on him more responsibilities.

It is very important that we pray very much for all bishops, for they will have a great account to render in the judgment for the faithful entrusted to them.

516 The pallium

I was very interested to read an article on an archbishop receiving the pallium from the papal nuncio but was wondering why my own archbishop doesn't wear one and what exactly the significance of the pallium is.

For those not familiar with the pallium, it is a band of white wool some five centimetres wide forming a circle, with a strip hanging down in front and in back with black silk at the bottom of each. It is decorated with six crosses of black silk and has three gold jewelled pins. The pins were originally used to hold the pallium in place but are now merely decorative. The pallium is worn by the archbishop over his chasuble when he celebrates Mass and it is the symbol of his authority.

Since it is made of wool the pallium is the symbol of the bishop as the good shepherd and also of the Lamb of God crucified for the salvation of mankind. Pope Benedict XVI elaborated on this symbolism in the Mass for the inauguration of his pontificate on 24 April 2005: "The symbolism of the pallium is even more concrete: the lamb's wool is meant to represent the lost, sick or weak sheep which the shepherd places on his shoulders and carries to the waters of life."

The Pope too wears the pallium, although his has red crosses instead of black, and thus the pallium of an archbishop symbolises his union with the Pope. The pallium is used only by what is known as a metropolitan archbishop; that is, the archbishop of the principal diocese within a group of dioceses which make up an ecclesiastical province. In Australia the metropolitan archdioceses are those of Sydney, Brisbane, Melbourne, Adelaide and Perth. The other dioceses within those provinces, known as suffragan dioceses, are all the other dioceses in the respective state. The diocese of Darwin is a suffragan diocese of the province of Adelaide. The archdioceses of Canberra-Goulburn and Hobart have no suffragan dioceses and are therefore not metropolitan archdioceses, so that their archbishops do not use the pallium.

According to the *Code of Canon Law*, a metropolitan archbishop must request the pallium within three months of his appointment and he may wear it only in the territory of his own diocese and in the other dioceses of his ecclesiastical province (Can. 437).

Until 2014, it was the custom for the Pope himself to confer the pallium on all newly appointed metropolitan archbishops in a ceremony in Rome on the feast of Saints Peter and Paul, June 29, each year. In 2015 Pope Francis decided that he would bless the pallia in Rome but it would be the papal nuncio, the Pope's representative in each country, who would confer the pallium on the archbishop in a ceremony in the local cathedral in the presence of the other bishops of the province. This allows the people of the province to be present at this important ceremony and it highlights both the union of the archbishop with the Holy Father and the authority of the metropolitan archbishop in his province.

In recent times the Trappist monks of the abbey of Tre Fontane outside Rome raise the lambs for the wool, and on the feast of St Agnes, January 21, two lambs are blessed by the Pope. On Holy Thursday the lambs are shorn by the Benedictine nuns of the Monastery of St Cecilia in Rome and from this wool the pallia are made.

The use of the pallium goes back to the early centuries of the Church. The *Liber Pontificalis* (Pontifical Book), which was compiled in the fifth and sixth centuries in the Roman Curia, records that Pope St Mark, who died in 336, conferred the pallium on the bishop of Ostia, who was one of the consecrators of the Roman Pontiff. In 513 Pope Symmachus granted the privilege of the pallium to St Caesarius of Arles and since then the granting of the pallium by the Pope to the bishops of Italy and other countries has increased greatly.

So the pallium has a long history and a rich symbolism. When we see an archbishop wearing it we should pray that he may fulfil well his mission of being a good shepherd for the flock entrusted to him and that he may always be in full communion with the Pope.

Matrimony

517 The Pauline and Petrine privileges

A friend recently said something about the Petrine privilege in conjunction with marriage. Can you tell me what this is, and whether it has anything to do with the Pauline privilege?

The two privileges, named of course after St Peter and St Paul, involve the dissolution of a non-sacramental marriage "in favour of the faith", so that someone can enter into a marriage with a Catholic. The term Petrine privilege is not official and is not used by the Holy See.

It should be remembered that a marriage between two baptised persons is always a sacrament and it cannot be dissolved once the marriage has been consummated by a conjugal act. Only if the marriage is non-sacramental, that is a marriage in which one of the spouses is not baptised, can it be dissolved in favour of the faith of one of the partners.

The Pauline privilege has its origin in Scripture in St Paul's first letter to the Corinthians. He writes: "To the rest I say, not the Lord, that if any brother has a wife who is an unbeliever, and she consents to live with him, he should not divorce her. If any woman has a husband who is an unbeliever, and he consents to live with her, she should not divorce him... But if the unbelieving partner desires to separate, let it be so; in such a case the brother or sister is not bound" (*1 Cor* 7:12-15).

The Church has interpreted these words to mean that if someone who was not baptised converts to the faith and their unbaptised spouse does not want to live with them in harmony and leaves, the convert is no longer bound by the marriage and is free to marry another person.

This has been regulated by Canon Law in Canon 1143, which says:

§1. "In virtue of the Pauline privilege, a marriage entered into by two unbaptised persons is dissolved in favour of the faith of the party who received baptism, by the very fact that a new marriage is contracted by that same party, provided the unbaptised party departs. §2. The unbaptised party is considered to depart if he or she is unwilling to live with the baptised party, or to live peacefully without offence to the Creator, unless the baptised party has, after the reception of baptism, given the other just cause to depart."

In simple terms, if the marriage of two unbaptised persons breaks up after the baptism of one of the spouses because the other spouse does not want to live peacefully without offence to God, the baptised person is free to marry someone else. The canons require that the two persons be questioned about a number of issues before permission can be given for the baptised person to marry. As is stated, it cannot be the baptised person who wants to depart or who gives the other spouse cause to depart. Once permission has been given for a new marriage, the marriage bond with the unbaptised person is dissolved by the law itself when the new marriage takes place.

The so-called Petrine privilege is similar but it differs in that the original marriage was between a baptised person and an unbaptised one. The privilege is sometimes called Petrine because it is the Pope as the successor of St Peter who dissolves the bond of the first marriage.

With the increasing number of marriages between Catholics and unbaptised persons in the twentieth century and the increasing number of divorces, the Holy See began to issue norms regarding their dissolution. The first norms, from the Holy Office in 1934, were subsequently amended by the Congregation for the Doctrine of the Faith in 1973 and 2001.

In accordance with the latest norms, if the person requesting the privilege was a Catholic at the time of the original marriage, he or she must be able to practise the faith and bring up the children in it in the proposed new marriage. If the petitioner is a non-Catholic he or she must intend to enter the Church and marry a baptised person. In this way it is clear that the dissolution of the first marriage is in favour of the faith of the person requesting it.

A thorough investigation of the case is conducted by the local bishop, who forwards the documentation to the Congregation for the Doctrine of the Faith. The Congregation can then recommend the dissolution of the marriage to the Holy Father, who is the only one who can dissolve the bond.

518 Are most marriages null?

I was surprised to read recently that Pope Francis said most marriages are in fact null because the spouses are caught up in the culture of the provisional and are incapable of committing themselves for life. How could the Pope say that? Is it true that most marriages are invalid?

Pope Francis did say something to that effect in answer to a question after his opening address to the Ecclesial Congress of the Diocese of Rome, on 19 June 2016. What he said aroused considerable surprise in the secular and even the Catholic media, so it is very important to understand both the context and the content of what he said. Then we can interpret it in a proper light.

The Congress was dealing with the theme "'The joy of love': the way of the families of Rome in light of the Apostolic Exhortation *Amoris laetitia* of Pope Francis". After his opening address, the Pope answered three questions put to him by participants in the Congress. The third questioner began by saying that today we hear talk of the crisis of marriage, and asked how we can educate young people in love and in sacramental marriage, overcoming their resistance, their scepticism, disillusionment and fear of the definitive.

The Pope took up the last phrase and said that today we are living in a culture of the provisional. As an example, he spoke of a bishop who had been approached by a university graduate who said he wanted to become a priest, but only for ten years. This culture of the provisional is widespread even in priestly and religious life. The Pope went on to say, according to the official Vatican version released later, that therefore some of our sacramental marriages are null, because the spouses say, "Yes, for the whole of our life", but they do not know what they are saying, because they have a different culture. They say it, and they have good will, but they lack true understanding.

The Pope gave examples from Argentina when he was a bishop there. He had forbidden people to marry in the Church when they were expecting a baby because they were not really free and several years later he had seen them come back for a sacramental marriage, truly understanding what they were doing. He also mentioned that in pre-marriage courses the priest would ask the couples how many of them were living together and the majority would raise their hands. He said that instead of asking them immediately to get married in the Church the priests should accompany them, wait and allow them to mature in fidelity. For this we need a lot of patience.

In this broader context of the Pope's remarks, we can see a true pastoral approach that recognises that many couples are not ready to enter into a definitive, indissoluble marriage when they first approach the Church, and that it is better to accompany them while they mature and come to a better understanding of what true sacramental marriage is. This is wise and the fruit of much pastoral experience.

Is it fair to say that because of this culture of the provisional and spouses' lack of understanding of the definitive nature of marriage, some marriages are null? Undoubtedly it is, although determining which marriages fall into this category is not easy.

What aroused the surprise of many journalists at what the Pope said was the fact that the video footage shows the Pope saying in reality that the "great majority" of marriages are null for this reason. That is obviously an exaggeration and so the official Vatican version has "some" marriages. The Holy Father would naturally have agreed to the change.

Even in a secular country like Australia, where three quarters of couples live together before marriage and a similar percentage marry before a civil celebrant, there are forty-three divorces granted for every one hundred marriages celebrated each year, so most marriages stay together and are valid.

What we can learn from the Pope's answer is the need to help couples prepare very well for marriage so that they are mature and well formed enough to understand the permanence of marriage and so enter into a valid marriage from the outset. What we should not do is seize on an off-the-cuff comment and use it to criticise the Pope as if he does not know what he is talking about. And, as always, we should pray for him.

519 The validity of marriage

Following up what Pope Francis said about many marriages being null because the spouses are caught up in the culture of the provisional and are unable to commit to permanence, would this really be a cause of nullity?

The first thing to say is that marriage, before being a sacrament, is a natural institution which has existed since Adam and Eve and which people of all civilisations and cultures down the ages have had. As described in Australian law, it is the union of a man and woman to the exclusion of all others voluntarily entered into for life. Anyone can enter into a valid marriage and the Church regards the marriage of any two non-Catholics of whatever religion as valid, provided it was celebrated in some civilly valid way and there is no natural impediment to it, such as being bound by the bond of a prior marriage. In short, it is not difficult for someone to enter into a valid marriage.

This applies all the more to Catholics. The Church does not set the standard for validity so high that only highly educated, well informed and strong willed people can reach it. You don't need a degree in theology to marry validly! The Church wants everyone to be able to marry validly and so the requirements are easy to meet. The spouses must simply not positively reject any of the essential elements of marriage.

For example, as regards knowledge of what marriage is, Canon 1096, 1 of the *Code of Canon Law* says that in order for consent to exist the contracting parties must be "at least not ignorant of the fact that marriage is a permanent partnership between a man and a woman, ordered to the procreation of children through some form of some sexual cooperation." This is very basic knowledge and everyone who has reached puberty is presumed to have it (cf. Can 1096, 2). After all, the phrases "until death do us part" and "all the days of my life" given in the exchange of consent in the wedding are well known and are accepted by all couples marrying in the Church.

Even if someone is in error about the indissolubility of marriage, they can still consent validly as long as their error does not "determine the will" (cf. Can. 1099). That is, only if this error causes the person to choose something other than true marriage will it lead to invalid consent. Thus there is a difference between merely thinking that marriage can be dissolved by divorce and marrying with the express intention and condition that it be dissoluble by divorce. In this latter case error determines the will, so that if the marriage broke up and it could be proved that the person had expressed this condition at the time of the wedding, the marriage would be invalid.

Most people marrying in the Church do not have such an intention and, indeed, if the priest or deacon preparing the couple for the wedding were aware that they did, he could not proceed with the wedding. The person or persons with that intention would be denying an essential property of marriage, its indissolubility, and so the marriage would be invalid and it could not go ahead.

This is made clear in Canon 1101, 2, which says that if either of the parties "should by a positive act of the will exclude marriage itself or any essential element of marriage or any essential property, such party contracts invalidly." Indissolubility is an essential property of marriage. So simply marrying in error about the permanence of marriage does not make it invalid. A positive act of the will to exclude it is needed.

What about the situation Pope Francis describes, where there is a widespread culture of the provisional and, as he said, "the spouses say 'Yes, for the whole of our life', but they do not know what they are saying, because they have a different culture. They say it, and they have good will, but they lack true understanding." Would their marriage be null on this ground? Not easily. The couple do understand that marriage is for life even though they are confused about what this means.

Perhaps nullity could be proved under Canon 1095, 2, which says that among those incapable of contracting marriage are "those who suffer from a grave lack of discretion of judgment concerning the essential matrimonial rights and obligations to be mutually given and accepted." Here the couple accept the indissolubility of marriage in theory but they suffer from a grave lack of understanding about what this means in practice and they would be incapable of contracting a true marriage. Some marriages might be null on this ground but certainly not a great majority.

520 The internal forum and the validity of marriage

In the recent meeting of the Synod of Bishops on marriage there were proposals to allow people who are divorced and remarried civilly to resolve in the internal forum the matter of the validity of their marriage and the reception of Communion. What is this and is it acceptable?

As you say, there were proposals by some bishops to use the internal forum to resolve the question of the validity of one's first marriage and the consequent reception of Communion by the divorced and remarried civilly. Nonetheless, in the final report agreed upon by the synod fathers there is no express mention of these people being admitted to Communion, although some might interpret certain statements in it as being open to this possibility.

What is meant by the internal forum in this context? In Church law we distinguish between the external forum, which is the publicly observable realm of human actions, such as the fact that a couple were married, that someone was ordained a priest, etc., and the internal forum, which is the forum of conscience, where everything is between the individual person and God. This is the forum, for example, of the sacrament of penance and spiritual direction.

The internal forum solution in the matter of the reception of Communion by someone who is divorced and remarried civilly would involve the person coming to a judgment in their conscience that their first marriage was invalid, even though for whatever reason there was no declaration to that effect by a marriage tribunal. Would this be acceptable?

In 1994 Cardinal Ratzinger, then Prefect of the Congregation for the Doctrine of the Faith, with the approval of Pope John Paul II answered the question in the negative in a "Letter to the bishops of the Catholic Church concerning the reception of Holy Communion by the divorced and remarried members of the faithful". It is extremely relevant to the present situation.

Cardinal Ratzinger wrote: "In recent years, in various regions, different pastoral solutions in this area have been suggested according to which, to be sure, a general admission of the divorced and remarried to Eucharistic communion would not be possible, but the divorced and remarried members of the faithful could approach Holy Communion in specific cases when they consider themselves authorised according to a judgment of conscience to do so. This would be the case, for example, when they had been abandoned completely unjustly, although they sincerely tried to save the previous marriage, or when they are convinced of the nullity of their previous marriage, although unable to demonstrate it in the external forum or when they have gone through a long period of reflexion and penance, or also when for morally valid reasons they cannot satisfy the obligation to separate. In some places, it has also been proposed that in order objectively to examine their actual situation, the divorced and remarried would have to consult a prudent and expert priest. This priest, however, would have to respect their eventual decision to approach Holy Communion, without this implying an official authorisation" (n. 3).

"With respect to the aforementioned new pastoral proposals, this Congregation deems itself obliged therefore to recall the doctrine and discipline of the Church in this matter. In fidelity to the words of Jesus Christ (cf. *Mk* 10:11-12), the Church affirms that a new union cannot be recognised as valid if the preceding marriage was valid. If the divorced are remarried civilly, they find themselves in a situation that objectively contravenes God's law. Consequently, they cannot receive Holy Communion as long as this situation persists" (n. 4).

"The mistaken conviction of a divorced and remarried person that he may receive Holy Communion normally presupposes that personal conscience is considered in the final analysis to be able, on the basis of one's own convictions, to come to a decision about the existence or absence of a previous marriage and the value of the new union. However, such a position is inadmissible" (n. 7).

It is clear from this that an internal forum personal decision about the invalidity of one's first marriage is not acceptable. Couples in this situation should have recourse to the marriage tribunal, where the new norms given recently by Pope Francis will make the process much quicker. Or, if they cannot separate, they should live as brother and sister, abstaining from marital intimacy.

521 Involvement of the divorced in the life of the Church

If divorced and civilly remarried people cannot be admitted to Communion, in what ways can they be involved in the life of the Church?

The final report of the synod of bishops on marriage held in October 2015 spoke at some length, and very positively, about the involvement in Church life of persons who have been divorced and are now remarried civilly. It did not specify the exact form this involvement might take.

The report contains three paragraphs on the matter. To be sure, these paragraphs received the largest number of negative votes when they were voted on by the synod fathers, because they were seen to be ambiguous. While the paragraphs did not make express mention of the divorced receiving Communion, some feared they might be interpreted to mean that.

Paragraph 84 of the final report is the most comprehensive on the matter. It reads in part: "The baptised who are divorced and civilly remarried should be better integrated into Christian communities in the various ways possible, avoiding every occasion of scandal. The logic of integration is the key to their pastoral accompaniment, not only so that they know they belong to the Body of Christ which is the Church, but so that they may have a joyous and fruitful experience in it. They are baptised, they are brothers and sisters, the gifts and charisms of the Holy Spirit flow into them for the good of all. Their participation can express itself in various ecclesial services: so the Church must discern which of the various forms of exclusion practised in liturgical, pastoral, educational and institutional life might be overcome. Not only should they not consider themselves excommunicated, but they ought to be able to live and mature as living members of the Church, experiencing her as a mother who also accompanies them, who cares for them with affection, and who encourages them on the way of life and of the Gospel.

"This integration is also necessary for the care and Christian education of their children, which is the most important consideration. For the Christian community to care for these people does not weaken [the Church's] faith and its witness to the indissolubility of marriage; rather, in this care the Church properly expresses her charity."

While the report does not go into specifics as to how the divorced and remarried might be involved in the life of the Church, Pope St John Paul II did mention some specific ways in his Apostolic Exhortation *Familiaris consortio*, which followed the earlier synod of bishops on the family held in 1980. There he wrote: "The Church, which was set up to lead to salvation all people and especially the baptised, cannot abandon to their own devices those who have been previously bound by sacramental marriage and who have attempted a second marriage. The Church will therefore make untiring efforts to put at their disposal her means of salvation...

"Together with the Synod, I earnestly call upon pastors and the whole community of the faithful to help the divorced, and with solicitous care to make sure that they do not consider themselves as separated from the Church, for as baptised persons they can, and indeed must, share in her life. They should be encouraged to listen to the word of God, to attend the Sacrifice of the Mass, to persevere in prayer, to contribute to works of charity and to community efforts in favour of justice, to bring up their children in the Christian faith, to cultivate the spirit and practice of penance and thus implore, day by day, God's grace" (*FC* 84).

In practice, the divorced and remarried should be encouraged to pray and do penance, to read the Scriptures, to attend Mass along with their children, to have their children baptised and brought up in the faith, to send their children to a Catholic school if they wish, to participate in works of charity and justice, etc. On the other hand, for obvious reasons it would not be appropriate for them to be readers in Mass or extraordinary ministers of Communion, although they could certainly be invited to sing in the choir. A good rule of thumb would be to invite them to assume those roles that could be assumed by a non-Catholic. In general, they should be welcomed into the family of the Church to which they belong and, as St John Paul II concludes the paragraph cited above, "Let the Church pray for them, encourage them and show herself a merciful mother, and thus sustain them in faith and hope" (*FC* 84).

522 New procedures for marriage cases

Pope Francis recently announced new procedures to make marriage nullity cases quicker and more affordable. What are the changes and do they really safeguard marriage?

The new procedures, which took effect on 8 December 2015, the first day of the Jubilee Year of Mercy announced by Pope Francis, are spelled out in the Pope's Apostolic Letters *Mitis iudex Dominus Iesus* (The Lord Jesus, meek judge) for the Latin Rite and *Mitis et misericors Iesus* (Meek and merciful Jesus) for the Eastern Churches. I will comment on the former document.

As the Pope explains at the beginning, the reform responds to a request from a majority of the bishops in the Extraordinary General Assembly of the Synod of Bishops which met in Rome in October 2014 calling for a quicker and more accessible process. In response to the request Pope Francis appointed a commission to draft new norms headed by the Dean of the Roman Rota, the Vatican's tribunal which handles marriage cases. Also on the commission was the President of the Pontifical Council for Legislative Texts. So the new norms are the work of some of the best canonists in the Church today.

The Pope explains that the supreme norm of the salvation of souls and the principle of the indissolubility of marriage remain intact in the new regulations, which replace canons 1671-1691 of the 1983 *Code of Canon Law*. Among the protections surrounding the marriage bond, as in the past, is the figure of the defender of the bond, who is to present all the possible arguments in favour of the validity of the marriage (cf. Can. 1676).

What is new in the process? One of the biggest changes is the provision that there need be only one judgment of nullity, unlike in the former process, where the declaration of nullity by the first tribunal had to be confirmed by a second appeals tribunal (cf. Can. 1679). Nonetheless if one of the partners in the marriage, or the promoter of justice or defender of the bond, is not satisfied with the declaration of nullity they can still appeal against the judgment to a higher tribunal (cf. Can. 1680 §1).

Another big change is the provision, in addition to the ordinary process, of a "shorter process" when the nullity of the marriage is supported by particularly strong arguments. The Pope says he is aware that the shorter process might put at risk the indissolubility of the marriage, so he has determined that in those cases the diocesan bishop himself is to be the judge.

The shorter process can be used only when both partners in the marriage, or only one of them with the consent of the other, request the judgment of possible nullity of their marriage and there are circumstances which do not require a more thorough investigation and which render the nullity obvious (cf. Can. 1683). The Procedural Regulations that accompany the Apostolic Letter give a list of possible circumstances that would allow the case to be judged via the shorter process. Among them are the lack of faith in one or both parties to give full consent to a Catholic marriage, the brevity of their married life together, extramarital relations at the time of the wedding or shortly thereafter, the deceitful hiding of one's sterility or of a serious contagious illness or of the existence of children from a previous relationship, etc. (cf. Art. 14 §1).

If the bishop, in coming to his judgment after consulting those who have drawn up the case, reaches moral certainty of the nullity of the marriage, he gives his judgment, which is final. If he cannot reach this certainty he refers the case back to be decided by the ordinary process (cf. Can. 1687 §1). In the ordinary process there are to be three judges, presided over by a cleric, or if this is not possible, one judge who must be a cleric (cf. Can. 1673 §§3-4). It is possible that the shorter process could be completed in as little as a few months.

The Pope expresses the wish that, as far as possible, the partners not be charged anything for having their case heard, although he acknowledges that those working in the tribunal must be paid. So he has certainly made marriage cases simpler, quicker and more accessible to the faithful.

We give thanks to the Holy Father for giving the Church these new norms and we pray that those carrying them out will always respect the truth of the marriage and the indissolubility of the bond.

523 More on new procedures for marriage cases

Talking with several people, including a priest, I have the impression that the new procedures for marriage nullity cases may be too brief and may not sufficiently safeguard the permanence of Christian marriage. Is this concern well founded?

We should say at the outset that concern for the permanence of Christian marriage is very important. After all, Christian spouses promise to be faithful to each other "until death do us part" or "all the days of my life". This is a serious commitment and it is for the good of the spouses, the children and the whole of society. We are all aware of the harm, indeed the havoc, that the breakup of marriage can cause. The effects are seen very quickly in workplaces, in schools, on the roads – everywhere. Not for nothing did Our Lord say, "What therefore God has joined together, let no man put asunder" (*Mt* 19:5-6). For this reason the Church has always done everything possible to support married couples and safeguard the marriage bond.

But the breakup of marriage is a reality, in great part caused by human weakness and the effects of original sin. In Australia, for example, in 2016 there were forty-three divorces granted for every one hundred marriages celebrated. Divorce is a reality which the Church has always confronted in a motherly, pastoral way. She has shown pastoral concern for all those in broken marriages and has examined marriages that have broken up to see if there are possible grounds for judging that the marriage was null from the outset, thereby allowing the spouses to marry again.

Up until now this examination of a marriage could take a long time, even years, and would entail some financial cost to the spouses. It involved an investigation of the facts of the marriage and a first judgment at the level of the diocesan or regional tribunal, followed by a second judgment by a higher appeals tribunal. Only when both these tribunals agreed that the marriage was null from the outset were the spouses free to contract a second marriage in the Church.

The length of the process or its financial cost could lead some people to give up and simply marry outside the Church or not approach the tribunal in the first place. To shorten the process and, if possible, make it free of charge to the spouses, Pope Francis has now given the Church the new norms. He has done so moved above all by his concern for the salvation of the souls of the many people who feel distant from the juridical structures of the Church.

The new norms have been well received by canonists and others working in marriage tribunals. The scrapping of the second judgment, leaving only the first judgment by the local tribunal, might appear to make it too easy to obtain a decree of nullity. But it should be remembered that in most cases the second judgment simply confirms the first one, so that doing away with it does not change the outcome in most cases and it speeds up the process considerably. In any case, with the new norms there is still the possibility of having the judgment of nullity reviewed by an appeals tribunal as in the past.

What is more, Pope Francis has retained the centuries-old practice of examining the validity of marriage by a judicial process, not a merely administrative one. In the latter case the bishop or his vicar could declare a marriage null without a full investigation and judgment. And the Pope has certainly not accepted the proposal of some to have a mere "pastoral process" in which the spouses would simply tell their story to a priest, who would come to a decision about their suitability to receive the sacraments.

It should also be remembered that the "shorter process", which might take only a few months, can be used only when there are obvious grounds for nullity that do not require a more thorough investigation. In many cases, perhaps most, the ordinary process will still be followed, leading to a judgment by the diocesan tribunal. But this judgment will now be final and does not need to be appealed, thereby speeding up the process.

All in all, the new norms do safeguard the marriage bond provided that those who work on the case do so with diligence and respect for the permanence of marriage.

524 Same-sex marriage – why not?

Now that same-sex marriage is in the news again, everyone is talking about it and many of my friends are in favour. Can you remind me of the reasons why the Church is opposed to it? Shouldn't gay people be entitled to the same respect and rights as others?

Marriage is not just a "social construct", a concept invented by man that can change with time at the whim or even the vote of the people. It is a reality deeply rooted in human nature and it has been in existence from the beginning. All civilisations have had the institution of marriage as the union of a man and a woman destined to bring forth children.

God created humans male and female and gave them an attraction for each other that leads them to want to spend their lives together, expressing their love among other ways in the act of marital intimacy through which children are born into the world. This was God's plan for the fulfilment of individuals and for the continuation of the human race. The *Catechism of the Catholic Church* sums it up: "The matrimonial covenant, by which a man and a woman establish between themselves a partnership of the whole of life, is by its nature ordered toward the good of the spouses and the procreation and education of offspring" (*CCC* 1601).

Marriage comes from God himself, as the Second Vatican Council teaches: "The intimate community of life and love which constitutes the married state has been established by the Creator and endowed by him with its own proper laws... God himself is the author of marriage" (*GS* 48). Marriage between a man and a woman is written in human nature, as Aristotle observed hundreds of years before Christ: "Between man and wife, friendship seems to exist by nature; for man is naturally inclined to form couples – even more than to form cities" (*Nicomachean Ethics* 8.12).

The Australian Marriage Act 1961, in clarifying the terms used in the Act, gives us the traditional definition of marriage: "the union of a man and a woman to the exclusion of all others, voluntarily entered into for life." This definition has stood the test of time. It is founded on human nature.

We cannot change the nature of marriage by an act of parliament any more than we can change the nature of person so as to extend the term to dogs, cats or chimpanzees. Animals, by nature, cannot be persons. Two persons of the same sex, by nature, cannot call their union marriage. Marriage is the union of a man and a woman.

What is more, as we have seen, marriage is intended by God for the procreation and education of children. Love between a man and a woman naturally tends to bring children into the world. It is naturally fertile. Two people of the same sex, on the contrary, cannot bring forth children from their love. Their union is naturally sterile. If they have children by artificial means or they adopt them, these children will grow up without the complementary care of their natural father and mother, which is God's plan for their wellbeing. Indeed, studies have shown that children of same-sex couples do not fare as well as those of natural families.

But shouldn't people with same-sex attraction be shown respect and given the same rights as others? They should always be shown respect, for they too are human beings, children of God and redeemed by Jesus Christ. And they can live together if they want and even commit themselves to remain together for life, taking into account of course that any acts of sexual intimacy with each other would be mortally sinful. But there can be no right to call that relationship marriage. Marriage, as instituted by God and written in human nature, is the union of a man and a woman.

If people of the same sex want legal recognition of their union, they already have access to it. For example, the New South Wales Relationships Register, which commenced operation in 2010, provides legal recognition for a couple, regardless of their sex, by registration of the relationship.

Looking further down the track, if the definition of marriage were changed by law to include the union of two persons of the same sex, there is no reason why sometime later it might not be broadened further to include more than two persons or a relationship between persons and animals. The best way to destroy marriage is to call everything marriage. When everything is marriage, nothing is marriage. We must do everything possible to protect this institution.

525 Consequences of legalised same-sex marriage

I was talking recently with a workmate who said that even if same-sex marriage is legalised, it really won't make much difference to the rest of us. We will go on with our life and same-sex couples with theirs. Is this the case?

I agree that for most people life will go on as it did before. Men will continue to marry women in great numbers, as they always have. A tiny percentage of "marriages" will be between two persons of the same sex. But there are other consequences of which we should be aware.

The first casualty of course is the very concept of marriage. Until recent times the word referred only to a union between a man and a woman. Now it will be extended to unions of persons of the same sex and who knows to what other arrangements. In some countries they are already talking about "trouples", a union of three persons, and Brazil has legalised polygamy.

A good place to see the consequences of legalised same-sex marriage is Canada, a country in many ways similar to ours, where same-sex marriage has been legal for ten years. What percentage of all registered couples there are same-sex? According to Statistics Canada, the national census of 2011 showed that same-sex couples constituted only .8 percent of all couples. This compares with .7 percent in both Australia and New Zealand.

What percentage of these same-sex couples in Canada have in fact "married" under the legislation? One might think that practically all such couples would rush to do so. In fact by 2011, the most recent census for which figures are available, only about thirty percent were married, making up only .24 per cent of all registered couples. Of these, 54.5 percent were male and 45.5 percent female. Female couples were much more likely to have children living with them: 7,700 children aged 24 and under as against 1,900 with male couples.

What then has happened in Canada over the last ten years? The first thing is that these almost 10,000 children have grown up without a father or a mother to nurture them, something that is always detrimental to their wellbeing.

The website "REAL Women of Canada" reports other consequences. It mentions the well known fact that sexual faithfulness is not usually regarded as a requirement in same-sex relationships, as it is in opposite-sex marriages. Moreover, these relationships are notoriously short lived, averaging some two to three years, with obvious harmful consequences for the children.

Another effect is seen in the Netherlands, where same-sex marriage has been legal for fifteen years. The out-of-wedlock birth rate there has increased by an average of two percent a year, more than in any other country in Western Europe. It reflects a marked decrease in the desire for legal marriage and an increase in cohabitation.

There can also be legal repercussions for those opposed to same-sex marriage. In Canada, religion-based social services, such as counselling and adoption services, are now required to conform to the same-sex marriage law and the tax-exempt status of Churches has been questioned. For example, Bishop Fred Henry of Calgary was threatened by the Canada Revenue Agency with removal of the Catholic Church's tax-exempt status if he persisted in speaking out against same-sex marriage during a federal election.

Within school boards, teachers and other individuals are required to support same-sex marriage and to refrain from publicly opposing it. Because of a complaint to the British Columbia Human Rights Tribunal, the government of British Columbia announced that the school curriculum from Kindergarten to Year 12 would be revised to include positive homosexual instruction. Likewise, school boards in

Quebec and Ontario, especially in Toronto, Hamilton and London, now require homosexual "education" in their school systems and there is no opportunity for parents to withdraw their children if they disagree with it.

The Australian Bishops' Pastoral Letter "Don't mess with marriage" lists at the end a sample of fifteen instances like these of discrimination in many countries against people who oppose same-sex marriage. In short, the legalisation of same-sex marriage is not just about "marriage equality" for a handful of people. It is about a whole "Brave New World".

526 Children of same-sex parents

It seems to me that children of same-sex parents must suffer in some way from not having a mother or father to nurture them and that this would be an argument against allowing same-sex marriage. Is this the case?

There are sociological studies that bear out the truth of what you say and there are also personal testimonies of the children themselves. In this column I will comment on one of those testimonies and in the next I will refer to the results of sociological studies.

Katy Faust was raised by a lesbian couple and is now married with four children. On 2 February 2015 she wrote an open letter to Justice Kennedy of the U.S. Supreme Court, urging the court not to redefine marriage to include the union of two persons of the same sex.

Knowing first-hand what it is like to grow up in a same-sex household and also what it is like to raise children in a natural marriage, she writes that "when it comes to procreation and child-rearing, same-sex couples and opposite-sex couples are wholly unequal and should be treated differently for the sake of the children.

"When two adults who cannot procreate want to raise children together, where do those babies come from? Each child is conceived by a mother and a father to whom that child has a natural right. When a child is placed in a same-sex-headed household, she will miss out on at least one critical parental relationship and a vital dual-gender influence. The nature of the adults' union guarantees this. Whether by adoption, divorce, or third-party reproduction, the adults in this scenario satisfy their heart's desires, while the child bears the most significant cost: missing out on one or more of her biological parents. Making policy that intentionally deprives children of their fundamental rights is something that we should not endorse, incentivize, or promote."

She went on to say: "Now that I am a parent, I see clearly the beautiful differences my husband and I bring to our family. I see the wholeness and health that my children receive because they have both of their parents living with and loving them. I see how important the role of their father is and how irreplaceable I am as their mother. We play complementary roles in their lives, and neither of us is disposable. In fact, we are both critical. It's almost as if Mother Nature got this whole reproduction thing exactly right."

She says she has a great love for her mother and her partner, but observes: "If you ask a child raised by a lesbian couple if they love their two moms, you'll probably get a resounding 'yes!' Ask about their father, and you are in for either painful silence, a confession of gut-wrenching longing, or the recognition that they have a father that they wish they could see more often. The one thing that you will not hear is indifference."

With respect to studies showing that children of gay parents actually fare better than those raised by their biological father and mother, she comments: "If it is undisputed social science that children suffer greatly when they are abandoned by their biological parents, when their parents divorce, when one parent dies, or when they are donor-conceived, then how can it be possible that they are miraculously turning out 'even better!' when raised in same-sex-headed households? Every child raised by 'two moms' or 'two dads' came to that household via one of those four traumatic methods. Does being raised under the rainbow miraculously wipe away all the negative effects and pain surrounding the loss and daily deprivation of one or both parents?

"Redefining marriage redefines parenthood. It moves us well beyond our 'live and let live' philosophy into the land where our society promotes a family structure where children will *always* suffer loss. It will be our policy, stamped and sealed by the most powerful of governmental institutions, that these children will have their right to be known and loved by their mother and/or father stripped from them in *every* instance. In same-sex-headed households, the *desires* of the adults trump the *rights* of the child. Have we really arrived at a time when we are considering institutionalizing the stripping of a child's natural right to a mother and a father in order to validate the emotions of adults?"

This is powerful language based on personal experience. It deserves to be heard.

527 Studies on children of same-sex parents

A friend recently told me there are studies showing that children raised by same-sex couples actually fare better than those raised by their natural father and mother. Is this true?

Over the years there have been numerous studies to determine whether there is any difference between children raised by two persons of the same sex and those raised by their natural parents. As you say, some of these claim that the children fared better when raised by same-sex couples. But common sense and a little experience of life would tell us that such findings cannot possibly be valid.

The American Psychological Association, in a 2005 Policy Brief, cited 59 studies by its members which found that not one of those studies found children of lesbian or gay parents to be disadvantaged in any significant respect relative to children of heterosexual parents. But in an article published in the journal *Social Science Research* in July 2012, Professor Loren Marks of Louisiana State University analysed those studies and found that "not one of the 59 studies referenced in the 2005 APA Brief compares a large, random, representative sample of lesbian or gay parents and their children with a large, random, representative sample of married parents and their children." He observed that only four of the studies met the APA's own standards by providing evidence of statistical power.

Meanwhile, that same issue of *Social Science Research* published the results of the most rigorous and methodologically sound study ever conducted on the issue. Carried out by sociologist Mark Regnerus of the University of Texas at Austin, it surveyed almost 3000 people between the ages of 18 and 39 from both heterosexual and homosexual relationships. The study found that the children of gay or lesbian couples fared worse on 77 out of 80 outcome measures compared with those from biologically intact families.

Among the most important findings were that children of homosexual parents were much more likely to have received welfare, had lower educational attainment, reported less safety and security in their family of origin, reported more ongoing negative impact from their family of origin, were more likely to suffer from depression, had been arrested more often and, in the case of women, had more sexual partners, both male and female.

Children of lesbian mothers in particular were more likely to be cohabiting, almost four times more likely to be on welfare, more than three times more likely to be unemployed, nearly four times more likely to identify as something other than entirely heterosexual, ten times more likely to have been "touched sexually by a parent or other adult caregiver", more likely to have attachment problems related to the ability to depend on others, used marijuana more frequently, smoked more frequently, watched television for long periods more frequently and pled guilty to a non-minor offence more frequently. Children of lesbian mothers were 75% more likely to be in a same-sex romantic relationship and children of homosexual fathers three times more likely.

An article reporting these findings on the website of the Family Research Council by Peter Sprigg, Senior Fellow for Policy Studies, concluded: "The myths that children of homosexual parents are 'no different' from other children and suffer 'no harm' from being raised by homosexual parents have been shattered forever."

These findings are important and they deserve to be taken into account when considering whether same-sex marriage ought to be legalised.

III. MORAL LIFE IN CHRIST

General moral issues

528 Is morality objective?

At work we sometimes discuss issues like abortion and euthanasia and we always end up arguing. The others say I should follow my opinion and they will follow theirs. Is morality a matter for each person to decide or are there objective standards that apply to all?

You ask a very important question, about which there is much confusion. In preparing this column, I put the question "Is morality objective?" into a well-known search engine, and virtually all the articles that came up espoused the view that morality is not objective – the same for everyone – but subjective, a matter of personal opinion. So your question is relevant indeed.

Statements like the following abound. Morality is just a matter of personal choice. If I think abortion is acceptable, am I not entitled to my opinion and to have an abortion? If you think abortion is wrong, don't have one, but don't condemn me for holding a different opinion. There are no moral absolutes. Morality is a matter for each person to decide.

In fact, morality is not something for each person to decide. It is objective and there are moral absolutes. How can we be so sure of this? Some people base their argument on the Bible, which states very clearly as far back as the time of Moses that killing the innocent, committing adultery, stealing and lying are always wrong. The Ten Commandments say so. But many people do not believe in the Bible, so such arguments will not convince them.

Therefore, it is always better to base our reasoning on something more fundamental and universal than the Bible. This something is nothing other than human nature itself. To understand from the outset what we mean by human nature, it is simply what all humans have in common, just as dog nature is what all dogs have in common, and tree nature is what all trees have in common. It is what makes us humans rather than something else.

Now, as a result of being human, we have a fundamental dignity: we are someone, not something. We have an intellect and free will and we can weigh up alternative courses of action and, after considering the possible consequences of each, choose which to follow. And we are naturally social, called to live in communion with others, whether in marriage and the family or in the broader society. We need the presence of others at the same time as we are called to contribute to the good of others.

In view of our dignity and our social nature, we realise that certain forms of behaviour, or moral choices, are simply harmful to the wellbeing of individuals or of society. Actions like killing a child, whether when still in the womb or after birth, raping a woman, stealing others' property or burning down their house are always harmful to the good of the individual and of society. They do not contribute to human flourishing. They are intrinsically evil. They are objectively wrong, not a matter of personal opinion. They are moral absolutes.

Pope St John Paul II, in his Encyclical *Veritatis splendor* (1993), puts it like this: "Reason attests that there are objects of the human act which are by their nature 'incapable of being ordered' to God, because they radically contradict the good of the person made in his image. These are the acts which, in the Church's moral tradition, have been termed 'intrinsically evil' (*intrinsece malum*): they are such *always and per se*, in other words, on account of their very object, and quite apart from the ulterior intentions of the one acting and the circumstances" (*VS* 80).

The Pope goes on to quote the Second Vatican Council, which lists as examples of such acts, whatever "is hostile to life itself, such as any kind of homicide, genocide, abortion, euthanasia and voluntary suicide; whatever violates the integrity of the human person such as mutilation, physical and mental torture and attempts to coerce the spirit; whatever is offensive to human dignity, such as subhuman living conditions, arbitrary imprisonment, deportation, slavery, prostitution and trafficking in women and children..." (*GS* 27).

Acts such as these are wrong because they contradict the good of the human person and of society, not because they are forbidden by the Bible. Rather the Bible forbids them because they are wrong in themselves. So yes, morality is objective, not just a matter of personal opinion.

529 Cardinals' "dubia" on moral issues

I recently read an article reporting that four Cardinals had asked the Pope to clarify some of his teaching on marriage in Amoris Laetitia, *Chapter 8, and I was surprised by it. Is this disrespectful of the Pope or is it normal practice?*

Many people have commented on this matter so I take advantage of the opportunity to write about it.

The four Cardinals are all highly respected and senior: Walter Brandmüller, former President of the Pontifical Commission for Historical Sciences; Raymond Burke, former head of the Vatican's supreme tribunal the Signatura; Carlo Caffarra, retired Archbishop of Bologna; and Joachim Meisner, retired Archbishop of Cologne. In an interview published online in Catholic Action for Faith and Family on 14 November 2016 Cardinal Burke explained why the Cardinals sought this clarification.

He explained that when a doubt arises about some matter of faith or morals, or more specifically about the exact meaning of a particular text in a Vatican document, it is customary for bishops, priests or even the laity to seek clarification from the Holy See. This is a genuine desire for clarity, not in any way a lack of respect.

In fact, many statements from the Holy See are given in response to such queries. Over the years these statements have come from such bodies as the Pontifical Biblical Commission about the meaning of texts in the Bible, the Pontifical Council for Legislative Texts about the interpretation of the *Code of Canon Law*, and the Congregation for the Doctrine of the Faith about matters of faith.

Cardinal Burke said that *Amoris Laetitia* "has raised a number of questions and doubts in the minds of Bishops, priests and the faithful, many of which have already been presented to the Holy Father and discussed publicly. In the present case, four Cardinals have presented formally to the Holy Father five fundamental questions or doubts regarding faith and morals based on the reading of *Amoris Laetitia*." He acknowledged that even within the college of bishops there are contrasting interpretations of Chapter 8 of *Amoris Laetitia* and therefore the Cardinals were seeking an authoritative clarification. They sent a copy of the letter also to Cardinal Gerhard Müller, Prefect of the Congregation for the Doctrine of the Faith.

After some time had passed without a response, the Cardinals decided to make their questions known to the general public so that they could be discussed by all Catholics, especially bishops. The Cardinals asked five questions, expressed in very precise theological terms making reference to previous Church documents. They can be summarised as follows.

First, is it possible to grant absolution in the Sacrament of Penance and admit to Holy Communion people who are divorced and are in a new union and have marital relations with each other?

Second, are there still absolute moral norms that prohibit intrinsically evil acts and are binding without exception?

Third, is it still possible to affirm that a person who habitually lives in contradiction to a commandment of God's law, for instance the one that prohibits adultery, is in an objective situation of habitual grave sin?

Fourth, is it still the case that circumstances or intentions can never transform an act intrinsically evil by virtue of its object into an act subjectively good or defensible as a choice?

Fifth, is it still true that conscience can never authorise exceptions to absolute moral norms that prohibit acts which are intrinsically evil by virtue of their object?

The Cardinals felt that the wording of *Amoris Laetitia* left some of these basic principles of Catholic moral teaching open to question and so they were seeking an authoritative answer. It is not that the Pope had explicitly denied any of them but some of the interpretations of the Pope's document by bishops and theologians seemed to suggest that they were open to question.

Let us pray that the matter can be resolved in such a way that no doubt remains.

530 Conscience and moral absolutes

I am confused about whether there are some actions which are always wrong and can never be performed, no matter what the circumstances or motive, or whether it all depends on the circumstances and motive, which we have to judge with our conscience. Can you enlighten me?

This is an important question, which you phrase very well. It is the question of whether there are what theologians call "moral absolutes"; that is, actions which are always wrong, which are intrinsically evil and can never be done regardless of the circumstances or the intention of the person. Or, on the contrary, whether no action can be said to be wrong in all circumstances so that ultimately it depends on the circumstances and what our conscience tells us at the time.

Pope St John Paul II answered the question in his important Encyclical *Veritatis splendor* in 1993. He was writing in answer to the theories of consequentialism and proportionalism, according to which there are no moral absolutes, so that the morality of any action is determined by weighing up the consequences of acting or not acting, or on the proportion of good effects and bad effects in that particular choice.

In *Veritatis splendor* Pope John Paul tells us why there are moral absolutes: "The primary and decisive element for moral judgment is the object of the human act, which establishes whether it is *capable of being ordered to the good and to the ultimate end, which is God...* Reason attests that there are objects of the human act which are by their nature 'incapable of being ordered' to God, because they radically contradict the good of the person made in his image. These are the acts which, in the Church's moral tradition, have been termed 'intrinsically evil' (*intrinsece malum*): they are such *always and per se*, in other words, on account of their very object, and quite apart from the ulterior intentions of the one acting and the circumstances" (*VS* 79, 80).

Deep down we would all agree with this. There are actions like rape, killing an innocent person and stealing that are simply wrong in themselves. Pope John Paul gives a list of examples, quoting the Second Vatican Council: "Whatever is hostile to life itself, such as any kind of homicide, genocide, abortion, euthanasia and voluntary suicide; whatever violates the integrity of the human person, such as mutilation, physical and mental torture..." (*GS*, 27; *VS* 80).

These acts are intrinsically evil. They go against the good of the human person, whatever the circumstances, and so they can never be performed. Conscience, when faced with the possibility of carrying out any of these acts, can only judge that since the action is intrinsically evil it cannot be performed, no matter what the intention or the good that may come from it.

The Church has always taught this. Pope John Paul quotes St Augustine: "As for acts which are themselves sins like theft, fornication, blasphemy, who would dare affirm that, by doing them for good motives, they would no longer be sins, or, what is even more absurd, that they would be sins that are justified?" (*Contra Mendacium*, VII, 18; *VS* 81) If the Church did not hold to this traditional and fundamental teaching some serious consequences would follow.

First, we would have no clear guidelines to follow when making moral decisions. It would be in every case a matter of "do whatever you think best under the circumstances." But deep down we know that that cannot be, that there are some actions we can never perform because they are simply wrong. We humans crave clear guidance, certainty, when making choices.

Second, this teaching safeguards us from the harmful actions of others. If everything were a matter of "do whatever you think best", who would protect us from a neighbour who judges it appropriate under the circumstances to steal our property, burn down our house or rape our teenage daughter? Granted, these sins are being committed now, but there would be no end to them if the Church abandoned her teaching on moral absolutes. Moral chaos would reign.

Third, moral absolutes set a clear standard, a high bar toward which to strive. Without them we would not make the effort we make now to live up to this demanding moral code: not to tell lies, not to steal, not to gossip, not to indulge in impure thoughts and actions… In a word, we thank God for the Church's clear teaching on moral absolutes.

531 The role of conscience

I have a friend with four young children who had herself sterilised because she couldn't cope with more. She says she knew the Church disapproved of it but felt that in her circumstances it was the right thing to do. Can a good conscience make a choice like this?

This relates to what I wrote in my last column about moral absolutes. There I showed that the Church has always taught that there are some acts which are simply wrong in themselves and can never be performed, no matter what the circumstances or the intention. They are intrinsically evil. Among them are killing an innocent person, abortion, stealing, rape, adultery, torture... And yes, direct sterilisation as a means of avoiding having another child is one of them, as is the use of contraception for that purpose (cf. *CCC* 2399, 2370).

These acts are wrong in themselves because they go against the good of the human person. Whatever goes against the good of the human person is not good for the person, no matter how good it may seem at the time. It always hurts the one who does it, and often harms others as well. We may not understand this at the time but it is the case.

Where does that leave someone who knows that the Church teaches that a particular act is wrong yet feels that in their personal circumstances it would be permissible, even advisable, to do it? This is a moral dilemma that many people face at one time or another.

It comes back to the role of conscience. Conscience is defined in the Catechism as "a judgment of reason whereby the human person recognises the moral quality of a concrete act that he is going to perform, is in the process of performing, or has already completed" (*CCC* 1778). The wording is important. The role of conscience is to "recognise" the moral quality of an act. That is, it is presupposed that acts have a moral quality in themselves; that is, they are in conformity with God's law and the good of the person or not. The Catechism expresses it like this: "It is by the judgment of his conscience that man perceives and recognises the prescriptions of the divine law" (*CCC* 1778).

When a person recognises through the Church's teaching that a proposed act is contrary to God's law, the role of conscience is to apply that judgment to the case at hand and decide that, in spite of the difficulty involved, he or she cannot perform the act. This can sometimes be a very difficult decision to make. As the Catechism puts it, "Man is sometimes confronted by situations that make moral judgments less assured and decision difficult. But he must always seriously seek what is right and good and discern the will of God expressed in divine law" (*CCC* 1787).

When all the circumstances seem to be pushing the person to do something he or she knows is against the law of God, a good thought process is to remember that God is truly a loving Father who wants what is best for his children and has given us the commandments as his fatherly instruction to help us find happiness, both here and hereafter. And the Church, which passes on the commandments to us, is a loving Mother, who also wants to help us along the way through her motherly teaching. If she teaches that something is intrinsically evil and never to be done, it is because that act will hurt us and hinder our journey to true happiness.

We may not understand this at the time, but we should follow our Father and our Mother's teaching nonetheless. It is similar to a mother telling her children never to accept a ride from strangers or watch a particular television program. Even though the children do not understand why, if they are sensible they will follow their mother's advice.

In these matters we should remember too that God does not ask for the impossible and he always gives us the grace to do what he is asking. Very often we find that in going against our human judgment and following what God is asking, everything works out much better than we had thought possible. For the woman to have another child instead of being sterilised or instead of having an abortion often turns out to be the best thing that ever happened to her.

Let us learn to trust in God and do what he is asking. That way we avoid serious sin and we grow in holiness – and happiness.

532 Formation of conscience

I have often heard people say, "It's up to you. It's a matter for your conscience" as if we could do virtually anything as long as our conscience approved it. Somehow that doesn't seem right to me. Can you please shed some light on this?

You are right. Conscience is not a law unto itself, an inner voice that we can follow willy nilly. First we must form it.

To see how this is so we can go to the definition of conscience in the *Catechism of the Catholic Church*: "Conscience is a judgment of reason whereby the human person recognises the moral quality of a concrete act that he is going to perform, is in the process of performing, or has already completed" (*CCC* 1778).

Conscience is not just a voice within us that somehow mysteriously tells us what to do or not do. It is a judgment of our reason, of our intellect. A judgment involves weighing up a number of factors in order to arrive at a conclusion. In the case of the judgment of conscience the intellect weighs up the objective truth about the morality, the rightness or wrongness, of the act in question in order to decide whether the act is obligatory, permissible or forbidden.

A good analogy for conscience is the sextant which a sailor uses to determine his position on the high seas. The sailor points the sextant at some heavenly body, a fixed point of reference, in order to know where he is on the globe. Without the stars or some other heavenly body, the sextant is useless. Similarly, without the light of God's law, as taught by the Church, conscience has nothing by which to guide itself. It is blind.

So before we are able to make a proper judgment of conscience we need to learn what is right and wrong, to form our conscience. The Catechism speaks of the importance of this: "The education of conscience is indispensable for human beings who are subjected to negative influences and tempted by sin to prefer their own judgment and to reject authoritative teachings" (*CCC* 1783). How true this is! When faced with a difficult moral decision, we are all tempted to choose the easy way, to prefer our own judgment and not to seek the truth as taught by the Church.

How do we do form our conscience? The Catechism answers: "In the formation of conscience the Word of God is the light for our path; we must assimilate it in faith and prayer and put it into practice. We must also examine our conscience before the Lord's Cross. We are assisted by the gifts of the Holy Spirit, aided by the witness or advice of others and guided by the authoritative teaching of the Church" (*CCC* 1785).

We see here five ways. First, the Word of God, which we find in the scriptures and the tradition of the Church. We should read the Bible attentively and assimilate its teachings in prayer so that we can put them into practice. It is always a strong, clear light for our path. Second, the Cross of Christ, where we see Our Lord's determination to do what was right, even if it cost him his life. He did not seek the easy way, but the right way. Third, the gifts of the Holy Spirit – wisdom, understanding, knowledge, counsel, fortitude, piety and fear of the Lord – which assist us in knowing what is right and in having the fortitude and piety to carry it out. Fourth, the witness and advice of others, especially of those who know their faith well and endeavour to live it out to the full. And finally and most importantly, the authoritative teaching of the Church. Whenever we have doubts about the right course of action to follow we can open the Catechism. There we find the authoritative answer of the Church, our mother, who teaches with the guidance of the Holy Spirit.

The Second Vatican Council, in the Declaration *Dignitatis humanae*, emphasises the importance of listening to the Church: "In forming their consciences the Christian faithful must give careful attention to the sacred and certain teaching of the Church. For the Catholic Church is by the will of Christ the teacher of truth. Her charge is to announce and teach authentically that truth which is Christ, and at the same time with her authority to declare and confirm the principles of the moral order which derive from human nature itself" (*DH*, 14)

When we have a well formed conscience and we follow it, we have the certainty that we are acting in accordance with God's loving will and that we are on the way to holiness, to heaven.

533 Erroneous conscience

I was talking recently with a friend who habitually commits serious sins but says his conscience allows it. I tried to convince him he was wrong but he said he stood by his conscience. My question is, can someone's conscience be wrong?

Yes, someone can definitely have an erroneous conscience. St John Paul II puts it very succinctly in his Encyclical *Veritatis splendor*: "Conscience *is not an infallible judge*; it can make mistakes" (*VS* 62). We need to form our conscience so that it is a true guide. We begin when we are little, learning first from our parents, then from our teachers, priests, friends, books, etc. It is possible that along the way we are told, or we read, something that is simply wrong and we come to believe it.

For example, over the years I have heard people say they were told, by people whom they trusted very much, that we don't need to attend Mass on Sundays if we don't feel like it, or that masturbation is not a sin, or at least not a mortal sin. These teachings are clearly wrong, yet they were being taught by people in positions of authority.

The *Catechism of the Catholic Church* deals with the topic of the erroneous conscience, saying it can happen that "moral conscience remains in ignorance and makes erroneous judgments about acts to be performed or already committed" (*CCC* 1790). This can happen in two ways: through one's own fault or without personal fault. That is, culpably or inculpably.

Regarding the former, the Catechism teaches: "This ignorance can often be imputed to personal responsibility. This is the case when a man 'takes little trouble to find out what is true and good, or when conscience is by degrees almost blinded through the habit of committing sin.' In such cases, the person is culpable for the evil he commits" (*CCC* 1791; *GS* 16).

For example, someone might not pay attention when moral truths are being taught in class, he might have doubts about the morality of a particular action and not make an effort to find out the truth, or through repeated sins he may convince himself there is nothing wrong with what he is doing. In all these cases the person is responsible for having an erroneous conscience and God will hold him to account for the sins he commits as a result.

The Catechism goes on to mention other examples of how one can have an erroneous conscience: "Ignorance of Christ and his Gospel, bad example given by others, enslavement to one's passions, assertion of a mistaken notion of autonomy of conscience, rejection of the Church's authority and her teaching, lack of conversion and of charity: these can be at the source of errors of judgment in moral conduct" (*CCC* 1792).

Alternatively, someone can have an erroneous conscience through no fault of their own: "If – on the contrary – the ignorance is invincible, or the moral subject is not responsible for his erroneous judgment, the evil committed by the person cannot be imputed to him. It remains no less an evil, a privation, a disorder. One must therefore work to correct the errors of moral conscience" (*CCC* 1793).

The Catechism, like many moral theology texts, calls this ignorance *invincible*, ignorance that cannot be overcome. It cannot be overcome simply because the person does not realise that he or she is ignorant or in error. How does this come about? One way is simply through never having been told a particular moral truth. Many people are in this situation, at least as regards some moral issues. They may be committing sins habitually without being aware that what they are doing is wrong.

An inculpably erroneous conscience can also come about through the person being misled by someone they trust and then naturally believing what they have been taught. It can be a friend, a teacher, a priest, a book… Here it is not a matter of ignorance but of error, inculpable error. But again the error is invincible in the sense that the person does not realise he or she is in it.

As the Catechism says, this situation "remains no less an evil, a privation, a disorder" (*CCC* 1793). Whenever a person is doing what is objectively wrong they will always be hurt by it, even if they are completely unaware that it is wrong. So if we know someone in this situation we should try to explain the Church's teaching on the issue and show them how with the grace of God they can do what is right, even if they fail at times. God is merciful and will always forgive them.

534 Following our conscience

I have two questions about conscience. First, are we always sinning when we don't do what our conscience is telling us? And second, must we follow our conscience even when it is wrong?

These are very good questions and it is important that we understand the answers. We should understand first how our conscience works. We tend to think that it is always telling us to do or not to do something. For example, it tells us to get out of bed because it is time to get up, to go to Mass because it is Sunday, etc. And it can tell us not to do something: not to watch a particular television program or access some site on the internet because it will lead us into sin, not to tell a lie, not to steal someone else's property, etc. In all of these instances, conscience is commanding or forbidding us to do something.

But it can also simply allow or suggest us to do something, without imposing any obligation. For example, it can allow us to watch this or that television program, to read this or that book, to eat this or that breakfast cereal... Or it might suggest that we consider saying a rosary, attend Mass during the week, do some spiritual reading... In all of these cases there is no sense of strict obligation but merely one of permission or suggestion.

Coming back to your question, there are instances in which yes, we are sinning when we don't follow our conscience. This is the case whenever our conscience is certain and it is commanding or forbidding an action. As we have seen, conscience doesn't always command or forbid, but when it does we are obliged to follow it, and if we don't we are committing sin. The reason is simply that it is through the judgments of conscience that we recognise the moral quality of our actions. When we recognise that some action is to be done or not done, we understand that it is God who wants us to do it or not do it and to go against his law is to sin.

The *Catechism of the Catholic Church* confirms this: "A human being must always obey the certain judgment of his conscience. If he were deliberately to act against it, he would condemn himself" (*CCC* 1790). What is the importance of the word "certain"? Implied in the use of this word is the possibility that conscience, instead of being certain, might be doubtful. When it is certain we have no doubts about what is to be one or not done and we must act accordingly.

When conscience is doubtful, we hesitate and are unsure. In that case, our conscience is really telling us to resolve the doubt by seeking advice, reading up on the matter, consulting the Catechism, etc. We should always do this when we are in doubt, for fear of offending God in a grievous matter and endangering our eternal salvation, or at least spending longer in purgatory.

What happens when our conscience is certain but in fact wrong? For example, we think a particular feast day in the Church is a holyday of obligation and so our conscience is telling us to attend Mass, when in fact it is not a holyday at all. If we miss Mass that day we will have a sense of guilt for having offended God in missing Mass on a holyday of obligation, and God will hold us to account for the corresponding sin. This is a very important teaching and we all understand the reasoning behind it. This answers your question about whether we must follow our conscience even when it is wrong. Usually in these circumstances we do not know that our conscience is wrong, yet our conscience is certain and obliging us to do something so we should do it, for fear of sinning.

What is our obligation when our conscience is merely advising or suggesting us to do something? Obviously we are then under no strict obligation to do or not do it. We are not sinning if we ignore what our conscience is telling us. But it is still good to listen to our conscience and endeavour to follow it. For example, someone's conscience may be suggesting, advising, that they seek holiness in a more real way by attending Mass some days during the week. There is no pain of sin if they do not attend those Masses but they will grow more in love for God and their neighbour if they do, and they will store up a greater treasure in heaven. If everyone ignored these suggestions they would not be committing sin but the Church and the world would be the less for it.

So let us be attentive to the voice of our conscience, especially when it is commanding or forbidding some action, but also when it is merely suggesting or advising.

535 Freedom of conscience

I have often heard people use the expression "freedom of conscience" but have wondered exactly what it means. Can you enlighten me?

While each person may have their own understanding of it, there are two senses in which conscience is not free and another in which it is.

If freedom of conscience means freedom to form your own judgment, to decide what is right and wrong for you no matter what the Church teaches about the issue, then conscience is certainly not free. Conscience is a judgment about the morality of an act and as such is bound by the objective truth of the matter. For example, once we come to understand that two plus two equals four, our mind naturally adheres to that truth. We know we are not free to say that two plus two equals five because it is simply not the case.

Similarly, once we come to know, for example, that killing an innocent person is gravely immoral our conscience is bound by that truth. It is not free to judge otherwise. We know that if we say it is not a grave sin for us we are simply wrong. So with respect to moral truth, which is as objective as the truths of mathematics, the judgment of conscience is not free.

The Second Vatican Council teaches this in the Declaration on Religious Liberty *Dignitatis humanae* (1965): "For this reason everybody has the duty and consequently the right to seek the truth in religious matters so that, through the use of appropriate means, he may prudently form judgments of conscience which are sincere and true … Moreover it is by personal assent that men must adhere to the truth they have discovered" (*DH* 3).

Freedom of conscience can also be understood to mean freedom to do whatever one wants, even when their conscience is telling them not to do it. Their conscience can tell them, for example, that procuring an abortion is a serious sin, but they still feel free to go ahead and terminate the pregnancy. While they can talk of freedom, deep down they know they are not free, that they are doing something very wrong. This would be in a sense freedom *from* conscience, freedom to go against one's conscience. There can be no such freedom. God will always hold us responsible for acting against the judgment of our conscience. And we will hurt ourselves and others along the way.

The sense in which there is freedom of conscience is that of freedom to follow one's conscience. If there can be no freedom to go against one's conscience there must always be freedom to follow it, provided of course the use of that freedom does not infringe the rights of others or harm the common good. In a very important statement, that same Declaration of the Second Vatican Council teaches: "It is through his conscience that man sees and recognises the demands of the divine law. He is bound to follow this conscience faithfully in all his activity so that he may come to God, who is his last end. Therefore, he must not be forced to act contrary to his conscience. Nor must he be prevented from acting according to his conscience, especially in religious matters. The reason is because the practice of religion of its very nature consists primarily of those voluntary and free internal acts by which a man directs himself to God. Acts of this kind cannot be commanded or forbidden by any merely human authority" (*DH* 3).

The Declaration goes on to specify particular rights of religious communities to religious freedom: the freedom to organise themselves according to their own principles, to engage in public worship, to train and appoint their own ministers, to own property and build places of worship... (cf. *DH* 4). When we consider the many times in human history when individuals and communities have been prevented from worshipping God according to their own conscience, or coerced into worshipping in a way contrary to their conscience on pain of death, we can understand how important this freedom is.

So while there can never be freedom to make up one's own

mind about what is right and wrong, or freedom to act against one's conscience, there must always be freedom to act in accordance with it. Let us pray that this freedom will always be respected.

536 Conscience "at peace with God"

I have a friend who has been divorced and is now remarried civilly to a man with whom she has three children and they receive Communion with the approval of their parish priest because they are "at peace with God." Is this acceptable?

Would that we all had a conscience at peace with God! That is, that we had peace of soul, based on the knowledge that we are doing what God is asking of us, even if at times we fail! When we strive to do the will of God, we generally have peace of soul and this is a great blessing.

Of course, it can happen too that someone does not have a well-formed conscience and they think they are doing the will of God when objectively they may be offending him grievously. Think, for example, of someone who has been told by her parish priest that in her circumstances it would be acceptable to use contraception and she does so with complete peace of soul. Even though the advice is inappropriate, the woman will be at peace with God and can follow what her conscience is telling her.

Coming back to your friend, she is now living in an obviously happy relationship with her new partner, they have three children together, she attends Mass and receives the sacraments with the approval of her parish priest. She will be at peace with God and acting in good faith, even though objectively she is living in a state of grave sin. Our Lord was very clear about this: "Whoever divorces his wife and marries another, commits adultery against her; and if she divorces her husband and marries another, she commits adultery" (*Mk* 10:11-12). And Pope St John Paul II wrote in *Familiaris consortio* that "the

Church reaffirms her practice, which is based upon Sacred Scripture, of not admitting to Eucharistic Communion divorced persons who have remarried" (*FC* 84).

While an individual may be at peace with God even though objectively they are living in a state of grave sin, another matter is the responsibility of pastors in helping these people. There are two principal scenarios, to which the response may be very different.

The first is exemplified by the case I mentioned above of a person who is using contraception in good faith, having been misinformed by a priest or a friend, or out of sheer ignorance. If she happens to mention this fact in passing to another priest sometime later, for example in her first confession after many years, he might very well decide not to say anything about it in order not to spoil her "homecoming". He judges that now is not the opportune time to tell her that her use of contraception is a grave sin, and intends to let time pass and bring it up later when her faith is stronger and she is better prepared to change her life. This is an accepted pastoral practice and is known as leaving the person in good faith. This can be done especially when the person's sin is a private matter between them and God and is not known to the wider community.

The other scenario involves a situation like that of your friend who is divorced and remarried civilly, where her irregular marriage situation is public and known to others. If the couple approach a priest and ask if they can go to Communion, pastoral charity demands that he explain to them the reality of their situation, based on Our Lord's words and the constant practice of the Church of not admitting to Communion people in their situation. To do otherwise would be a lack of real concern for their soul, given that their marital acts would be acts of adultery and these always bring great harm to the soul. But in addition, because their irregular marital situation is publicly known, to admit them to Communion would cause scandal in the parish, where there are many people struggling to be faithful to their marriage commitments and now see someone in an irregular situation receiving Communion along with them.

What the priest should do is sit down with them, listen to them, and help them realise that they should not continue to commit grave sins and that they can endeavour to live as brother and sister. If they say this would be too hard, he can explain that they only need agree to try, and that if they fail from time to time they can be forgiven. As Pope Francis wrote in *Amoris laetitia,* "the law is itself a gift of God which points out the way, a gift for everyone without exception; it can be followed with the help of grace" (*AL* 295).

537 Sin always hurts the sinner

I recently heard a priest say that sin always hurts the sinner. Is this true? If so, can you please explain why?

It is most certainly true that sin always hurts the sinner, and in two ways: humanly and supernaturally. We can begin by reminding ourselves what sin is. The *Catechism of the Catholic Church* defines it in the words of St Augustine as: "an utterance, a deed, or a desire contrary to the eternal law" (*CCC* 1849; *Contra Faustum* 22). Or, more simply, sin is a wilful violation of God's law. How do we know what God's law is? We know it in two ways: through reason reflecting on human nature in what we call the natural law, and through God's revelation in Scripture and tradition.

Simply by reflecting on human nature we can know that such acts as killing an innocent person, stealing, lying, etc., are wrong. And we realise that each of these acts harms the person who does them as well as harming the fabric of society. For this reason the laws of all countries forbid them and punish them. In short, all peoples realise that certain forms of behaviour are harmful to society as well as to the individual. They are contrary to the natural moral law.

In addition to the natural law, we also find God's law in his revelation. The most obvious instances are the Ten Commandments given by God to Moses on Mount Sinai (cf. *Ex* 20:1-17) and Jesus' commentary on the Ten Commandments in the Sermon on the Mount (cf. *Mt* 5:17-48). There are of course many other moral precepts throughout the Scriptures. What we find when we study the Ten Commandments is that they are all based on fundamental principles of the natural law: the need to worship God, to honour our parents, not to kill, not to commit adultery, not to steal, etc. God gave us the Ten Commandments to make clear through revelation what was already written on the human heart. As St Irenaeus puts it, "From the beginning, God had implanted in the heart of man the precepts of the natural law. Then he was content to remind him of them. This was the Decalogue" (*Adv. Haeres.* 4, 15).

We might be inclined to ask, "Why did God give us all these commandments? Was he arbitrarily making up some rules to make our life difficult so that he could test us and see if we were worthy of eternal life? He was most certainly not making up arbitrary rules. As a true Father who wants the best for his children, he was pointing out things we should not do because they will only hurt us and hurt our relations with others (you shall not kill, you shall not commit adultery, you shall not steal…), and things we should do if we want to find the happiness and flourishing we desire (remember to keep holy the Sabbath, honour your father and mother…).

Parents do the same thing. Because they love their children and don't want them to get hurt and suffer, they tell them not to eat certain foods, not to watch certain television programs, not to tell lies, not to cheat, not to disobey their parents and teachers, not to accept rides from strangers, etc. This is only natural. It is a consequence of true love. With God it is the same. He knows better than we do what behaviours will hurt us in the short term and in the long term and he wants to avoid us doing them and finding out the hard way.

In addition to hurting us humanly, sin also hurts us supernaturally.

It offends God and weakens our love for him. It makes us less Christ-like. Little by little it predisposes us to commit bigger sins until we end up committing them and sometimes give up hope and stop praying and going to confession altogether. In that state we could very well end up in hell unless we repent (cf. *CCC* 1033). In addition, every sin requires that we do something to make up for it, what we call temporal punishment. We can make up for it either here on earth through penance, prayer, good deeds, reception of the sacraments and indulgences, or in purgatory. In a sense through sin we are sending our spiritual bank account more and more into debt, and it must be in balance before we can go to heaven.

So yes, sin always hurts the sinner. Very much. It is not that sin is wrong because God has forbidden it, but rather that God has forbidden it because it is wrong, because it hurts us.

538 Soul and spirit

In one of his letters St Paul makes a distinction between "soul" and "spirit". I thought they were the same thing. Can you please explain the difference, if there is one?

St Paul makes this distinction in two of his letters; that is, if we attribute the *Letter to the Hebrews* to St Paul, which is not certain. In his first letter to the Thessalonians he writes: "May the God of peace himself sanctify you wholly; and may your spirit and soul and body be kept sound and blameless at the coming of our Lord Jesus Christ" (*1 Thess* 5:23). In the *Letter to the Hebrews* we read: "For the word of God is living and active, sharper than any two-edged sword, piercing to the division of soul and spirit, of joints and marrow, and discerning the thoughts and intentions of the heart" (*Heb* 4:12).

We should understand that the Greek word for spirit is *pneuma* which, like its Hebrew equivalent *ruah*, has an original meaning of breath or wind. Thus it can refer to one's life or breath. It is in this sense that we understand Our Lord's words from the Cross: "Into your hand I commit my spirit" (*Ps* 31:5; cf. *Lk* 23:46). And of course the word is applied to the Holy Spirit, who came down on the apostles at Pentecost with the sound of wind (cf. *Acts* 2:2).

Over time the word spirit came to apply to the intellectual life of man, to his reason, consciousness, acts of the will, and especially to his spiritual life in the sense of his relationship with God. In this latter sense the person can be either spiritually alive, living in the grace and love of God, or spiritually dead, through serious sin.

The word for soul (*nephes* in Hebrew, *psyche* in Greek, *anima* in Latin) refers to the life principle in any living thing. It is distinguished from the body, and it allows the being to live. In this sense we say that every living thing, whether plant, animal or human, has a soul. Man, of course, has a spiritual soul which can exist in its own right, unlike that of animals and plants. When the body of the living thing is altered to a degree where it can no longer sustain life (e.g. it is crushed, burned, broken) the soul is no longer there and the being dies. In humans, the soul, as a spiritual substance, continues to live on after death and it passes to heaven, purgatory or hell. And it is through our spiritual soul that we can think, love, and relate to God.

Returning to your question, how should we understand the distinction St Paul makes between soul and spirit? The various Catholic commentaries on scripture tend to agree that by *soul* is to be understood the life and lower functions of the person, such as those of the bodily senses, whereas by *spirit* is to be understood the higher intellective functions of knowing and loving and especially the spiritual life of relationship with God.

Thus Dom Bernard Orchard OSB, in his *Catholic Commentary on Holy Scripture* says that the sword mentioned in *Hebrews* 4:12 divides "sensitive soul from thinking spirit". The *Navarre Bible* commentary on *1 Thess* 5:23 says: "'Spirit and soul and body': three aspects which go to make up a well-integrated human person. Spirit and soul are in fact two forms of the same principle. Here soul refers to the principle of sensitive life, whereas 'spirit' is the source of man's higher life; his intellectual life derives from his spirit, and this intellectual life, once enlightened by faith, is open to the action of the Holy Spirit (cf. *Rom* 1:9)".

Commenting on the same text, Scott Hahn in his *Ignatius Catholic Study Bible* says: "Paul is emphasizing the wholeness of the person without intending to make precise distinctions between his component parts. A certain distinction can be made, however, if we understand the *body* as the material frame, the *soul* as its immaterial principle of life, and the *spirit* as the human capacity for prayer and worship (*Rom* 1:9, *1 Cor* 14:15, *CCC* 367).

The *Catechism of the Catholic Church* sums it up: "Sometimes the soul is distinguished from the spirit: St Paul for instance prays that God may sanctify his people 'wholly', with 'spirit and soul and body' kept sound and blameless at the Lord's coming (*1 Thess* 5:23). The Church teaches that this distinction does not introduce a duality into the soul. 'Spirit' signifies that from creation man is ordered to a supernatural end and that his soul can gratuitously be raised beyond all it deserved to communion with God" (*CCC* 367).

539 The fruits of the Holy Spirit

Recently my daughter asked me about the fruits of the Holy Spirit, but I was not exactly sure what they were. I get them confused with the gifts. Are they different?

The fruits of the Holy Spirit are very different from the gifts. The gifts, in the words of the *Catechism of the Catholic Church*, are "permanent dispositions which make man docile in following the promptings of the Holy Spirit" (*CCC* 1830). They are received in the soul along with sanctifying grace and remain in us as permanent dispositions to help us follow the promptings of the Holy Spirit. We lose them only when we lose the state of grace through mortal sin. There are seven gifts: wisdom, understanding, counsel, fortitude, knowledge, piety and fear of the Lord. I wrote about them in an earlier column (cf. J. Flader, *Question Time 2,* q. 218).

The fruits, on the other hand, are the effects in us of living a life according to the spirit, according to the will of God, a life of holiness. The Catechism describes them as "perfections that the Holy Spirit forms in us as the first fruits of eternal glory" (*CCC* 1832).

In order to understand them better it is helpful to go to the passage in the letter to the Galatians where St Paul lists them. He contrasts the fruits, in this case the bitter fruits, of living according to the flesh with the fruits of living according to the spirit. He begins: "But I say, walk by the Spirit, and do not gratify the desires of the flesh. For the desires of the flesh are against the Spirit, and the desires of the Spirit are against the flesh; for these are opposed to each other, to prevent you from doing what you would" (*Gal* 5:16-17). We all understand how we are pulled in two directions: downwards by the pull of the flesh to seek bodily and earthly pleasures, and upwards by the Spirit to seek the things of God.

St Paul goes on to list the effects of living according to the flesh: "Now the works of the flesh are plain: immorality, impurity, licentiousness, idolatry, sorcery, enmity, strife, jealousy, anger, selfishness, dissension, party spirit, envy, drunkenness, carousing, and the like" (*Gal* 5:19-21). He goes on to warn about the possible loss of eternal life for those who indulge in them: "I warn you, as I warned you before, that those who do such things shall not inherit the kingdom of God" (*Gal* 5:21).

Immediately afterwards he lists the effects of living according to the spirit: "But the fruit of the Spirit is love, joy, peace, patience, kindness, goodness, faithfulness, gentleness, self-control; against such there is no law" (*Gal* 5:22-23). It is from this passage that the Church derives the list of fruits of the Holy Spirit. Although the Greek New Testament lists nine fruits, Christian tradition, following St Jerome's Latin Vulgate edition, has given us twelve, adding generosity, modesty, and chastity. The complete list is thus charity, joy, peace, patience, kindness, goodness, generosity, gentleness, faithfulness, modesty, self-control and chastity. Even though St Paul uses the word "fruit" in the singular, the word should be understood as a genus which has many species, which he then lists.

So the fruits of the Holy Spirit are the good habits, the virtues, the good deeds that come from living as a child of God. They are the fruits of a holy life. While we see in ourselves many of these fruits, we also see some of the works of the flesh. Our spiritual life is always a struggle to live more in the spirit and less in the flesh, and to return to God through the sacrament of Penance when we have failed.

St Basil has a beautiful description of the effects of living according to the Spirit: "Through the Holy Spirit we are restored to paradise, led back to the Kingdom of heaven, and adopted as children, given confidence to call God 'Father' and to share in Christ's grace, called children of light and given a share in eternal glory" (*De Spiritu Sancto*, 15, 36; *CCC* 736).

The Catechism adds: "By this power of the Spirit, God's children can bear much fruit. He who has grafted us onto the true vine will make us bear 'the fruit of the Spirit: ... love, joy, peace, patience, kindness, goodness, faithfulness, gentleness, self-control'" (*Gal* 5:22-23; *CCC* 736).

540 The morality of dreams

Is a person guilty of sin who has unchaste nightmares or dreams and wakes up realising what just went through their mind was a dream?

The first thing to say about dreams is that they are something that happens to us when we are asleep and we have no control over them. We do not choose what we are going to dream or what we are going to do in a dream. Often dreams make no sense when we think back over them since they involve a series of totally unconnected events and places. They sometimes involve real people, places and events in our lives but usually what happens in the dream has little relationship with reality. Dreams are simply a natural phenomenon, part of our psychological makeup.

On the other hand they do have something to do with our real person, especially when they involve people or places we have known. Thus a football player is likely to dream from time to time about football and a singer about singing, a truck driver about driving and a mother about raising children. In this way dreams are in some way a reflection of our real life, especially of our subconscious.

In view of this, what can we say about the moral significance of what we do in dreams? For any act to have moral significance, whether sinful or meritorious, we must be aware of what we are doing and we must freely choose to do it. This is the case with most of our actions. There are some actions, however, even while we are awake that lack this moral significance. For example, we may sneeze in Mass or we may become distracted in prayer through no fault of our own. Similarly, while asleep we may snore or talk or even walk. In all these cases there is no moral fault because we are not in control of what we are doing.

Passing to dreams, it is clear that while asleep we cannot be consciously aware of what we are doing nor can we freely choose to do or not do something. Even though the dream may seem very real at the time, and we may seem to be in control and to be acting knowingly and willingly, when we wake up we realise that we were not acting at all. It was only a dream. In view of this, it is clear that there can be no guilt or merit for what we did or did not do in a dream. If in the dream we did something that in a waking state would have been a sin, we are not guilty of a sin, even though we may have a certain sense of shame or remorse for even having dreamed it. And if in the dream we did something meritorious, there is no merit.

Nonetheless, dreams do reveal to some extent where our heart is in real life. Thus if we find ourselves frequently dreaming of committing certain sins, it is likely that we have been thinking consciously of those sins or even desiring to commit them when we were awake. Alternatively, if in our dreams we were tempted to commit a sin and we did not commit it, that could be a sign that in real life we would not have committed it either. Or if we often dream of working hard to spread the Gospel in some other country or of dedicating ourselves to feed the poor, our heart is probably in those activities. Thus the subject matter of our dreams can show us at least the tendencies of our heart. A virtuous person will tend to be virtuous in dreams and a sinful person sinful. While we are not responsible for what we do in dreams, we are responsible for what we think about and desire when we are awake.

It was probably the connection between dreams and desires that moved the Roman emperor Dionysius to have his subject Marsyas decapitated because Marsyas had dreamed of cutting the emperor's throat. Foolish though it was, Dionysius undoubtedly thought that if Marsyas considered killing him in his dreams, he would have carried it out in real life.

The popular saying "I wouldn't even dream of doing such a thing" reflects the notion that our dreams do reveal something of our character and that, even though we might consider doing certain things which are wrong, there are others that are so abhorrent that we wouldn't even dream of doing them.

In short, what we do in dreams has no moral guilt or merit it itself, but it may reveal something of our character.

541 The enneagram

A friend recently invited me to a program on the enneagram and I didn't know anything about it. Is this something that can be recommended for Catholics?

First, what is an enneagram? The name comes from the Greek words for *nine* and *written* or *drawn*, and it refers to a tool for analysing one's personality based on nine interconnected personality types, represented by nine points on a geometric figure called an enneagram. Supposedly with its origins in the mystical Sufi sect of Islam, it was developed by an Armenian occultist, George Ivanovich Gurdjieff, who lived in Russia from 1877 to 1947. It was further developed and brought to the West in the 1960s by Chileans Oscar Ichazo and Claudio Naranjo.

The Sufi religion provides the background for the enneagram. Sufis believe in the "Design", which is God's plan for mankind. The "Design" cannot be known by all but only by the initiated, in this case by Sufi masters who have direct access to it. In this sense, it is a form of gnosticism, the belief in a higher, hidden knowledge accessible only to a privileged few.

How does the Church look on the enneagram? In 2000 the United States Conference of Catholic Bishops' Committee on Doctrine prepared a draft statement entitled "A Brief Report on the Origins of the Enneagram". The report identified areas of concern and stated: "While the enneagram system shares little with traditional Christian doctrine or spirituality, it also shares little with the methods and criteria of modern science."

In 2003 the Vatican document *Jesus Christ, Bearer of the Water of Life*, which dealt with the dangers of New Age practices, said that gnosticism "has always existed side by side with Christianity ... more often assuming the characteristics of a religion or a para-religion in distinct, if not declared, conflict with all that is essentially Christian. An example of this can be seen in the enneagram, the nine-type tool for character analysis, which when used as a means of spiritual growth introduces an ambiguity in the doctrine and the life of the Christian faith" (1.4).

In 2004 the U.S. Conference of Catholic Bishops' Committee on Doctrine released a "Report on the Use of the Enneagram: Can it Serve as a True Instrument of Christian Spiritual Growth?" for the internal use of the bishops. The report states: "An examination of the origins of enneagram teaching reveals that it does not have credibility as an instrument of scientific psychology and that the philosophical and religious ideas of its creators are out of keeping with basic elements of Christian faith on several points. Consequently, the attempt to adapt the enneagram to Christianity as a tool for personal spiritual development shows little promise of providing substantial benefit to the Christian community".

Fr Mitch Pacwa S.J. writes: "Besides these scientific and psychological problems with the enneagram, Christians have many theological difficulties with it. The frequent use of such occult practices as divination and spiritism in Gurdjieff and Ichazo immediately throws up a red flag. In Deuteronomy 18:9-15 and many other Scripture passages, God our Lord forbids such pursuits. Most of the 'experts' I know, however, avoid the occult or know nothing about its presence in the enneagram's background. Despite this avoidance or ignorance, theological problems appear in enneagram workshops across the country" ("Tell Me Who I Am, O Enneagram", *Christian Research Journal,* Fall 1991, p. 14).

In 2011 Archbishop Thomas Wenski of Miami wrote an online column titled "New Age is Old Gnosticism" (10 February 2011). He described the enneagram as a "pseudo-psychological exercise supposedly based on Eastern mysticism, [which] introduces ambiguity into the doctrine and life of the Christian faith and therefore cannot be happily used to promote growth in an authentic Christian spirituality." He says that the enneagram program redefines sin by associating faults with personality types, and that it encourages an unhealthy self-absorption with one's own type, so that the type is at fault rather than the person, thus undermining personal freedom and responsibility.

With all these warnings, I would certainly not recommend attending an enneagram program.

Relations with God

542 Loving God above all things

I know we are supposed to love God above all things, but sometimes I think I have more love for my husband and children than for God. This worries me. What exactly does it mean to love God above all things?

There are different ways we can love someone more than another. One is by the intensity of feelings we have for one over the other. In this way we may often experience a greater feeling of love for our family or friends than for God. After all, these people are in our lives in a tangible way, and they show their love for us in obvious ways which move us to feel a strong love for them. God, on the other hand, we do not see with our eyes or hear with our ears, and so it is only natural that we do not feel the same intensity of love for him that we do for some human beings.

Not even the saints experienced a strong feeling of love for God at all times. It is well known that St Teresa of Calcutta experienced a great spiritual dryness, a feeling of the absence of God, a dark night of the soul, for the last fifty years of her life. True love for God is not experienced in feelings but in deeds, in loving God "in deed and in truth", as St John writes (*1 Jn* 3:18). Jesus himself invites us to love him in this way: "If you love me you will keep my commandments" (*Jn* 14:15). If the saints did not always feel a strong love for God, they did always show their love in generous deeds, in doing God's will.

The other way of loving one person more than another is by what we call love of preference. Here it is not a matter of the intensity of feelings but rather of preferring love for one person to love for another in our will. Even though we might love a human being with more intensity of feeling than we experience in our love for God, we would prefer to lose the love of that person rather than lose the love of God, and with it eternal life with him.

Our Lord himself speaks of this love of preference: "He who loves father or mother more than me is not worthy of me; and he who loves son or daughter more than me is not worthy of me" (*Mt* 10:37). It is clear that Jesus is referring here to love of preference, not to feelings of love. To be sure, he wants us to love our family members just as we love God – "You shall love the Lord your God with all your heart, and with all your soul, and with all your strength, and with all your mind; and your neighbour as yourself" (*Lk* 10:27; *Deut* 6:5). But he clearly wants us to love him more than we love our neighbour, even our family members.

What he says immediately before this makes it clear. "For I have come to set a man against his father, and a daughter against her mother, and a daughter-in-law against her mother-in-law; and a man's foes will be those of his own household" (*Mt* 10:35-36). When someone begins to take his faith more seriously it can happen that even his father or mother or other family members turn against him. If that happens the person must choose between loving God, being prepared to do whatever he asks, and loving one's family members. It is then that Jesus says: "He who loves father or mother more than me is not worthy of me" (*Mt* 10:37). It is a choice most people do not have to make, but should we need to make it, we should prefer love for God to love for our fellow man.

St John Vianney, the Curé of Ars, comments: "If we had rather offend the good God than deprive ourselves of a passing satisfaction, than renounce those guilty meetings, those shameful possessions, we do not love the good God with a love of preference, since we love our pleasures, our passions, better than the good God himself. Let us go down into our own souls; let us question our hearts, my children, and see if we do not love some creature more than the good God. We are permitted to love our relations, our possessions, our health, our reputation; but this love must be subordinate to the love we should have for God, so that we may be ready to make the sacrifice of it if he should require it…" (Exhortation 15, *The Love of God*).

The martyrs bore witness to this love of God above all things, sacrificing their love for their family members and friends, their possessions and even life itself, rather than offend God and lose his love for all eternity. The more we show our love for God by being constant in our prayer and penance, by the reception of the sacraments and by doing his will in all things, the more we too will be prepared to sacrifice everything rather than lose the love of God.

543 Respect for the Holy Name of Jesus

When I was growing up I was taught to bow my head whenever I said or heard the name "Jesus". I have noticed that some priests still bow their heads in Mass but no one else seems to do it anymore except for some of us oldies. How has this come about?

I too belong to the generation that learned to bow our heads at the name of Jesus, but, as you say, the custom seems to be falling into disuse. So important is respect for the divine name that God chose to give us a separate commandment regarding it: "You shall not take the name of the Lord your God in vain" (*Deut* 5:11). Elsewhere in the Old Testament there are numerous passages that speak of the holiness of God's name, among them: "O Lord, our Lord, how majestic is your name in all the earth!" (*Ps* 8:1; cf. *Zach* 2:13; *Ps* 29:2; 96:2; 113:1-2).

In the New Testament St James denounces those "who blaspheme that honourable name by which you are called" (*Jas* 2:7). And St Paul, referring to Jesus emptying himself to take the form of a servant and then becoming obedient unto death, writes: "Therefore God has highly exalted him and bestowed on him the name which is above every name, that at the name of Jesus every knee should bow, in heaven and on earth and under the earth, and every tongue confess that Jesus Christ is Lord, to the glory of God the Father" (*Phil* 2:9-11).

By way of concretising respect for the name of Jesus in a formal way the Second Council of Lyons in 1274 decreed that "at the name of Jesus every knee should bow; whenever that glorious name is recalled, especially during the sacred mysteries of the Mass, everyone should bow the knees of his heart, which he can do even by a bow of his head."

As regards what is to be done in Mass today, the *General Instruction of the Roman Missal* says: "A bow of the head is made when the three Divine Persons are named together and at the names of Jesus, of the Blessed Virgin Mary and of the saint in whose honour Mass is being celebrated" (*GIRM* 275).

The importance of honouring the holy name of Jesus is seen too in the feast of that name, which has been celebrated, at least at the local level, since the end of the fifteenth century. The feast of the Holy Name of Jesus was inserted into the universal calendar by Pope Innocent XIII in 1721. Although it was removed when the calendar was revised in 1969, it was restored under Pope John Paul II in 2002 and is now celebrated on January 3.

The Divine Praises we say in Benediction are another manifestation of respect for the divine name, with the words "Blessed be his Holy Name." The Divine Praises were originally written in 1797 to make reparation for blasphemy and profanity against God.

Another testimony to the importance of honouring the name of Jesus is the existence of the Holy Name Society in many countries. The Society has its origins in the Second Council of Lyons in 1274, which prescribed that the faithful should have special devotion to the holy name of Jesus and that reparation should be made for the insults against that name by the Albigenses and other heretics of the time. Pope Gregory X, in 1274, entrusted to the newly-founded Dominicans the task of preaching the devotion. The Holy Name Society today has as its aim to promote respect for the name of God and Jesus and to make reparation for the many blasphemies and other sins against that name.

Given the widespread misuse of the names of God and Jesus today in ordinary life, as well as on television, in films and in other forms of entertainment, it is especially important to do all we can to restore respect for the name of God. Bowing our head when we pronounce or hear the name of Jesus is a very good way to do this. Also important is to make an internal act of reparation whenever we hear the name of God or Jesus blasphemed. It should hurt us that the object of our love is mistreated in this way.

It may very well be that the custom of bowing the head at the name of Jesus will pass out of general use, as have other laudable customs in recent times, but that does not prevent us personally from continuing to live it and passing on to our children this ancient custom.

544 Freedom of worship

In my suburb the Muslims have proposed to build a mosque. This has the people completely divided, most of them being against it. Is building a mosque something that should be allowed in a predominantly Christian society? How does the Church look on this?

The Second Vatican Council answered your question in several documents, among them the Dogmatic Constitution on the Church *Lumen gentium* and the Declaration on Religious Liberty *Dignitatis humanae*. These documents spoke not only about Muslims but about people of all religions and how Catholics should respect their freedom of worship.

Before the Council there was a widespread attitude that only the Catholic religion was true and that other religions, including other

Christian denominations, were false. From this it followed that Catholics had a right to build churches and to worship in accordance with their beliefs but those of other religions did not.

Thank God the Council looked at the question in a totally different light. In the Council's documents other religions were considered not to be false but rather to have elements of truth and goodness, which indeed they do. For example, the Council's document on the Church *Lumen gentium*, after examining the relationship of people of other religions and of none with the Church, says: "Whatever good or truth is found amongst them is considered by the Church to be a preparation for the Gospel" (*LG* 16). In other words, the fact that someone belongs to another religion can be considered to be positive. It is a preparation for finding the fullness of truth in the Catholic Church.

Similarly, the Declaration on the Relation of the Church to Non-Christian Religions *Nostra aetate* says: "The Catholic Church rejects nothing of what is true and holy in these religions. She has a high regard for the manner of life and conduct, the precepts and doctrines which, nevertheless often reflect a ray of that truth which enlightens all men" (*NA* 2).

With respect to Muslims in particular it says: "The Church has also a high regard for the Muslims. They worship God, who is one, living and subsistent, merciful and almighty, the Creator of heaven and earth, who has also spoken to men. They strive to submit themselves without reserve to the hidden decrees of God, just as Abraham submitted himself to God's plan, to whose faith Muslims eagerly link their own. Although not acknowledging him as God, they worship Jesus as a prophet, his virgin Mother they also honour, and even at times devoutly invoke. Further, they await the day of judgment and the reward of God following the resurrection of the dead. For this reason they highly esteem an upright life and worship God, especially by way of prayer, alms-deeds and fasting" (*NA* 3).

In view of this, the Council's Declaration on Religious Liberty

Dignitatis humanae teaches that, based on their dignity as human persons, all people have the right to follow their conscience in matters of worship. It teaches: "The Vatican Council declares that the human person has a right to religious freedom. Freedom of this kind means that all men should be immune from coercion on the part of individuals, social groups and every human power so that, within due limits, nobody is forced to act against his convictions, nor is anyone to be restrained from acting in accordance with his convictions in religious matters in private or in public, alone or in association with others. The Council further declares that the right to religious freedom is based on the very dignity of the human person as known through the revealed word of God and by reason itself. This right of the human person to religious freedom must be given such recognition in the constitutional order of society as will make it a civil right" (*DH* 2).

In other words, people of all religious persuasions have the right to worship according to their beliefs, and therefore to build temples and whatever other buildings are needed to exercise this right. As good Christians, we should respect this right, even though we may disagree with the religious beliefs of those concerned. At the same time, we hope that authorities in other countries, including Muslim ones, will respect the right of Catholics and people of other faiths to build churches and worship God in them.

545 The Resurrection and the Lord's Day

When and why did the early Christians change their day of worship from Saturday to Sunday?

Your question of course refers to the third commandment: "Remember to keep holy the Sabbath" or "Remember to keep holy the Lord's Day." The Sabbath for the Jews was the seventh day of the week, Saturday, and a day of rest. God explained to Moses, "Six days shall work be done, but the seventh day is a Sabbath of solemn rest, holy to the Lord" (*Ex* 31:15). The reason for it goes back to God's work of creation: "And on the seventh day God finished his work which he had done, and he rested on the seventh day from all his work which he had done. So God blessed the seventh day and hallowed it, because on it God rested from all his work which he had done in creation" (*Gen* 2:2-3).

When did Christians change their day of rest and worship to Sunday? It came about almost immediately and spontaneously. Already in the *Acts of the Apostles*, written by St Luke sometime before the year 70, we read: "On the first day of the week, when we were gathered together to break bread..." (*Acts* 20:7). The first day of the week was Sunday and the breaking of the bread was of course the celebration of the Eucharist, or Mass. Similarly in the *Didache*, written probably late in the first century, we find: "But every Lord's day gather yourselves together, and break bread, and give thanksgiving" (14, 1a). We note here the early use of the term "Lord's day" for Sunday. The phrase also appears in the book of *Revelation*, written by St John toward the end of the first century: "I was in the Spirit on the Lord's day..." (*Rev* 1:10).

Even though the first Christians gathered on Sundays to celebrate the Eucharist, at the beginning many of them continued to attend the synagogue on Saturdays as well. St John Paul II writes in his Apostolic Letter *Dies Domini* (1998): "The apostles, and in particular Saint Paul, continued initially to attend the synagogue so that there they might proclaim Jesus Christ, commenting upon 'the words of the prophets which are read every Sabbath' (*Acts* 13:27). Some communities observed the Sabbath while also celebrating Sunday. Soon, however, the two days began to be distinguished ever more clearly, in reaction chiefly to the insistence of those Christians whose origins in Judaism made them inclined to maintain the obligation of the old Law" (*DD* 23).

The principal reason for gathering together on Sundays and calling it the Lord's day was of course that Christ rose from the dead on that day, the first day of the week (cf. *Jn* 20:1). Likewise the coming of the Holy Spirit at Pentecost took place on a Sunday. But the early Christians went further and associated the first day with the first day of creation. St John Paul II writes: "Christian thought spontaneously linked the Resurrection, which took place on "the first day of the week", with the first day of that cosmic week (cf. *Gen* 1:1-2:4) which shapes the creation story in the Book of Genesis: the day of the creation of light (cf. 1:3-5). This link invited an understanding of the Resurrection as the beginning of a new creation, the first fruits of which is the glorious Christ, "the first born of all creation" (*Col* 1:15) and "the first born from the dead" (*Col* 1:18; *DD* 24). It is significant that as light was created on the first day, Christ is "the light of the world" (*Jn* 8:12).

In the middle of the second century St Justin takes up this theme, commenting on the significance of the first day of the week being named after the sun in Latin: "We all gather on the day of the sun, for it is the first day [after the Jewish Sabbath, but also the first day] when God, separating matter from darkness, made the world; and on this same day Jesus Christ our Saviour rose from the dead" (*1 Apol.* 67). The early Christians referred to Christ as the "sun of justice" (cf *Mal* 4:2) and so it was fitting that they would honour him on this day rather than worship the sun as the pagans did.

But Sunday is also the eighth day and as such it calls to mind the day without end which is eternal life, eternal rest, with God. St Augustine in his *Confessions* asks God to grant us "the peace of quietness, the peace of the Sabbath, a peace with no evening" (*Conf.* 13, 50). And St John Paul II, quoting St Basil, explains that "Sunday symbolises that truly singular day which will follow the present time, the day without end which will know neither evening nor morning, the imperishable age which will never grow old; Sunday is the ceaseless foretelling of life without end which renews the hope of Christians and encourages them on their way" (cf. *On the Holy Spirit,* 27, 66; *DD* 26).

So Sunday is the weekly celebration of Easter, "the day of days", and it should have great importance in the lives of all.

546 Keeping the Lord's Day holy

I have a number of Catholic friends who no longer attend Mass regularly on Sundays. Some say they are too busy, or they have children's sport or they have to work. This disturbs me because they are such good people and they used to practise regularly. How can I help them?

You point to a problem which is becoming increasingly common and worrisome. In the survey conducted in 2011, only 12.2 per cent of Australian Catholics were attending Mass at least three times a month. Fifty years ago it was closer to 60 per cent. This is not a healthy situation. After all, God is our beginning and our end. He made this universe out of nothing, he made us in his image and likeness, he loves us so much that he became man and died on the cross to redeem us, and he has a place waiting for us in heaven. We cannot live without him and we certainly do not want to die without him.

As you say, your friends are good people. About half of Australian Catholic families send their children to Catholic schools. They want a Catholic education for their children because they value the faith and values in which they were brought up themselves. Many of them were attending Mass regularly only a few years ago. What has happened is that over time they have let other influences take over so that, without bad will, God has come to mean less and less to them.

Pope St John Paul II spoke about this in his Apostolic Letter *Dies Domini*: "Until quite recently, it was easier in traditionally Christian countries to keep Sunday holy because it was an almost universal practice and because, even in the organisation of civil society, Sunday rest was considered a fixed part of the work schedule. Today, however, even in those countries which give legal sanction to the festive character of Sunday, changes in socio-economic conditions have often led to profound modifications of social behaviour and hence of the character of Sunday. The custom of the 'weekend' has become more widespread, a weekly period of respite, spent perhaps far from home and often involving participation in cultural, political or sporting activities which are usually held on free days. This social and cultural phenomenon is by no means without its positive aspects if, while respecting true values, it can contribute to people's development and to the advancement of the life of society as a whole. All of this responds not only to the need for rest, but also to the need for celebration which is inherent in our humanity. Unfortunately, when Sunday loses its fundamental meaning and becomes merely part of a 'weekend', it can happen that people stay locked within a horizon so limited that they can no longer see 'the heavens'. Hence, though ready to celebrate, they are really incapable of doing so" (*DD* 4).

The problem with letting Sunday Mass slip out of our life is that it is usually accompanied by letting God slip out of our life. And life without God is sad indeed. God brings the light, the hope, the joy, the love, the certainty we all need and seek. And when we have young children, especially when they are in Catholic schools, the children see the contradiction between what they learn in school and what they live at home. If parents are not inclined to attend Mass themselves, they should think of the good of their children. Bringing them up with the celebration of Sunday as the Lord's Day, where the family puts attendance at Mass as a priority, is a good way to instil in them the virtues of faith, hope and love for God which provide the foundation on which to build their lives.

It can be helpful too to reflect on Our Lord's words to the apostles when they fell asleep in the garden of Gethsemane: "Can you not watch one hour with me?" (*Mt* 26:40) Can we not give God one hour a week, when he is watching over us and blessing us twenty-four hours a day, seven days a week? When people return to attendance at Sunday Mass after some time away, they appreciate the great value of putting the Lord once again in his day, and of putting their own lives in God's care. And they realise how much they get out of Mass as well: hearing God's word in the readings, receiving some helpful advice in the homily, praying for all their intentions, and especially receiving Christ once again in holy Communion. Let us do all we can to help our friends and loved ones experience this great joy.

If we really want, we can make Sunday Mass compatible with our work, sport and relaxation, going on Saturday evening or Sunday evening if need be. It will make a big difference.

547 Sunday, a day of rest

I know we are not supposed to work on Sundays but this is not always easy. Can you tell me what sorts of things we can do and what we should avoid?

The *Catechism of the Catholic Church* gives the general criterion for how we are to live the obligation of Sunday rest: "On Sundays and other holy days of obligation, the faithful are to refrain from engaging in work or activities that hinder the worship owed to God, the joy proper to the Lord's Day, the performance of the works of mercy, and the appropriate relaxation of mind and body. Family needs or important social service can legitimately excuse from the obligation of Sunday rest. The faithful should see to it that legitimate excuses do not lead to habits prejudicial to religion, family life, and health" (*CCC* 2185).

As the Catechism says, family needs can require doing some work on Sundays. Meals need to be prepared and the house tidied up, nappies need to be changed, etc. Nonetheless, one should avoid doing jobs which take greater amounts of time and which could be done on other days, like the laundry, shopping, painting the house, gardening, etc. For some people Sunday is the only day on which they can do some of these tasks, and so of course they may do them.

As regards public activities, the Catechism goes on to say: "Traditional activities (sport, restaurants, etc.), and social necessities (public services, etc.), require some people to work on Sundays, but everyone should still take care to set aside sufficient time for leisure" (*CCC* 2187). It is obvious that hotels, restaurants, places of amusement and recreation, sporting events, etc., require staff to work on Sundays, as do social services such as police, ambulance services, fire departments, hospitals, aged care facilities, etc. Catholics, if rostered on, may thus do these jobs even on Sundays but they should try not to make it a regular, or especially a weekly occurrence. And of course they should attend Mass at some time on Saturday evening or Sunday.

It is important too to observe what the Catechism also teaches: "Every Christian should avoid making unnecessary demands on others that would hinder them from observing the Lord's Day" (*CCC* 2187). This refers to employers, who should make up their rosters so as to allow their employees to be able to rest at least on some Sundays each month. It can also refer to individuals, who should not require tradesmen and others to do jobs for them on Sundays. Even if the tradesmen want to work on a Sunday, it is good at least to suggest that they rather spend the day with their family.

We are all aware how, over the years, more and more businesses and shops are open on Sundays and Our Lord is increasingly pushed out of his day. It is up to us to resist this growing secularisation and to defend our time for rest and the worship of God. The Catechism teaches: "[Christians] have to give everyone a public example of prayer, respect, and joy and defend their traditions as a precious contribution to the spiritual life of society. If a country's legislation or other reasons require work on Sunday, the day should nevertheless be lived as the day of our deliverance which lets us share in this 'festal gathering,' the 'assembly of the first-born who are enrolled in heaven'" (*Heb* 12:22-23; *CCC* 2188).

What activities should we try to foster on Sundays? Apart from attending Mass, which is the most important, we should spend time with our family and relatives, something which is often difficult on other days of the week. In addition, "Sunday is a time for reflection, silence, cultivation of the mind, and meditation which furthers the growth of the Christian interior life" (*CCC* 2186). And of course "Sunday is traditionally consecrated by Christian piety to good works and humble service of the sick, the infirm, and the elderly" (*CCC* 2186). In other words, it is a good opportunity to practise works of mercy.

St John Paul II sums it up: "Through Sunday rest, daily concerns and tasks can find their proper perspective: the material things about which we worry give way to spiritual values; in a moment of encounter and less pressured exchange, we see the true face of the people with whom we live. Even the beauties of nature – too often marred by the desire to exploit, which turns against man himself – can be rediscovered and enjoyed to the full" (*DD* 67).

Relations with our neighbour

548 What exactly is mercy?

We have heard much about mercy of late with the Jubilee Year of Mercy about to begin, but, although I think I understand it somewhat, can you tell me exactly what mercy is?

The word mercy comes from the Latin *misericordia*, which in turn comes from the two words *miseria*, meaning wretchedness, misery or affliction, and *cor*, meaning heart. Thus etymologically mercy means a heart for the wretchedness or affliction of another. Or, as we understand it in English, it means compassion or pity.

St Thomas Aquinas comments in his *Summa Theologiae*: "To say that a person is merciful is like saying that he is sorrowful at heart (*miserum cor*), that is, he is afflicted with sorrow by the misery of another as though it were his own. Hence it follows that he endeavours to dispel the misery of the other person as if it were his own; and this is the effect of mercy. God cannot feel sorrow over the misery of others, but it does most properly belong to him to dispel that misery, whatever form that shortcoming or deprivation takes" (*STh* I, q. 21, a. 3).

Mercy is a beautiful virtue and, according to St Thomas Aquinas, "In itself, mercy takes precedence over other virtues, for it belongs to mercy to be bountiful to others, and, what is more, to succour others in their wants, which pertains chiefly to one who stands above. Hence mercy is accounted as being proper to God: and therein his omnipotence is revealed to the highest degree" (*STh* II-II, q. 30, a. 4). The reason St Thomas sees omnipotence, or almighty power, in God's mercy is undoubtedly that in the creation of the universe God began with nothing, whereas in his mercy he goes even further and begins with our sinfulness, which was offensive to him, reconciling us to himself by forgiving our sins.

Pope Francis comments in his Bull *Misericordiae Vultus* proclaiming the Jubilee Year: "Saint Thomas Aquinas' words show that God's mercy, rather than a sign of weakness, is the mark of his omnipotence. For this reason the liturgy, in one of its most ancient collects, has us pray: 'O God, who reveal your power above all in your mercy and forgiveness...' Throughout the history of humanity, God will always be the One who is present, close, provident, holy, and merciful" (*MV* 6).

We see God's mercy especially in his becoming man in Jesus Christ and dying on the Cross in order to reconcile us with him after the original sin of our first parents. He didn't need to do that, but he "so loved the world that he gave his only-begotten Son, that whoever believes in him should not perish but have eternal life" (*Jn* 3:16). And he shows his mercy time and again when he forgives us our sins through the sacrament of mercy, the sacrament of penance.

Not for nothing are the Scriptures full of passages which speak of God's mercy. Already at the beginning of the Old Testament God reveals his mercy when he responds to the original sin of Adam and Eve by promising a redeemer. He says to the serpent: "I will put enmity between you and the woman, and between your seed and her seed; he shall bruise your head, and you shall bruise his heel" (*Gen* 3:15). Then when the Israelites had offended him by worshipping a golden calf, God renewed his covenant with his people and said to Moses: "The Lord, the Lord, a God merciful and gracious, slow to anger, and abounding in mercy and faithfulness, keeping merciful love for thousands, forgiving iniquity and transgression and sin..." (*Ex* 34:6-7).

The Psalms too have many passages referring to God's mercy. For example: "Bless the Lord, O my soul, and forget not all his benefits, who forgives all your iniquity, who heals all your diseases, who redeems your life from the pit, who crowns you with mercy and compassion..." (*Ps* 103:2-4). Likewise: "Happy is he whose help is the God of Jacob ... who executes justice for the oppressed; who gives food to the hungry. The Lord sets the prisoners free; the Lord opens the eyes of the blind. The Lord lifts up those who are bowed down; the Lord loves the righteous" (*Ps* 146:5-8).

Pope Francis comments: "In short, the mercy of God is not an abstract idea, but a concrete reality through which he reveals his love as that of a father or a mother, moved to the very depths out of love for their child" (*MV* 6).

549 Showing mercy

I often feel I should help someone in need and then don't follow through with it. Is this a serious matter before God or is it alright sometimes not to help someone?

We shouldn't become scrupulous about these works of charity, or mercy, as if it were a mortal sin or even a venial sin not to help someone in need. We are not always required to help them. But wherever possible we should be generous towards others, remembering that whatever we did to the least of our brethren we did to Our Lord himself (cf. *Mt* 25:40).

When the person in need is in our own family – a sick child, a hungry husband, a child without a clean school uniform – naturally we are obliged to provide for their needs. This is a matter of justice more than of mercy, since parents have a duty to provide for their children. At the same time, children have a duty to provide for their parents, especially when the parents are elderly and unable to care for themselves.

When the person in need is in our extended family – an in-law, aunt or uncle, nephew or niece, cousin... – or is a close friend, the duty is less, but greater than if it were a complete stranger. As they say, "Charity begins at home", so those closest to us have the first claim on our love. But we should be charitable to strangers too, whenever possible.

Our Lord praises those who do these works of mercy and promises them eternal life: "Come, O blessed of my Father, inherit the kingdom prepared for you from the foundation of the world; for I was hungry and you gave me food, I was thirsty and you gave me drink, I was a stranger and you welcomed me..." (*Mt* 25:34-35). At the same time, he threatens with eternal punishment those who never do them: "Depart from me, you cursed, into the eternal fire prepared for the devil and his angels; for I was hungry and you gave me no food, I was thirsty and you gave me no drink..." (*Mt* 25:41-42). It should be understood that it is only those who fail to help someone they had an obligation to help in a serious matter and are unrepentant that will be punished forever.

Commenting on this passage St Augustine explains that when we give to others we are only giving from what God has already given to us: "Give from your riches. From whose riches do you give except from his? If you gave from your own riches it would be bounty, but if you give from his, it is only a repayment. For what have you that you did not receive?" (*On Psalm 95,* 14, 15).

Our Lord himself promises to show mercy to those who are merciful to others: "Blessed are the merciful, for they shall obtain mercy" (*Mt* 5:7). St Caesarius of Arles comments: "Sweet is the name of mercy, dearest brethren; and if the name is sweet, how much sweeter is the quality itself? Yet though all men would wish to receive it, alas their own conduct is not such as to deserve it. All wish to receive mercy; few are ready to show mercy to others. What effrontery to want to receive what you neglect to give! You must show mercy in this life if you hope to receive it in the next" (*Sermon* 25, 1).

In what way does God show mercy in the next life to those who show it to others in this one? St Caesarius continues: "There are two kinds of mercy then: mercy on earth and mercy in heaven, human mercy and divine mercy. What is human mercy like? It makes you concerned for the hardship of the poor. What is divine mercy like? It forgives sinners. Whatever generosity human mercy shows during our life on earth divine mercy repays when we reach our fatherland. In this world God is cold and hungry in all the poor, as he himself said: 'As you did it to one of the least of these my brethren, you did it to me.' God then is pleased to give from heaven, but he desires to receive on earth. What sort of people are we – when God gives, we want to receive, when he asks, we refuse to give? When a poor man is hungry, Christ is in need, as he said himself: 'I was hungry and you gave me no food.' Take care not to despise the hardship of the poor, if you would hope, without fear, to have your sins forgiven" (*ibid*).

In summary, while it is not always a sin to fail to help someone in need, it is good to be generous here on earth as much as possible so that God will repay us with eternal life in heaven.

550 The corporal works of mercy

Can you please remind me what the works of mercy are, and how I might live them in practice?

The Church has traditionally taught that there are seven corporal works of mercy that refer to helping our neighbour in his or her bodily needs, and seven spiritual works of mercy that refer to our neighbour's spiritual needs. In this column I will write about the corporal works and in the next about the spiritual works.

Pope Francis in *Misericordiae Vultus* speaks of the importance of doing the works of mercy: "It is my burning desire that, during this Jubilee, the Christian people may reflect on the *corporal and spiritual works of mercy*. It will be a way to reawaken our conscience, too often grown dull in the face of poverty. And let us enter more deeply into the heart of the Gospel where the poor have a special experience of God's mercy. Jesus introduces us to these works of mercy in his preaching so that we can know whether or not we are living as his disciples. Let us rediscover these *corporal works of mercy*: to feed the hungry, give drink to the thirsty, clothe the naked, welcome the stranger, heal the sick, visit the imprisoned, and bury the dead" (n 15).

The corporal works of mercy, with the exception of the last, are mentioned by Jesus himself in his description of the Last Judgment: "Then the King will say to those at his right hand, 'Come, O blessed of my Father, inherit the kingdom prepared for you from the foundation of the world; for I was hungry and you gave me food, I was thirsty and you gave me drink, I was a stranger and you welcomed me, I was naked and you clothed me, I was sick and you visited me, I was in prison and you came to me'" (*Mt* 25:34-36).

How can we live these works of mercy in practice? We tend to limit our thinking to the relatively few opportunities we may have to help the truly down and out: those begging on a street corner, those in hostels for the homeless, refugees, the poor in other countries through international charities, etc. We should most certainly do all we can to help people in these ways, seeing Jesus in them and knowing that he will reward us for our generosity. But we should not forget that charity begins at home and we have abundant opportunities to live the works of mercy within our family and extended family and in our neighbourhood.

Mothers of families and all who help them in domestic chores are living most of these works all the time. Simply preparing the family meal, setting the table and cleaning up afterwards are examples of *feeding the hungry* and *giving drink to the thirsty*. If visitors come, especially if they arrive unexpectedly, there is an opportunity to *welcome the stranger*. Moreover, we can invite a lonely person or a whole family to join us from time to time, extending our hospitality to them.

These works can also be done to help the family of a relative or friend in special circumstances, such as a death or serious illness, financial hardship, moving into a new home, etc. Taking them a meal when we know it would be difficult for them to prepare it themselves is always greatly appreciated at these difficult times. Similarly, helping an infant or an elderly or handicapped person to get dressed, and doing the laundry with all it entails are ways to *clothe the naked*. We can also give unused clothing to the St Vincent de Paul Society or some other charity, making sure that it is clean and in a good state of repair.

We can make sure that we visit regularly friends and relatives in hospitals and nursing homes, and those confined to their own homes, as ways of *visiting the sick*. If we know someone *in prison, we should endeavour to visit them* too or at least write to them. And of course we should attend funerals whenever we can, showing the bereaved our love and support, thus living out the work of *burying the dead*.

In short, we don't have to cross oceans to find the poor, "For you always have the poor with you" (*Mt* 26:11).

551 The spiritual works of mercy

I am familiar with the corporal works of mercy, which Jesus himself preached but can you remind me what the spiritual works of mercy are, and how I can live them in practice?

The Church has traditionally taught that there are seven corporal works of mercy and seven spiritual works. All of them relate to helping our neighbour who is in need in some way, and hence they are works of mercy.

The corporal works, with the exception of the last – to bury the dead – are mentioned, as you say, by Jesus in his description of the Last Judgment (cf. *Mt* 25:35-36). The spiritual works, on the other hand, are not found all in one place in the Scriptures, but have been put together by the tradition of the Church.

They refer to various ways of helping our neighbour in his or her spiritual needs: to counsel the doubtful, instruct the ignorant, admonish sinners, comfort the afflicted, forgive offences, bear wrongs patiently and pray for the living and the dead. As with the corporal works, we have many opportunities to live them, practically on a daily basis.

We *counsel the doubtful* whenever someone confides their doubts to us, within the family, in our workplace, a friend... These doubts may be about minor matters or occasionally about serious ones: whether to engage in dishonest practices to make more money, whether to marry a particular person or stay in a marriage, whether to have an abortion, whether to end their life because they are seriously depressed... It is clear that God has put us in their life to help them in these situations and our sound advice can help them make the right choice – and sometimes even save their life or their immortal soul.

We have many opportunities to *instruct the ignorant*, ranging from teaching our own children the truths of the faith, to answering questions about the faith in our workplace, becoming a catechist and teaching children in state schools or Catholic schools, imparting the faith in an RCIA program, getting together with other adults to study the faith using DVDs or books...

We can *admonish sinners* when someone confides to us that they are doing something wrong and we gently point out that God loves them and that their way of acting is no way to treat God, that their behaviour will not lead to the happiness they desire and there are other solutions to their problem, or we remind them that one day they will have to give an account of their life to God in the judgment. And we should take advantage of every opportunity to invite them back to the sacrament of penance, the sacrament of mercy.

We *comfort the afflicted* when we spend time with someone going through a hard time and we show them that we really care for them, listening to them, giving thoughtful advice, praying with them and helping them get through the difficulty insofar as possible.

We should always *forgive offences* from the heart, praying for those who have hurt us, wishing them well, telling them we forgive them and asking God to forgive them. After all, we pray in the Our Father, "forgive us our trespasses as we forgive those who trespass against us". Moreover, Jesus went on to say: "For if you forgive men their trespasses, your heavenly Father also will forgive you; but if you do not forgive men their trespasses, neither will your Father forgive your trespasses" (*Mt* 6:14-15). These words are an urgent call to forgive everyone.

We can *bear wrongs patiently* within the family when our children or spouse really upset us and we remain calm and patient, in our workplace when someone gets on our nerves and we don't say anything, on the roads when another driver does something foolish or dangerous and we don't fly into a rage.

And we should always *pray for the living and the dead*: for the living in all their needs, especially when they are far from God so that they come back to him, and for the dead, that God may take them to heaven as soon as possible.

As is clear, we have many opportunities to practise the spiritual works of mercy and we should take advantage of every opportunity to do so.

552 Vaccination of children

I know couples who prefer not to have their children vaccinated against certain illnesses because of the dangers these vaccinations can represent for the child. I was considering whether to do the same myself. Do you have any thoughts on this?

There are some parents who prefer not to take the risk of having their children vaccinated against various illnesses because of the dangers, sometimes serious, that these vaccinations can represent. That is their choice. But they should take into account a number of considerations.

Practically everything we do has some element of risk, from carrying a child in the womb and giving birth to him or her, to undergoing surgery, to taking certain medications, to eating at a restaurant, to travelling by train or bus, to driving a car or crossing the street... In all these cases we understand that there are risks but on balance we make the judgment that the benefits outweigh the risks.

Something similar can be said for vaccinating a child. Here there may be risks associated with the vaccination itself but if the child is not vaccinated the risks associated with the child, or later the adult, coming down with the illness are far greater. For example, diseases such as measles and whooping cough are serious and potentially fatal. Likewise, parents may worry that the measles-mumps-rubella vaccine can cause encephalitis, but that risk is about one in a million, whereas the risk of encephalitis if the child catches measles is one in two thousand. Of those with encephalitis one in ten will die and four in ten will have permanent brain damage.

What is more, the program of virtually universal vaccination of children in many countries has lowered the incidence of childhood illnesses dramatically, and if the level of vaccination were to fall significantly, epidemics of these diseases could reappear, with serious consequences.

In 2003 the Pontifical Academy for Life was asked by the Congregation for the Doctrine of the Faith to undertake a study of the morality of using vaccines produced from aborted foetuses in the vaccination of children (cf. J. Flader, *Question Time 3*, q. 408). In its report the Academy spoke of the importance of children's vaccinations in general. It mentioned, for example, the effects of German measles, or rubella, which it described as "one of the most pathological infective agents for the embryo and foetus." When a pregnant woman catches rubella, especially during the first trimester, the risk of foetal infection is very high (approximately 95%), leading to the foetus contracting congenital rubella with a host of severe consequences. For example, during a severe epidemic of German measles in the United States in 1964 there were 20,000 cases of congenital rubella resulting in 2,100 neonatal deaths, 11,600 cases of deafness, 3,580 cases of blindness and 1,800 cases of mental retardation.

It was this epidemic that brought the push for the development of a vaccine against rubella. The report said that the severity of congenital rubella and the handicaps which it can cause "justify systematic vaccination against such a sickness" since it is almost impossible to avoid the infection of a pregnant woman if she comes in contact with someone with rubella. "Therefore, one tries to prevent transmission by suppressing the reservoir of infection among children who have not been vaccinated, by means of early immunisation of all children (universal vaccination). Universal vaccination has resulted in a considerable fall in the incidence of congenital rubella, with a general incidence reduced to less than 5 cases per 100,000 live births."

In a footnote the report warned that the foetus could contract congenital rubella if the pregnant woman entered into contact, even briefly with a child who had not been immunised and was carrying the virus. "In this case, the parents who did not accept the vaccination of their own children become responsible for the malformations in question, and for the subsequent abortion of foetuses, when they have been discovered to be malformed." In many cases the pregnant woman could be the very mother who did not want her child to be vaccinated.

All of this should be taken into account when considering whether or not to have one's children vaccinated. It is a decision not to be taken lightly.

553 The Church and the death penalty

With the sad news that two Australians have been executed overseas for drug trafficking, I would like to ask whether the Church has an official position on the death penalty.

The Church does have an official position which has changed somewhat over the years, becoming more and more firmly against it, while still allowing for it in very limited circumstances.

We should remember that the Old Testament lists at least thirty-six different offences punishable by death. They include murder (*Gen* 9:6), kidnapping (*Ex* 21:16), striking or cursing one's parents (Ex 21:15), stubborn disobedience to a priest or even to one's parents (*Deut* 17:12, 21:18-21), idolatry (*Ex* 22:20), violating the Sabbath (*Ex* 35:2), blasphemy (*Lev* 24:10-16), human sacrifice (*Lev* 20:2), divination which applied to witches, sorcerers, wizards, mediums, soothsayers, diviners, etc. (*Ex* 22:18), adultery (*Lev* 20:10-21), bestiality (*Ex* 22:19), incest (*Lev* 18:6-17), homosexual acts (*Lev* 18:22), premarital sex (*Lev* 21:9) and rape (*Deut* 22:25-27).

In the New Testament we find two passages which imply the admissibility of the death penalty. The first is in the *Acts of the Apostles,* where St Paul, when brought before the Roman tribunal, says: "If then I am a wrongdoer, and have committed anything for which I deserve to die, I do not seek to escape death" (*Acts* 25:11). The second is in St Paul's letter to the Romans: "But if you do wrong, be afraid, for he [the civil ruler] does not bear the sword in vain; he is the servant of God to execute his wrath on the wrongdoer" (*Rom* 13:4). That is, the state, as the minister of God, bears the sword and can legitimately punish with death.

Jesus himself, when faced with a woman who had committed adultery, for which the law of Moses commanded that she be stoned to death, did not challenge the law but in his mercy forgave her (cf.

Jn 8:3-11). Likewise, he himself invoked the law of Moses involving the death penalty when he said to the scribes and Pharisees: "For God commanded, 'honour your father and your mother' and 'He who speaks evil of father or mother, let him surely die'" (*Mt* 15:4).

Later the Fathers and Doctors of the Church were virtually unanimous in their support for capital punishment. In the Middle Ages a number of canonists taught that ecclesiastical courts should refrain from using the death penalty and that civil courts should impose it only for major crimes. St Thomas Aquinas and Duns Scotus invoked the authority of Scripture and tradition in favour of it, and they also gave arguments based on reason.

In the first half of the twentieth century there was a consensus of Catholic theologians in favour of capital punishment for serious offences. Even the Vatican City State from 1929 to 1969 had the death penalty in its penal code for the attempted assassination of the Pope.

Since then the Church has tightened her position to a point where, acknowledging the legitimacy of the death penalty, she limits its use to only a few exceptional cases. The *Catechism of the Catholic Church* says: "Assuming that the guilty party's identity and responsibility have been fully determined, the traditional teaching of the Church does not exclude recourse to the death penalty, if this is the only possible way of effectively defending human lives against the unjust aggressor" (*CCC* 2267). The clause "if this is the only possible way..." effectively limits the use of the death penalty to very few cases.

The Catechism goes on: "If, however, non-lethal means are sufficient to defend and protect people's safety from the aggressor, authority will limit itself to such means, as these are more in keeping with the concrete conditions of the common good and more in conformity with the dignity of the human person" (*ibid.*) Surely, it is more in keeping with the dignity of the human person not to execute him or her.

Finally, the Catechism says: "Today, in fact, as a consequence of the possibilities which the state has for effectively preventing crime, by rendering one who has committed an offence incapable of doing harm – without definitively taking away from him the possibility of redeeming himself – the cases in which the execution of the offender is an absolute necessity 'are very rare, if not practically non-existent'" (*ibid.;* John Paul II, Enc. *Evangelium vitae* 56). So the death penalty should be reserved for cases of absolute necessity. And these are rare indeed.

554 What to do with cremated remains

We recently had a family member cremated and we now have the ashes in our home. Can we keep them here or is it better to do something else with them?

As regards the Church's teaching on cremation itself, I wrote a column on it some years ago (cf. *Question Time 2*, q. 241). The Church's position is summarised in the 1983 *Code of Canon Law*: "The Church earnestly recommends that the pious custom of burial be retained; but it does not forbid cremation, unless this is chosen for reasons which are contrary to Christian teaching" (Can. 1176, §3).

More recently, on 15 August 2016 the Congregation for the Doctrine of the Faith issued an Instruction on burial and cremation entitled *Ad resurgendum cum Christo*. It says with respect to burial: "By burying the bodies of the faithful, the Church confirms her faith in the resurrection of the body, and intends to show the great dignity of the human body as an integral part of the human person whose body forms part of their identity. She cannot, therefore, condone attitudes or permit rites that involve erroneous ideas about death, such as considering death as the definitive annihilation of the person, or the moment of fusion with Mother Nature or the universe, or as a stage in the cycle of regeneration, or as the definitive liberation from the 'prison' of the body" (*AR* 3).

Whether it is buried or cremated, the body should always be treated with great respect. The *Order of Christian Funerals* says in this regard: "Since in Baptism the body was marked with the seal of the Trinity and became the temple of the Holy Spirit, Christians respect and honour the bodies of the dead and the places where they rest..." (*OCF,* 19).

St Paul explains why we treat the body with so much respect: "Do you not know that your bodies are members of Christ? ...Do you not know that your body is a temple of the Holy Spirit within you, which you have from God? You are not your own; you were bought with a price. So glorify God in your body" (*1 Cor* 6:15, 19-20).

The *Catechism of the Catholic Church* teaches: "In expectation of that day [the Last Day], the believer's body and soul already participate in the dignity of belonging to Christ. This dignity entails the demand that he should treat with respect his own body, but also the body of every other person, especially the suffering" (*CCC* 1004).

The *Order of Christian Funerals,* in its Appendix on cremation, adds the following: "Moreover, the body which lies in death naturally recalls the personal story of faith, the loving family bonds, the friendships, and the words and acts of kindness of the deceased person. Indeed the human body is inextricably associated with the human person, which acts and is experienced by others through that body. It is the body whose hands clothed the poor and embraced the sorrowing. The body of the deceased Catholic Christian is also the body once washed in baptism, anointed with the oil of salvation, and fed with the Bread of Life. Thus, the Church's reverence for the sacredness of the human body grows out of a reverence and concern both natural and supernatural for the human person" (*OCF,* 411, 412).

The document goes on to say: "The cremated remains of a body should be treated with the same respect given to the human body from which they come. This includes the use of a worthy vessel to contain the ashes, the manner in which they are carried, the care and attention to appropriate placement and transport, and the final disposition" (*OCF* 417). This way of acting is easy to understand. The cremated remains, the ashes, are what remain of the human body and they should be treated with the same respect with which one treats the body of a recently deceased person before it is buried.

What then is to be done with the ashes? The *Order of Christian Funerals* stipulates: "The cremated remains should be buried in a grave or entombed in a mausoleum or columbarium" (n. 417). One option is bury them in a family grave, along with another person or persons' remains. Another is to bury them in a special niche garden for these remains at the cemetery or parish. Still another is to enclose them in a niche wall or in a mausoleum or in a special vault designed for urns containing cremated remains, sometimes called a columbarium. Interestingly, the word columbarium means literally a dovecot, since it contains small niches or recesses similar to those for doves. Most cemeteries and some parishes have special places for these remains.

The new Instruction explains that the reason for laying the ashes to rest in a sacred place is that it "ensures that they are not excluded from the prayers and remembrance of their family or the Christian community. It prevents the faithful departed from being forgotten, or their remains from being shown a lack of respect, which eventuality is possible, most especially once the immediately subsequent generation has too passed away. Also it prevents any unfitting or superstitious practices" (*AR* 5).

The ashes should not be kept at home or scattered on the sea or ground. The *Order of Christian Funerals* says: "The practice of scattering cremated remains on the sea, from the air, or on the ground, or keeping cremated remains in the home of a relative or friend of the deceased are not the reverent disposition that the Church requires. Whenever possible, appropriate means for recording with dignity the memory of the deceased should be adopted, such as a plaque or stone which records the name of the deceased" (*OCF* 417). The new Instruction repeats this criterion and gives a further reason for it: "In order that every appearance of pantheism, naturalism or nihilism be avoided, it is not permitted to scatter the ashes of the faithful departed in the air, on land, at sea or in some other way, nor may they be preserved in mementos, pieces of jewellery or other objects" (*AR* 7).

555 What is lust?

We often hear about the sin of lust, but can you tell me exactly what it is? Is it the same as impure thoughts? Is it a mortal sin?

The *Catechism of the Catholic Church* says: "Lust is disordered desire for or inordinate enjoyment of sexual pleasure. Sexual pleasure is morally disordered when sought for itself, isolated from its procreative and unitive purposes" (*CCC* 2351).

As this point implies, there can be a legitimate desire for and enjoyment of sexual pleasure. This is the case when their object is the act of intimacy within marriage. In this act, the procreative aspect of intimacy, that is its openness to life, and the unitive aspect, the one-flesh union of husband and wife, are respected. Thus, when husband and wife desire to give themselves to one another in an act of love open to life, and they desire the pleasure that accompanies this act, they are acting honourably and there is no suggestion of the sin of lust. The same could be said of engaged couples who desire the act of intimacy they will have when they are married.

As regards the pleasure experienced in the act, Pope Pius XII said: "The Creator himself ... established that in the [generative] function, spouses should experience pleasure and enjoyment of body and spirit. Therefore, the spouses do nothing evil in seeking this pleasure and enjoyment. They accept what the Creator has intended for them. At the same time, spouses should know how to keep themselves within the limits of just moderation" (Address, 9 October 1951). By the expression "within the limits of just moderation", the Pope is implying that there could be even for married couples a possible sin of lust in their expression of love if they sought the pleasure merely for pleasure's sake or they sought to maximise it in a disordered way.

As the Catechism puts it, "The acts in marriage by which the intimate and chaste union of the spouses takes place are noble and honourable; the truly human performance of these acts fosters the self-giving they signify and enriches the spouses in joy and gratitude" (*CCC* 2362).

Lust, then, is the desire for sexual pleasure outside the marriage act, or in a marriage act not open to life. It is one of the seven capital sins, or capital vices, mentioned by St Gregory the Great: pride, avarice, envy, wrath, lust, gluttony and sloth" (cf. *CCC* 1866). These sins are called capital, from the Latin word for head, because they are the heads or principles which lead to other vices and sins.

Lust is very much related to the ninth commandment: You shall not covet your neighbour's wife (cf. *Ex* 20:17). Our Lord spoke strongly against it: "You have heard that it was said, 'You shall not commit adultery.' But I say to you that every one who looks at a woman lustfully has already committed adultery with her in his heart" (*Mt* 5:27-28). Looking at a woman lustfully in this context means desiring to have sexual relations with a woman other than one's wife. The very desire, if it is more than just a passing thought, is already the sin of adultery in the heart, and it would be a mortal sin.

Pope St John Paul II, in one of his Theology of the Body addresses, spoke about how lust reduces the natural attraction of men for women, and vice versa, to an attraction merely for the body: "When compared with the original mutual attraction of masculinity and femininity, lust represents a reduction. In stating this, we have in mind an intentional reduction, almost a restriction or closing down of the horizon of mind and heart. It is one thing to be conscious that the value of sex is a part of all the rich storehouse of values with which the female appears to the man. It is another to 'reduce' all the personal riches of femininity to that single value, that is, of sex, as a suitable object for the gratification of sexuality itself" (Address, 17 Sept. 1980).

St Thomas Aquinas says that the consequences of lust are "blindness of mind, thoughtlessness, inconstancy, rashness, self-love, hatred of God, love of this world and abhorrence or despair of a future world" (*STh* II-II, q. 153, art. 5). We see here how damaging lust can be.

Thus lust is a particularly serious form of impure thought and it can certainly be a mortal sin if the person deliberately retains it and takes pleasure in it. It debases man and how he looks upon women. We are called to something higher, to holiness, to purity of heart: "Blessed are the pure in heart, for they shall see God" (*Mt* 5:8).

556 Sex before marriage

I have several friends who engage in sex before marriage and see nothing wrong with it. "Everyone is doing it" or "We love one another", they say. I am having trouble convincing them that this is wrong. How can I help them?

The first thing is to remind them of the reason for sexuality in God's plan. God willed to share with men and women the power through sexuality of bringing new human beings into the world. This is an awesome gift. Through their sexuality, expressed in an act of loving union in marriage, spouses cooperate in God's creative power, bringing into existence a new human being who otherwise would not exist. Not for nothing do we call this gift "procreation". Sexuality then is something to be used only in marriage, where a child conceived can be properly cared for.

The Second Vatican Council teaches that the moral goodness of the use of sexuality "does not depend solely on sincere intentions or on an evaluation of motives. It must be determined by objective standards. These, based on the nature of the human person and his acts, preserve the full sense of mutual self-giving and human procreation in the context of true love" (*GS* 51). That is, for the use of sexuality to be in keeping with God's plan, it must be an expression of mutual self-giving, not self-seeking, open to life and in the context of true love in marriage. Sex is not merely a "recreational activity" to give those who engage in it a passing pleasure. This is to trivialise it.

What is more, this mutual self-giving implies a true commitment between the persons. Sex, after all, is a very intimate act in which the persons reveal themselves to one another and come together in a one-flesh union. This involves and fosters an emotional bond which can be deep and lasting. If, after having had sexual relations for a time a man and a woman break off their relationship, it can have serious repercussions, especially for the woman. She can feel betrayed, and even used by the man. This is not love but selfish gratification at the expense of another person. And of course sex outside of marriage is always seriously sinful.

The Pontifical Council for the Family, in its document *The Truth and Meaning of Human Sexuality* (1995), goes so far as to say that "the disordered use of sex tends progressively to destroy the person's capacity to love by making pleasure, instead of sincere self-giving, the end of sexuality and by reducing other persons to objects of one's own gratification" (n. 105).

Since pre-marital sex often involves the use of contraception to prevent pregnancy, it can have harmful consequences on the attitude to life. The document goes on to say: "Moreover, this subsequently leads to disdain for the human life which could be conceived, which, in some situations, is then regarded as an evil that threatens personal pleasure" (n. 105). Thus instead of looking on pregnancy and new life as a beautiful gift, the couple can consider the child conceived as an evil, often to be got rid of through abortion.

As for those who say they have sex because they love each other, they should know that this is not love. Love is to seek the good of the other, not of oneself. And to lead the other into mortal sin, endangering their eternal salvation, is not the way we treat someone we love. It is the antithesis of love.

Moreover, when a couple engage in pre-marital sex they are getting each other used to having sexual relations with someone to whom they are not married. If they later marry, they should not be surprised if their spouse is unfaithful since, after all, they got him or her used to sleeping with someone to whom they were not married. To be faithful in marriage it is therefore fundamental to be faithful to God and to each other before marriage. Couples who have lived chastity before marriage are much more likely to be faithful in marriage.

A good question to ask a single person who is sleeping with others is, "Would you consider marrying someone who would sleep around before marriage?" When they think about it, many would answer no, that they want to find someone who is chaste and will make a faithful spouse and a good parent for their children. "But then", we can say, "do you think that that chaste person would want to marry someone like you, who is sleeping around?" As they say, if you want to make a good catch, be a good catch.

Apart from using arguments like these, we should always pray very much for those who engage in pre-marital sex so that they will see the harm they are doing and change their ways.

557 Is the use of contraception sometimes allowed?

I have a Catholic friend who uses the oral contraceptive pill to treat a medical condition and she says this is permitted by the Church. Is this correct?

We should first clarify what we mean by contraception, as there can be misunderstandings on this point. It can be taken to mean broadly the use of some substance or method with the intention of preventing the sexual act from leading to the conception of a child. This includes such substances as the oral contraceptive pill, the intrauterine device (IUD), condoms, spermicidal gels, etc.

As your friend says, the use of the oral contraceptive pill to treat a medical condition is not forbidden. Pope Paul VI said as much in his Encyclical *Humanae vitae*: "The Church, on the contrary, does not at all consider illicit the use of those therapeutic means truly necessary to cure diseases of the organism, even if an impediment to procreation, which may be foreseen, should result therefrom provided such impediment is not, for whatever motive, directly willed" (*HV* 15). Here the person is taking a medication not to prevent the conception of a child but to treat a medical condition, even though she knows that the medication would also prevent conception. When an oral contraceptive is used this way, since the intention is to treat a medical condition, its use is morally justified. The contraceptive effect is a consequence which is not sought in itself but is merely accepted, justifiably in this case. Naturally, as the Pope says, the woman cannot directly will the contraceptive effect.

In this way, many single women living chaste lives and even nuns may be using the contraceptive pill. If a married woman of childbearing age is using an oral contraceptive to treat a medical condition she can engage in acts of marital intimacy with her husband, but it is often recommended that she abstain from marital acts during the fertile period of her cycle in order to avoid a possible abortion caused by the medication, should conception occur.

558 Why is the Church opposed to contraception?

I am a recent convert and a mother of five children. My husband and I are open to life and we have no intention of using contraception, but I have Catholic friends who use it and see nothing wrong with it. Why is the Church opposed to it?

To answer your question we can go back to the beginning, to God's plan for marriage. In the book of *Genesis* we read: "So God created man in his own image, in the image of God he created him, male and female he created them. And God blessed them, and God said to them, 'Be fruitful and multiply, and fill the earth and subdue it.'" (*Gen* 1:27-28). This was, in a sense, God's first commandment to human beings: to be fruitful and have children. The very words "God blessed them" are significant. Throughout the Scriptures, children are always regarded as a blessing, and for a couple to be sterile was seen as a sign of divine disfavour. For example, we read in one of the psalms: "Your wife will be like a fruitful vine within your house; your children will be like olive shoots around your table. Thus shall the man be blessed who fears the Lord" (*Ps* 128:3-4; cf. *Lk* 1:25).

Indeed, to bring children into the world is to cooperate with God in his wonderful work of creation by bringing into being a new human life. Not for nothing do we call it *procreation*. Except in the case of sterility, spouses have the power to give life to someone who otherwise would not exist. In one of his Theology of the Body addresses, Pope St John Paul II said that in the act of marital union, "there is renewed, in a way, the mystery of creation in all its original depth and vital power" (Address, 21 November 1979). It is truly an awesome gift and responsibility to be able to cooperate with God in this way. Therefore, the Church from the beginning has forbidden the use of contraception, understood as anything intended to prevent the conception of a child.

In the Encyclical *Humanae vitae* Pope Paul VI explained why the use of contraception is forbidden: "That teaching, often set forth by the Magisterium, is founded upon the inseparable connection, willed by God and unable to be broken by man on his own initiative, between the two meanings of the conjugal act: the unitive meaning and the procreative meaning. Indeed, by its intimate structure, the conjugal act, while most closely uniting husband and wife, capacitates them for the generation of new lives, according to laws inscribed in the very being of man and of woman. By safeguarding both these essential aspects, the unitive and the procreative, the conjugal act preserves in its fullness the sense of true mutual love and its ordination towards man's most high calling to parenthood" (*HV* 12).

Thus, the one-flesh union of husband and wife (the unitive aspect), must always be open to life (the procreative aspect). When open to life, this union is truly an act of love, which is a total self-giving of the spouses to each other, without holding anything back. If they use contraception, on the contrary, the couple do not give themselves totally to one another. They give their bodies but they withhold their fertility by using a physical or chemical barrier to avoid offspring, thus altering the very nature of the act. Not only is this contrary to God's plan for the use of sexuality, it is not true love.

Pope St John Paul II explains this in his Apostolic Exhortation *Familiaris consortio*: "Thus the innate language that expresses the total reciprocal self-giving of husband and wife is overlaid, through contraception, by an objectively contradictory language, namely, that of not giving oneself totally to the other. This leads not only to a positive refusal to be open to life but also to a falsification of the inner truth of conjugal love, which is called upon to give itself in personal totality" (*FC* 32).

An act of marital union using contraception is an act of sex, but not of love. Couples who have been using contraception and later give themselves completely to one another without any barriers appreciate the difference keenly. If they have a serious reason to avoid a child for the time being or indefinitely, the couple can use natural family planning, abstaining from marital acts by mutual agreement during the fertile period each month. Those who use this method often find that their love for each other actually grows, as do their respect for each other and their self-mastery.

Finally, some people think the reason why contraception is forbidden is that it is artificial. If that were the case, we could not take medicine to cure a cold or a headache! The reason why it is forbidden, as we have seen, is that it is used with the intention of avoiding pregnancy. If a couple practise withdrawal as a means of avoiding pregnancy, that too is forbidden even though it does not involve anything artificial. This was the sin of Onan, who spilled his seed on the ground and God put him to death (cf. *Gen* 38:8-10).

559 Can the Church's teaching on contraception change?

A friend recently said that since the Church has changed other teachings in the past it is just a matter of time until it changes the prohibition of contraception. Is this the case?

It is most certainly not the case. The teaching that the use of contraception goes against the very purpose of marriage and therefore against the natural law is not new but has been there since the beginning of the Church. It is a constant teaching that cannot be changed.

As early as the year 191 AD St Clement of Alexandria wrote that "to have coitus other than to procreate children is to do injury to nature" (*The Instructor of Children* 2:10, 91, 2).

A few years later, in 225 St Hippolytus decried the fact that "[Christian women with male concubines], on account of their prominent ancestry and great property, the so-called faithful want no children from slaves or lowborn commoners, [so] they use drugs of sterility or bind themselves tightly in order to expel a foetus which has already been engendered" (*Refutation of All Heresies* 9:12).

In the year 375 Epiphanius of Salamis also condemned the use of means to prevent conception. Speaking of certain Egyptian heretics he wrote: "They exercise genital acts, yet prevent the conceiving of children. Not in order to produce offspring, but to satisfy lust, are they eager for corruption" (*Medicine Chest Against Heresies* 26:5, 2).

A few years later, in 391 St John Chrysostom spoke strongly against spouses who prevented the conception of children: "Why do you sow where the field is eager to destroy the fruit, where there are medicines of sterility, where there is murder before birth? You do not even let a harlot remain only a harlot, but you make her a murderess as well... Indeed, it is something worse than murder, and I do not know what to call it; for she does not kill what is formed but prevents its formation. What then? Do you condemn the gift of God and fight with his laws? ... Yet such turpitude ... the matter still seems indifferent to many men – even to many men having wives. In this indifference of the married men there is greater evil filth; for then poisons are prepared, not against the womb of a prostitute, but against your injured wife. Against her are these innumerable tricks" (*Homilies on Romans* 24).

Writing in 419 St Augustine too was scathing in his criticism of spouses who engaged in marital intercourse while preventing conception: "I am supposing, then, although you are not lying [with your wife] for the sake of procreating offspring, you are not for the sake of lust obstructing their procreation by an evil prayer or an evil deed. Those who do this, although they are called husband and wife, are not; nor do they retain any reality of marriage, but with a respectable name cover a shame. Sometimes this lustful cruelty, or cruel lust, comes to this, that they even procure poisons of sterility... Assuredly if both husband and wife are like this, they are not married, and if they were like this from the beginning they come together not joined in matrimony but in seduction. If both are not like this, I dare to say that either the wife is in a fashion the harlot of her husband or he is an adulterer with his own wife" (*Marriage and Concupiscence* 1:15, 17).

St Augustine also wrote: "Sexual intercourse even with a lawful wife is unlawful and shameful if the conception of offspring is prevented. This is what Onan, the son of Juda, did, and on that account God put him to death" (*De conjug. adult.*, lib. ii, n. 12; cf. *Gen* 38:8-10).

A century later St Caesarius of Arles wrote in a similar vein: "Who is he who cannot warn that no woman may take a potion so that she is unable to conceive or condemns in herself the nature which God willed to be fecund? As often as she could have conceived or given birth, of that many homicides will she be held guilty, and, unless she undergoes suitable penance, she will be damned by eternal death in hell. If a woman does not wish to have children, let her enter into a religious agreement with her husband; for chastity is the sole sterility of a Christian woman" (*Sermons* 1:12).

As is clear, from the earliest centuries the use of contraception was looked upon as contrary to the very purpose of marriage. Indeed, all Christian denominations taught this until 1930, when the Lambeth conference of the Anglican church broke ranks and allowed the use of contraception. At the end of that year, by way of reaffirming the Catholic Church's centuries-old stand on the issue, Pope Pius XI wrote the Encyclical *Casti connubii*. After mentioning some of the reasons why couples may not want to have children, he wrote that the use of contraception goes against nature itself: "But no reason whatever, even the gravest, can make what is intrinsically against nature become conformable with nature and morally good. The conjugal act is of its very nature designed for the procreation of offspring; and therefore those who in performing it deliberately deprive it of its natural power and efficacy, act against nature and do something which is shameful and intrinsically immoral" (*CC* 54). He went on to say that "any use of matrimony whatsoever in the exercise of which the act is deprived, by human interference, of its natural power to procreate life, is an offence against the law of God and of nature, and that those who commit it are guilty of grave sin" (*CC* 56).

In 1968 Pope Paul VI repeated this teaching in his Encyclical *Humanae vitae*. After saying that abortion and sterilisation are excluded as lawful ways of regulating birth he added: "Similarly excluded is every action which, either in anticipation of the conjugal act, or in its accomplishment, or in the development of its natural consequences, proposes, whether as an end or as a means, to render procreation impossible" (*HV* 14).

Finally, the *Catechism of the Catholic Church*, quoting *Humanae vitae*, says that the use of contraception is "intrinsically evil" (*CCC* 2370). That is, it is simply wrong in itself and may never be used, for whatever reason. Given the constant teaching of the Church, from the very beginning until the present, that contraception goes against the very purpose of marriage and married love, it is clear that it is a teaching that cannot be changed.

560 Natural family planning

If the Church says we can't use contraception, where does that leave a couple who for one reason or another do not want to have another child? Do they have to abstain altogether from marital relations?

No, they don't have to abstain altogether. God forbid! As most people are aware, there are ways of determining the fertile days of the woman's monthly cycle so that the couple can have marital relations only during the infertile days, which are in fact most of the month. These ways are based on observing such signs as changes in body temperature, the viscosity of the cervical mucous and the cervix itself. These methods bear the generic name Natural Family Planning (NFP) and are very effective.

Naturally, since in God's plan marriage and the marriage act are the way of bringing new human beings into existence, the couple need a proportionate reason to use NFP if they want to avoid having a child. Pope Paul VI gives us the criterion in his Encyclical *Humanae vitae*: "With regard to physical, economic, psychological and social conditions, responsible parenthood is exercised by those who prudently and generously decide to have more children, and by those who, for serious reasons and with due respect to moral precepts, decide not to have additional children for either a certain or an indefinite period of time" (*HV* 10).

As the Pope explains, a proportionate reason is always necessary to use NFP. If the couple simply wish to delay the birth of the next child to give the wife time to recover because she is worn out after having had several children one after the other, that would be a sufficient reason. If on the other hand they do not want to have any more children at all, a more serious reason would be needed such as important physical or mental health issues, financial difficulties or the possibility of passing on a serious hereditary condition. It is up to the couple themselves to decide whether their reasons are sufficient.

The phrase "with due respect to moral precepts" means the couple cannot use such means as contraception or sterilisation, which go against the very purpose intended by God for the marriage act. Pope Paul explains: "The Church, nevertheless, in urging men to the observance of the precepts of the natural law, which it interprets by its constant doctrine, teaches that each and every marital act must of necessity retain its intrinsic relationship to the procreation of human life" (*HV* 11).

As regards the morality of having marital relations only during the infertile period of the cycle, Pope Paul VI says: "If therefore there are well-grounded reasons for spacing births, arising from the physical or psychological condition of husband or wife, or from external circumstances, the Church teaches that married people may then take advantage of the natural cycles immanent in the reproductive system and engage in marital intercourse only during those times that are infertile, thus controlling birth in a way which does not in the least offend the moral principles which we have just explained" (*HV* 16).

When the couple practise NFP each act of marital intimacy is open to the transmission of life, even if the couple know and expect that a new life will not arise from that act. They are living their sexuality and love in a way that is completely consistent with God's plan. Even if they were not consciously practising NFP so as to avoid the fertile periods, a couple would find that most of their acts of marital love would not result in a pregnancy anyway since there are only a few fertile days in each monthly cycle.

When, in spite of using NFP, the wife becomes pregnant, the couple should welcome this new manifestation of God's providence and love for them. Often they find that this unexpected child gives them great joy and makes a real contribution to the family and to society. They should accept this "unplanned" pregnancy as in fact "planned" by God.

As is clear, NFP is not something that a couple can practise at any time of the marriage without a good reason. They always need a proportionate reason. Especially at the beginning of the marriage it is important to be open to life.

561 Benefits of natural family planning

I know women who have been using natural family planning but have still conceived a child. Does the method really work?

The method really does work and, what is more, it brings many benefits to the couple. First, though, some studies on its effectiveness.

In 1993 the *British Medical Journal* published a study of natural family planning (NFP) involving 19,843 women in India. The study found that when the method was practised correctly in order to avoid pregnancy there was a 99.8% success rate; that is, two pregnancies for every one thousand women using the method for a year. That is even better than the approximately one pregnancy for every one hundred women using the oral contraceptive pill.

Another study, by the European Society of Human Reproduction and Embryology in 2007 involved 900 women and showed that the Sympto-Thermal Method had a 98.1% success rate in avoiding pregnancy. The Sympto-Thermal Method involves observing both the basal body temperature and the cervical mucous. Still another study of the Sympto-Thermal Method, a Hermann Study in 2007, showed the method to be 99.6% effective. So natural family planning, when used properly, is very effective. Usually when someone using NFP falls pregnant it is because they did not use the method properly.

As for the numerous benefits deriving from NFP the first and most obvious is that the method is completely natural. That is, it does not involve the woman taking in any chemicals or using devices that can have unpleasant or even harmful side effects. Many women who use the oral contraceptive pill, for example, experience such harmful side effects as reduced libido, more pronounced mood swings, higher incidence of depression, headaches, nausea, etc., not to mention the increased likelihood of blood clots, which can actually be fatal. It should not be forgotten either that the oral contraceptive pill, in most of its formulations, involves the use of a hormone that prevents implantation of the fertilised egg, should fertilisation occur, thus bringing about an abortion.

Normally we take medicine only when we are sick or when there is some bodily dysfunction. Fertility is not an illness or a dysfunction. It is rather a great blessing. So why take pills or use devices for it, especially when they can cause harmful side effects? The fact that

NFP is completely natural is one reason why increasing numbers of women, including many non-Catholics, are turning to it. Indeed, many teachers of NFP report that the great majority of those coming to them are not Catholic, reflecting the percentage of Catholics and non-Catholics in society at large. Moreover, many couples use NFP as a way of falling pregnant since it enables them to pinpoint the fertile period accurately.

In addition to these benefits, NFP has been shown to improve the relations between husband and wife, thus strengthening the marriage. Since both spouses must agree to use the method and to abstain from acts of marital intimacy during some days each month, they need to communicate effectively to know which those days are. In so doing they improve their communication and often grow closer to each other than before. Likewise, the very fact of needing to abstain during some days improves their self-control and helps them grow in the virtue of temperance. During those days they learn to express their love for each other in non-sexual ways, which helps them realise that there are many ways to express love. Having to abstain from sexual acts when otherwise they would engage in them also helps the spouses to respect each other more, to be more sensitive to their desires, and to show their love precisely by not engaging in physical acts of intimacy. When they do come together again in a sexual way their acts are more special and often more loving, as on their honeymoon.

As the fruit of all this, as might be expected, the divorce rate for couples practising NFP is much lower than for the general population. And yes, NFP involves sacrifice, but isn't that what love is all about?

562 Is gossip a sin?

At my workplace there is culture of gossip which I find distressing. We are constantly talking about one another's faults, especially those of our bosses. Is this a sin and is there anything I can do to help my workmates refrain from it?

Unfortunately gossip is a common phenomenon in workplaces, schools and universities, groups of friends and even families. There is somehow a morbid curiosity to know the sins and faults of others and to pass them on. Even as we engage in gossip, we recognise that it is toxic and disruptive of harmony and charity, yet we go on indulging in it.

Where does gossip fit into the moral law, especially the Ten Commandments? It is a sin principally against the eighth commandment: you shall not bear false witness against your neighbour. Everyone has a right to a good name and gossip undermines or even destroys another's reputation. In this area it is very helpful to apply the Golden Rule of not doing to others what we would not want them to do to us. If we would not want to have our good name ruined by others' malicious gossip – and none of us would – we should not indulge in gossip ourselves.

The term gossip is not a formal one in moral theology, but rather a colloquial one that refers in general to idle talk about others' affairs, especially their faults. There are two principal sins against the eighth commandment that fall under the general name of gossip: detraction and slander.

Detraction is disclosing without an objectively valid reason, another's faults and failings to persons who did not know them (cf. *CCC* 2477). In this case someone has committed an objective fault but it is not generally known. Gossip or detraction consists in revealing that fault to others without a valid reason. For example, it would be gossip or detraction to reveal that someone was drunk at a party, was caught speeding or was having an affair. We can all make mistakes but we don't want others to know about them. What is more, once a good reputation has been blackened it is almost impossible to restore it completely.

Only in exceptional circumstances would there be a valid reason to reveal another's hidden fault. For example, if we knew that someone was habitually using illicit drugs we could reveal this to a close family member of the person concerned so that they could help him or her. Or if we knew that someone had committed a crime, we would usually be obliged to report this to the police. But we do not disclose it to persons who have no need or right to know.

The other sin, slander, also called calumny, consists in telling lies that harm the good name of another (cf. *CCC* 2477). Here someone makes up a story that another was drunk or was caught speeding in order to discredit the person, when in fact nothing of the sort happened. This is obviously a more serious sin since it leads others to think that someone committed sins they never committed. It is a sin not only against charity and justice, since we all have a right to a good name, but also against the truth. Again, we can apply the Golden Rule and ask how we would like it if someone made up malicious lies about us.

In general we should always observe the popular saying that if we cannot say something good about another we should not say anything at all. Scripture is very clear about the evil of gossip. For example, we read in the book of Proverbs, "A perverse man spreads strife, and a whisperer separates close friends" (*Prov* 16:28). How often friendships have been broken when someone gossiped about another! At the very least, people who formerly thought well of another now think badly as a result of what they have heard through gossip. The precious good of a good name can be so easily lost through gossip.

What can we do to overcome this harmful custom? First, we should show no interest in listening to gossip, and we should certainly not pass on anything we have heard, some of which may turn out to be lies or at least exaggerations. And we should look for an opportunity to say something good about the person being maligned. In any case, we can often end the conversation by saying: "Let's pray for him, or her". In short, do unto others as you would have them do unto you.

IV. CHRISTIAN PRAYER

Prayer and devotions

563 Why doesn't God answer my prayers?

Other people tell me how God answers their prayers in remarkable ways, but he doesn't seem to answer mine. I have been praying for several intentions for a long time with no result. Does God always answer our prayers?

We can start with Jesus' familiar words in the Sermon on the Mount: "Ask, and it will be given you; seek, and you will find; knock, and it will be opened to you. For every one who asks receives, and he who seeks finds, and to him who knocks it will be opened" (*Mt* 7:7-8). It is clear from this that everyone who asks God for something will have their prayer answered. Everyone.

Our Lord goes on to explain that even earthly parents, with all their limitations, know how to give good things to their children: "Or what man of you, if his son asks him for bread, will give him a stone? Or if he asks for a fish, will give him a serpent? If you then, who are evil, know how to give good gifts to your children, how much more will your Father who is in heaven give good things to those who ask him!" (*Mt* 7:9-11)

In the example of parents giving good things to their children we find an initial answer to your question. First of all, parents are not going to give their children what is bad for them. They will not give them a stone instead of bread, or a snake instead of a fish. Neither does God ever give what is bad for us.

Here we might be inclined to answer: "Yes he does. God allows us to suffer: illness, failure, loss of property…" Indeed he does. But suffering is not bad for us. It can even be very good. Illness moves us to take better care of our health and to be detached from even life itself;

failure helps us to be more humble and aware of our weaknesses; the loss of property helps us to be more detached from the things of this world...

In allowing us to suffer, God is treating us as his children. He himself says so in the letter to the Hebrews: "And have you forgotten the exhortation which addresses you as sons? – 'My son, do not regard lightly the discipline of the Lord, nor lose courage when you are punished by him. For the Lord disciplines him whom he loves, and chastises every son whom he receives.' ... God is treating you as sons; for what son is there whom his father does not discipline? If you are left without discipline, in which all have participated, then you are illegitimate children and not sons. Besides this, we have had earthly fathers to discipline us and we respected them. Shall we not much more be subject to the Father of spirits and live? For they disciplined us for a short time at their pleasure, but he disciplines us for our good, that we may share his holiness" (*Heb* 12:5-10).

Yes, God allows us to suffer. He disciplines us, just as parents discipline their children because they love them and don't want to spoil them. While this can appear to the children to be bad, and even a lack of love, it is rather a manifestation of true love on the part of their parents. So, if in answer to our prayers for good things, or to be delivered from suffering, God allows us to suffer, this can be seen as an answer, a good answer. As the letter to the Hebrews says, it allows us to share in God's holiness. We shouldn't forget either, that our suffering unites us to the much greater suffering of Jesus himself, the beloved Son of the Father, and that too is a great good.

While God will never give us something bad, he doesn't always give us what we are asking for, as good as it may seem to us. Neither do earthly parents always give their children what they are asking for. When the child asks for a smart phone or a computer game, the parents, moved by love, may decide that this is not in the child's best interests, and may answer no, or not yet. Similarly, when God doesn't seem to answer our prayers, it may be that he knows that what we are asking for is not good for us. After all, we only see things from the human point of view and he sees them from the point of view of eternity. So God's answer to our prayer may be no, or not yet.

In any case, God always answers our prayers by uniting us with him through the prayer itself, which sanctifies us and gives us an increase of grace. In short, God gives us the Holy Spirit, as he himself says: "If you then, who are evil, know how to give good gifts to your children, how much more will the heavenly Father give the Holy Spirit to those who ask him!" (*Lk* 11 13) What better answer to prayer can there be than to receive holiness, grace, the Holy Spirit himself?

564 To whom can we pray?

Must we always pray to the Father through Jesus or can we pray directly to the Father? And can we also pray to Mary, the angels and the saints?

This question is more interesting than appears at first sight. We can start with the definition of prayer in the Catechism of the Catholic Church: "Prayer is the raising of one's mind and heart to God or the requesting of good things from God" (St John Damascene, *De fide orth.* 3, 24; *CCC* 2559). Here we see the classical understanding of prayer as words or thoughts addressed to God. It can be in the form of asking God for something, thanking him, telling him we are sorry, praising him, carrying on a conversation with him in meditation or mental prayer, or gazing on him with love in that more quiet and simple form of prayer known as contemplation.

When we say "God" in this sense we are normally referring to God in his unity, as the one God. Many prayers are directed to God in this way, among them the Act of Contrition: "O my God, I am heartily sorry for all my sins..."

But there is nothing to prevent us from praying to any one of the three divine persons individually. Thus we pray to the Father directly in the Our Father: "Our Father, who art in heaven, hallowed be thy name..." We pray to Jesus, the Son of God, directly in the Fatima prayer in the rosary – "O my Jesus, forgive us our sins, save us from the fires of hell..." – and in the "Jesus prayer" – "Lord Jesus Christ, son of God, have mercy on me, a sinner" (cf. *CCC* 2616). And we pray directly to the Holy Spirit in numerous prayers, among them: "Come, Holy Spirit, fill the hearts of the faithful and kindle in them the fire of your love..."

As regards praying through Jesus, we recall his words: "Whatever you ask in my name, I will do it, that the Father may be glorified in the Son; if you ask anything in my name, I will do it" (*Jn* 14:13-14). And again: "Truly, truly, I say to you, if you ask anything of the Father, he will give it to you in my name" (*Jn* 16:23). The Church in her liturgy does this. For example, the three so-called "Presidential prayers" in the Mass – the Collect, the Prayer over the Offerings, and the Prayer after Communion – are all addressed to the Father "through Christ our Lord".

The Catechism confirms this way of praying: "There is no other way of Christian prayer than Christ. Whether our prayer is communal or personal, vocal or interior, it has access to the Father only if we pray 'in the name' of Jesus. The sacred humanity of Jesus is therefore the way by which the Holy Spirit teaches us to pray to God our Father" (*CCC* 2664).

This does not mean that we must always mention Jesus expressly in our prayers if they are to be heard. We do not mention his name in the Our Father, and we are certain this prayer is pleasing to the Father. It is sufficient that we have an habitual intention of praying through Jesus, without needing to make this intention actual in every prayer. And even if we do not think of Jesus while praying, he is the mediator who presents our prayers to the Father.

Can we also pray to Mary, the angels and the saints? Of course we can. The Hail Mary is addressed to Our Lady: "Hail Mary, full of grace, the Lord is with thee..." Other Marian prayers like the Hail, Holy Queen, the Memorare, and many more are addressed directly to Mary. When in these prayers we ask for favours it is understood that Our Lady herself does not grant them but that she asks God to grant them. That is why we say, for example, "Pray for us sinners". It is understood that Mary prays for us to the Father through Jesus, and so the Church gives us the traditional expression "to Jesus through Mary".

And we can also pray to the angels and the saints. Among the most popular prayers to the angels are the prayer to the guardian angel and the prayer to St Michael, the archangel. There are numerous prayers addressed to the saints, from St Joseph through the long list of canonised saints in the history of the Church up to the present.

But we need not limit ourselves to praying to the canonised saints. We can pray to any deceased person, including our own parents, brothers and sisters and children. Even if they are in purgatory they can intercede for us. When a baptised infant dies we know with certainty that he or she is in heaven and so we can pray to them with complete trust that they are interceding powerfully for us. So we can pray to anyone and this prayer always reaches God through Jesus.

565 Prayer in the early Church

In the Acts of the Apostles we read that the apostles went to the temple at the hour of prayer, the ninth hour. Was this a custom at the time? Did the early Christians pray at set times of the day?

The reading to which you refer is: "Now Peter and John were going up to the temple at the hour of prayer, the ninth hour" (*Acts* 3:1). Another reference to prayer at a set time comes later in the Acts when "Peter went up on the housetop to pray, about the sixth hour" (*Acts* 10:9). The sixth hour, by the way, was 12 noon and the ninth hour 3 pm. The third hour was 9 am. As we can imagine, these hours for prayer stemmed from the Jewish customs of the time.

Jewish tradition has it that the Patriarchs Abraham, Isaac and Jacob introduced the custom of praying three times a day, and that Abraham introduced prayer in the morning, Isaac in the afternoon and Jacob at night. Moreover, each of the patriarchs had a special virtue or quality which Jews should live out in life and in prayer. Abraham served God with love and kindness, Isaac with justice and reverence and Jacob with truth and mercy. Thus Jews are taught to serve God and to pray to him with love, reverence and mercy.

While in the first centuries after receiving the Torah through Moses, individual Jews could pray at any time of the day, in the temple in Jerusalem there were fixed times for the sacrifices and prayers. The daily sacrifices were offered in the morning and evening, with the evening sacrifice extending into the night, and on special days there were additional sacrifices. Thus many individual Jews too prayed three times a day at these hours.

King David says in one of the psalms: "Evening and morning and at noon I utter my complaint and moan, and he will hear my voice" (*Ps* 55:17). And Daniel, during the exile in Babylon in the sixth century BC, "went to his house where he had windows in his upper chamber open toward Jerusalem: and he got down upon his knees three times a day and prayed and gave thanks before his God as he had done previously" (*Dan* 6:10).

During the exile in Babylon, when the Jews did not have the temple in which to offer sacrifice, they began to have synagogue services of prayer on Saturdays at fixed times of the day. These included readings from the Torah, psalms and hymns, much like the synagogue services today. This "sacrifice of praise" took the place of the sacrifice of animals which had been offered twice daily in the temple in Jerusalem.

When they returned to Jerusalem after the seventy years of exile, the Jews led by Ezra the scribe began to say certain prayers three times each day, corresponding to the hours of the daily sacrifices in the Temple, with additional prayers on the Sabbath and certain festivals. These are the *Shacarit* in the morning, *Mincha* in the afternoon and *Arvit* in the evening. The additional prayers are called *Mussaf* and a fifth prayer service, *Neila*, is recited only on *Yom Kippur*, the Day of Atonement. The *Mussaf* prayers were recited at noon, the hour at which St Peter went up to pray.

It is only natural that the first Christians, led by the apostles, would have continued to pray at those times, as we saw Peter and John do. The earliest reference to this outside the Bible comes in the *Didache*, a Christian document that dates to the end of the first century. It states that the Lord's Prayer should be said three times a day, although it does not specify any particular times for this prayer. Later the custom of praying at the third, sixth and ninth hours became established.

In the second and third centuries writers like St Clement of Alexandria, Origen and Tertullian wrote of the practice of morning and evening prayer, and of prayers at the third, sixth and ninth hours. In the fourth century the *Apostolic Constitutions* state: "Offer up your prayers in the morning, at the third hour, the sixth, the ninth, the evening, and at cock-crowing" (VIII, iv, 34).

Those familiar with the Liturgy of the Hours, or Breviary, will note that these are the hours specified for the recitation of the psalms and other readings. In this way the Church, through her sacred ministers and those in consecrated life, lives out St Paul's command to "pray constantly" (*1 Thess* 5:17).

566 The Divine Praises

Can you tell me the origin of the Divine Praises that we say in Benediction with the Blessed Sacrament?

I have searched far and wide to answer your question and I must say the information available is scanty. That could be because the origin is well known and there is not much more to say.

What is certain is that the Divine Praises in their original form were written by Fr Luigi Felici, S.J., in 1797 as a way to make reparation for blasphemies against the divine name. If blasphemy was common at the end of the eighteenth century, it is extremely common today. We see it in films, plays, workplaces, etc., where use of the name of Jesus Christ in a disrespectful way is widespread, as it is on the lips of many people in daily life.

Just to remind ourselves, the *Catechism of the Catholic Church* says that "Blasphemy ... consists in uttering against God – inwardly or outwardly – words of hatred, reproach, or defiance; in speaking ill of God; in failing in respect toward him in one's speech; in misusing God's name" (*CCC* 2148). As the Catechism says, blasphemy is not limited to spoken words against God. It can be committed inwardly, in our willful thoughts, and outwardly in such forms as books, plays and artworks that show contempt for God, Our Lady, the saints, the Church, the sacraments, etc.

As a way of making reparation for the blasphemies of his own day, Fr Felici (1736-1818) composed the Divine Praises, in which God, Jesus Christ, Our Lady, the angels and the saints are praised through a succession of prayers beginning with "Blessed be". In the original Divine Praises written by Fr Felici in Italian there were only eight praises, all beginning with the word "Blessed". Over the years various Popes added six more praises.

The present Divine Praises, with the papal additions indicated, are the following:

> Blessed be God.
>
> Blessed be his Holy Name.
>
> Blessed be Jesus Christ, true God and true man.

Blessed be the name of Jesus.

Blessed be his Most Sacred Heart (added by Pope Leo XIII before he asked for the whole world to be consecrated to the Sacred Heart of Jesus).

Blessed be his Most Precious Blood (added by St John XXIII in 1960).

Blessed be Jesus in the Most Holy Sacrament of the altar

Blessed be the Holy Spirit the Paraclete (added by Blessed Paul VI in 1964).

Blessed be the great Mother of God, Mary Most Holy.

Blessed be her holy and Immaculate Conception (added by Blessed Pius IX in 1851, three years before the proclamation of the dogma of the Immaculate Conception in 1854).

Blessed be her glorious Assumption (added by Pope Pius XII in 1952, two years after the proclamation of the dogma).

Blessed be the name of Mary, Virgin and Mother.

Blessed be St Joseph, her most chaste spouse (added by Pope Benedict XV in 1921).

Blessed be God in his Angels and in his Saints.

In 1801 Pope Pius VII granted an indulgence for the recitation of the Divine Praises. The Divine Praises are recited in many countries immediately after the blessing with the Blessed Sacrament in Benediction. It is a fitting time to praise, or bless, God, who blesses us with his presence in the Blessed Sacrament.

Over the years a number of musical settings of the Divine Praises have been written, so that they are often sung rather than merely recited. This is a splendid way to honour and praise God, since in the words of an ancient saying, "He who sings, prays twice".

When we hear or see God blasphemed, we can say some of the Divine Praises: "Blessed be God, Blessed be his Holy Name."

567 *Lectio divina*

In our Bible study group, someone suggested we do what she called Lectio divina. I hadn't heard of it before. Can you tell me what it is and whether it is a good thing?

Lectio divina, literally "divine reading", in the broad sense is simply praying with the Scriptures, or meditating on them. In this sense, anyone who prays with the Scriptures is in fact doing *Lectio divina*, whether or not they have ever heard the term.

The practice of praying with the Scriptures goes back to the early Church. The abundant collections of sermons and commentaries on the Scriptures of the early Church Fathers attest to the assiduous prayer that obviously went into their preparation. In the third century, Origen used the expression *lectio divina* in a letter to Gregory of Neocaesarea: "Devote yourself to the lectio of the divine Scriptures; apply yourself to this with perseverance. Do your reading with the intent of believing in and pleasing God. If during the lectio you encounter a closed door, knock and it will be opened to you by that guardian of whom Jesus said, 'The gatekeeper will open it for him'. By applying yourself in this way to *lectio divina*, search diligently and with unshakable trust in God for the meaning of the divine Scriptures, which is hidden in great fullness within. You ought not, however, to be satisfied merely with knocking and seeking: to understand the things of God, what is absolutely necessary is *oratio*. For this reason, the Saviour told us not only: 'Seek and you will find', and 'Knock and it shall be opened to you', but also added, 'Ask and you shall receive'" (*Epistola ad Gregorium*, 3).

The structured form of *Lectio divina* involving four distinct steps owes its origin to Guigo II, a Carthusian monk, in the twelfth century. Guigo gave these four steps the Latin names *lectio*, or reading, *meditatio*, or meditation, *oratio* or prayer, and *contemplatio* or contemplation.

In the following century the Carmelites gave great importance to the daily prayerful meditation on the Word of God, as did St Dominic, founder of the Dominicans. In the sixteenth century, St John of the Cross taught the four stages of Guigo II to his monks and even Protestant reformers like John Calvin and the Puritan Richard Baxter advocated the practice.

In the twentieth century the Second Vatican Council's Dogmatic Constitution on Divine Revelation *Dei verbum* recommended prayer with the Scriptures to all the faithful (cf. *DV* n. 25). On the fortieth anniversary of the approval of that document Pope Benedict XVI said: "I would like in particular to recall and recommend the ancient tradition of *Lectio divina*: the diligent reading of Sacred Scripture accompanied by prayer brings about that intimate dialogue in which the person reading hears God who is speaking, and in praying, responds to him with trusting openness of heart (cf. *Dei verbum*, n. 25). If it is effectively promoted, this practice will bring to the Church – I am convinced of it – a new spiritual springtime."

Five years later, in his Apostolic Exhortation *Verbum Domini* (2010), Pope Benedict explained the traditional four steps and added a fifth. *Lectio divina*, he wrote, "opens with the reading (lectio) of a text, which leads to a desire to understand its true content: what does the biblical text say in itself? Without this, there is always a risk that the text will become a pretext for never moving beyond our own ideas. Next comes meditation (*meditatio*), which asks: what does the biblical text say to us? Here, each person, individually but also as a member of the community, must let himself or herself be moved and challenged. Following this comes prayer (*oratio*), which asks the question: what do we say to the Lord in response to his word? Prayer, as petition, intercession, thanksgiving and praise, is the primary way by which the word transforms us. Finally, *lectio divina* concludes with contemplation (*contemplatio*), during which we take up, as a gift from God, his own way of seeing and judging reality, and ask ourselves what conversion of mind, heart and life is the Lord asking of us? ... We do well also to remember that the process of *Lectio divina* is not concluded until it arrives at action (*actio*), which moves the believer to make his or her life a gift for others in charity" (*VD* n. 87).

In summary, *Lectio divina* is indeed a good thing – for everyone, not just Bible study groups.

568 Chaplet of Divine Mercy

I was recently asked to join some friends in reciting the Chaplet of Divine Mercy and, although I had never recited it before, I liked it very much. Can you tell me the background and meaning of it?

This devotion is becoming increasingly popular and has its origin in revelations of Our Lord to St Faustina Kowalska, a Polish nun of the Sisters of Our Lady of Mercy. Born in 1905, she entered the sisters in 1925 and died of tuberculosis in 1938 at the age of 33. Pope St John Paul II canonised her in 2000. Beginning in 1931 Our Lord appeared to her many times, asking for devotion to the Divine Mercy to be established. This led to Pope John Paul II establishing the Sunday after Easter as Divine Mercy Sunday. Significantly, Pope John Paul died on 2 April 2005, the eve of the feast of Divine Mercy.

In 1933 St Faustina had a vision of Our Lord's mercy, which she described like this: "I saw a great light, with God the Father in the midst of it. Between this light and the earth I saw Jesus nailed to the Cross and in such a way that God, wanting to look upon the earth, had to look through Our Lord's wounds and I understood that God blessed the earth for the sake of Jesus." She had another vision on 13 September 1935: "I saw an Angel, the executor of God's wrath... about to strike the earth...I began to beg God earnestly for the world with words which I heard interiorly. As I prayed in this way, I saw the angel's helplessness, and he could not carry out the just punishment...."

The following day Jesus instructed her to say on ordinary rosary beads what is now known as the Divine Mercy Chaplet: "First say one 'Our Father', 'Hail Mary', and 'I believe'. Then on the large beads say the following words: 'Eternal Father, I offer you the Body and Blood, Soul and Divinity of your dearly beloved Son, Our Lord Jesus Christ, in atonement for our sins and those of the whole world.' On the smaller beads you are to say the following words: 'For the sake of his sorrowful Passion have mercy on us and on the whole world.' In conclusion you are to say these words three times: 'Holy God, Holy Mighty One, Holy Immortal One, have mercy on us and on the whole world'".

Jesus later told Sister Faustina: "Say unceasingly this Chaplet that I have taught you. Anyone who says it will receive great mercy at the hour of death. Priests will recommend it to sinners as the last hope. Even the most hardened sinner, if he recites this Chaplet even once, will receive grace from my infinite Mercy. I want the whole world to know my infinite Mercy. I want to give unimaginable graces to those who trust in my Mercy... When they say this Chaplet in the presence of the dying, I will stand between my Father and the dying person not as the just judge but as the Merciful Saviour".

St Faustina wrote that the prayers of the Chaplet have a threefold purpose: to obtain mercy, to trust in Christ's mercy and to show mercy to others. The Chaplet is traditionally said at 3 in the afternoon although it may be said at any time of the day or night.

On 13 June 2002 Pope John Paul II granted a plenary indulgence to those who on Divine Mercy Sunday attend the devotions in honour of Divine Mercy in any church or chapel, and also to those who in the presence of the Blessed Sacrament exposed or in the tabernacle recite the Our Father and the Creed and say a devout prayer to the merciful Jesus. This latter provision would of course include saying the Divine Mercy Chaplet in a church before the tabernacle.

Jesus himself asked that the Chaplet be said as a novena beginning on Good Friday and ending on the Sunday after Easter, which is now Divine Mercy Sunday. Different intentions are indicated for each day and on the last day it is for souls who have become lukewarm and indifferent in their faith. Of them Jesus said: "These souls cause me more suffering than any others; it was from such souls that my soul felt the most revulsion in the Garden of Olives. It was on their account that I said: 'My Father, if it is possible, let this cup pass me by.' The last hope of salvation for them is to flee to my Mercy."

The Chaplet is indeed a beautiful and powerful prayer. Would that many would take it up.

569 Perseverance in prayer

Nine years ago my son, who was brought up a Catholic and went to Catholic schools, got married in a registry office when neither he nor his wife was practising the faith. They now have three children, who are not even baptised. I have been praying for many years for their conversion but nothing has changed and I am tempted to give up. Is it worthwhile to keep on praying?

It is always worthwhile to keep on praying, for many years or even for a lifetime. There are some prayer intentions that are of short term realisation: praying for someone to get over a severe bronchitis, to be able to buy or sell a house, to find a job when out of work... Other intentions will take longer: for a couple to have a baby after years of marriage without children, for a young man or woman to find a suitable spouse... And other intentions require the prayer of many years: the conversion of someone who has given up the practice of the faith, the gift of faith for a non-Catholic, the return to marital life of a couple who have been separated for many years...

For how long should we keep on praying? St John Chrysostom gives us the answer: "When I tell someone, 'Pray to God for that, ask him, beg him,' they answer, 'I've already prayed for it once, or twice, or three, or ten, or twenty times, and got nothing.' Don't stop, my brother, until you get it; petition ends when you receive what you are asking for. Stop praying for it only when you receive it. Better still, don't even stop then. Until you get it, keep on praying for it; and when you have got it, thank God for it" (*Homily on the Canaanite woman*, 10).

We know that intentions like the conversion of someone or the return to married life of a separated couple can take many years and we should never give up praying for them. We should continue to pray daily, with great patience and perseverance, all our life if necessary. We can learn from St Monica, who for some fifteen years prayed and shed many tears for her son Augustine to give up his immoral lifestyle and become a Catholic. Finally her prayers were answered.

Our Lord himself urges us to persevere in prayer, giving us two parables in the Gospel of Luke. The first involves a man going at midnight to ask his neighbour for three loaves of bread because a friend has just arrived and he has nothing with which to feed him. The neighbour answers that he and his family are in bed and the door is shut so he cannot grant his request. Jesus goes on: "I tell you, though he will not get up and give him anything because he is his friend, yet because of his importunity he will rise and give him whatever he needs. And I tell you, Ask, and it will be given you..." (*Lk* 11:8-9). In other words, we should keep on insisting, pestering God until he grants us whatever is his will.

St Luke prefaces the second parable with the words: "And he told them a parable, to the effect that they ought always to pray and not lose heart" (*Lk* 18:1). He goes on: "In a certain city there was a judge who neither feared God nor regarded man; and there was a widow in that city who kept coming to him and saying, 'Vindicate me against my adversary.' For a while he refused; but afterward he said to himself, 'Though I neither fear God nor regard man, yet because this widow bothers me, I will vindicate her, or she will wear me out by her continual coming'" (*Lk* 18:2-5).

Jesus goes on to ask: "And will not God vindicate his elect, who cry to him day and night? Will he delay long over them? I tell you, he will vindicate them speedily. Nevertheless, when the Son of man comes, will he find faith on earth?" (*Lk* 18:7-8) The message is clear. We should continue praying day and night for as long as necessary. In this way we show Our Lord that yes, he will find faith on earth – in us. Not to continue praying is a lack of faith in the power and mercy of God.

So it is clear that that we should pray "without ceasing" as St Paul urges us (cf. *Col* 1:9, *1 Thess* 5:17) for whatever length of time – weeks, months, years, a lifetime. That is, to continue praying until our prayer is answered. God always hears and answers us. Even if we do not receive the answer we want, the longer we pray the more we grow in holiness by virtue of the prayer itself. This in itself is an answer to our prayer. Sometimes Our Lord may let us pray for a long time without giving us what we want, precisely because he sees how much good the prayer is doing us.

Seasons and feasts

570 Is Advent a season of penance?

I know that Advent is a season of hope and expectation of the coming of Christ in history and at the end of time, but is it also a season of penance? We don't hear much about this aspect, if indeed Advent is supposed to be a time of penance.

I agree that we don't hear much about the penitential aspect of Advent, but we can be sure that it is still there in the mind of the Church. This is seen most obviously in the colour purple, which is used for the vestments worn by the priest and for other decorations of the church. This colour is used in the two penitential seasons preceding the great feasts of the year: Lent preceding Easter and Advent preceding Christmas. On the third Sunday of Advent, *Gaudete*, or *Rejoice*, Sunday, the colour may be rose, suggesting a lessening of the penitential aspect as we pass the halfway point in our Advent discipline.

Moreover, the Vatican's *Directory on Popular Piety and the Liturgy* (2002) says that Advent is a time of "conversion, to which the Liturgy at this time often refers, quoting the prophets, especially John the Baptist, 'Repent for the kingdom of heaven is at hand'" (*Mt* 3:2; n. 96).

Indeed, it has been traditional in the Church since the beginning to have days or seasons of penance as a way of preparing for the big feasts. The history of Advent bears this out. In the fifth century Pope St Leo the Great (591-604) called for fasting on Wednesdays and Fridays in the weeks leading up to Christmas. In 581 the Synod of Mâcon in present-day France called for fasting on Mondays, Wednesdays and Fridays from 11 November, the feast of St Martin of Tours, up to and including Christmas Eve, 24 December.

When it was first celebrated, Advent began six Sundays before

Christmas. The number was reduced to four by Pope St Gregory the Great. Some Eastern Rite Catholic Churches and the Eastern Orthodox Churches still celebrate a longer Advent, beginning on 15 November, the day after they celebrate the feast of the Apostle Philip. Thus for them Advent, like Lent, has forty days and is sometimes referred to as the Little Lent. It is lived as a penitential season, known as the Nativity Fast or sometimes St Philip's Fast, although the penance required is not as strict as that for Lent. In the Melkite Catholic Church the fast now begins on 10 December.

During this season the strict Eastern tradition requires abstinence from all creatures with a backbone, including mammals, birds and fish, and from all products made from these creatures, including milk, cheese, yogurt and eggs. In some traditions only one meal is allowed each day and this cannot be eaten before noon.

So it is clear that Advent is traditionally a penitential season like Lent. It is understandable that this should be the case. If we are to pray "Come, Lord Jesus", as the liturgy invites us to do, we should make our soul more worthy to receive him. Like the Prodigal Son, we come before God in humility saying, "Father, I have sinned against heaven and before you; I am no longer worthy to be called your son" (*Lk* 15:21). This sense of unworthiness, which we rightly feel, leads to the desire to purify our soul from sin and the effects of sin by acts of penance. It is as if we are cleaning out the stable of our soul so that Our Lord can find it a more worthy dwelling place on Christmas Day when he comes. To this end it can be helpful to choose one or more of our usual Lenten penances to live during Advent. In this way we are reminded that we must deny ourselves in order to prepare well for Christmas.

In addition to acts of self-denial, it is good to make a greater effort in our spiritual life too through such acts as attending Mass more often, setting aside regular times for prayer, reading the Scriptures or some book about Advent or Christmas, etc. And of course we should practise more acts of charity and almsgiving, which are so much a part of the spirit of Christmas.

Also important in living this spirit of repentance is receiving the sacrament of Penance, the great sacrament of mercy and joy by which we are forgiven our sins by God. There can hardly be a "Happy Christmas" without being in the state of grace and being embraced by the Father.

571 Ash Wednesday

One thing I have always wondered about is the meaning of putting ashes on our forehead on Ash Wednesday. What does this have to do with Lent?

Lent, as we know, is a season of repentance for our sins and conversion in preparation for the celebration of our Redemption through Christ's death and resurrection. While we tend to think in terms of preparing for Easter, it is more than that. Mankind was estranged from God by the original sin of our first parents and, moved by love, the Son of God became man in order to reconcile us with God by his death and resurrection. The whole purpose of his becoming man was this. As the *Catechism of the Catholic Church* puts it, "The Word became flesh for us in order to save us by reconciling us with God, who 'loved us and sent his Son to be the expiation for our sins'" (*1 Jn* 4:10; *CCC* 457). So in Lent we prepare for the celebration of our Redemption, not only for Our Lord's resurrection on Easter Sunday.

Returning to your question, there are two different but related meanings of the ashes at the beginning of Lent. They are expressed in the words the priest or other minister of the ashes may use on imposing them on Ash Wednesday.

The first has to do with ashes as a sign of repentance While in modern times ashes in themselves are not associated with penance, in ancient times wearing sackcloth, a very rough garment, and sprinkling ashes on oneself were a common expression of repentance. One of the early references to it in the Bible comes in the book of Job, where Job, moved by sorrow for his sins, says to God, "therefore I despise myself, and repent in dust and ashes" (*Job* 42:6). Another example is that of Tamar, a daughter of King David, whose half-brother Amnon forced her to sleep with him. In shame, "Tamar put ashes on her head, and tore the long robe which she wore" (*2 Sam* 13:19).

Similarly, when King Ahasuerus ordered the killing of all the Jews in his kingdom in Babylon, Mordecai "tore his clothes and put on sackcloth and ashes, and went out into the midst of the city, wailing with a loud and bitter cry" (*Esther* 4:1). When the king's order became known throughout the provinces, "there was great mourning among the Jews, with fasting and weeping and lamenting, and most of them lay in sackcloth and ashes" (*Esther* 4:3). There are numerous other references to ashes in the prophets (cf. *Is* 61:3, Jer 6:26, *Ezek* 27:30, and *Dan* 9:3).

Jesus himself refers to this custom: "Woe to you, Chora'zin! woe to you, Beth-sa'ida! for if the mighty works done in you had been done in Tyre and Sidon, they would have repented long ago in sackcloth and ashes" (*Mt* 11:21).

So fasting and the use of sackcloth and ashes were a common expression of repentance in ancient times. Usually the ashes were sprinkled on the head. As a reminder of this meaning the priest or other minister may say on imposing the ashes on Ash Wednesday, "Repent, and believe in the Gospel".

The other meaning of ashes has to do with man's mortality. We recall that in the creation of Adam God "formed man of dust from the ground, and breathed into his nostrils the breath of life" (*Gen* 2:7). Later, after Adam and Eve committed the original sin, God told Adam that as punishment he would have to die: "In the sweat of your face you shall eat bread till you return to the ground, for out of it you were taken; you are dust, and to dust you shall return" (*Gen* 3:19).

On imposing the ashes the other formula the minister may use is these very words: "Remember that you are dust and to dust you shall return." Here we are reminded that we will not live forever on earth, and that we should be detached from earthly comforts and pleasures. Our Lenten penances can involve depriving ourselves of some of these comforts and pleasures so as to be purified from our sins and united with God in preparation for meeting him at our death.

The ashes are traditionally made from palm branches blessed on Palm Sunday the previous year. They may be either placed on the forehead with the thumb in the sign of the cross or sprinkled lightly on the head, as is the custom in Spain, Italy and parts of Latin America. In Rome it is the custom for the Pope to have the ashes sprinkled on his head after a short penitential procession from the church of St Anselm to the Basilica of Santa Sabina.

572 More about Ash Wednesday

In our parish a layman helped the priest distribute ashes on Ash Wednesday. Is this permitted? Also, has the Church been starting Lent with the imposition of ashes for a long time, or is this something new? Do other faiths have it?

In answer to your first question, there would seem to be nothing wrong with lay people assisting the priest in the distribution of ashes on Ash Wednesday. Even though nothing is said about it in the *Roman Missal*, the *Book of Blessings* has a rite for the blessing and distribution of ashes outside of Mass which includes the following indication: "This rite may be celebrated by a priest or deacon who may be assisted by lay ministers in the distribution of the ashes. The blessing of the ashes, however, is reserved to a priest or deacon (no. 1659)."

From this it would seem that lay people may assist the priest in the distribution of ashes within Mass as well so as not to prolong the ceremony unduly. Given that large numbers of people ordinarily attend the Ash Wednesday services and that anyone who wishes to receive the ashes may do so, including young children and others who cannot receive Communion, the distribution of ashes can take a long time and so extra ministers are often needed.

What is more, a lay minister may lead a service of distributing ashes previously blessed by a priest or deacon, for example in taking ashes to the sick or to another group of faithful who have not been able to attend the rite of blessing and distribution within Mass or outside of Mass. So as a principle lay people can distribute the ashes in certain circumstances. If lay faithful can be extraordinary ministers of Communion when there is a shortage of ordinary ministers, there would seem to be no reason why they cannot also be ministers of the ashes.

For how long has the Church begun Lent with the imposition of ashes? Ash Wednesday is mentioned in the earliest copies of the Gregorian Sacramentary, which dates to the late eighth century, so the custom goes back at least that far.

One of the earliest descriptions of Ash Wednesday is found in the writings of the Anglo-Saxon abbot Aelfric of Eynsham (955-1020) who writes in his Lives of the Saints: "We read in the books both in the Old Law and in the New that the men who repented of their sins bestrewed themselves with ashes and clothed their bodies with sackcloth. Now let us do this little at the beginning of our Lent that we strew ashes upon our heads to signify that we ought to repent of our sins during the Lenten fast."

It seems that by the end of the tenth century the custom of the faithful receiving ashes on the first day of Lent was common in Western Europe, although not in Rome. In 1091 Pope Urban II at the Council of Benevento ordered that the custom be extended also to the Church in Rome. Not long after that the name of the day was referred to in liturgical books as *Feria Quarta Cinerum*, or Wednesday of Ashes, Ash Wednesday.

The custom of beginning Lent with ashes stems from the practice of people who had committed grave sins beginning their final preparation for absolution at Easter by being sprinkled with ashes and putting on sackcloth on the first day of Lent. This form of public penance ceased towards the end of the tenth century but a vestige of it remained in the sprinkling of ashes on the heads of all the faithful on Ash Wednesday.

As regards the use of ashes in other faiths, the Eastern Orthodox generally do not use them, since the custom is not part of their tradition. As we have seen, Ash Wednesday was more of a Western tradition. Nonetheless, with the creation in 2012 of an Antiochian Orthodox Western Rite Vicariate in the United States, some Western Orthodox parishes have begun to observe Ash Wednesday.

The use of ashes among Protestants is varied, with a few denominations observing it. In more recent times the celebration of Ash Wednesday among Anglicans and Protestants has been on the increase as a gesture of unity with Catholics, spurred on by the ecumenical movement that followed the Second Vatican Council. It is observed by some Anglicans, Lutherans, Methodists, Episcopalians, Anabaptists and Reformed congregations.

573 Veiling statues in Lent

I recently visited a church at the end of Lent where all the statues and the crucifix were covered by purple veils. Why is the cross hidden from view at the very time when we should be meditating more on the passion of Christ?

The custom of covering the crucifix and other images in the church with purple veils from Passion Sunday, the fifth Sunday of Lent, until

Holy Saturday was once very common but now is much less so. After the Second Vatican Council there were moves to abolish the custom altogether but fortunately it has survived. Even more, the Bishops' Conference of each country can decide whether to make the custom obligatory in its territory.

Where the custom is lived the crucifix and all other statues in the church are covered with a purple cloth without ornamentation from First Vespers on Passion Sunday to before the Easter Vigil. The crucifix is unveiled after the Good Friday service, during which the cross is venerated by the faithful. The only images not covered by a veil are those of the Stations of the Cross and any stained glass windows. The statue of St Joseph, if outside the sanctuary, may remain uncovered during the month of March, when his feast occurs and he is specially honoured.

What is the origin of the custom? According to Fr Edward McNamara (cf. *Zenit* 050308), it may have derived from a practice in Germany in the ninth century of extending a large cloth before the altar from the beginning of Lent. This cloth, known as the "Hungertuch" or hunger cloth, hid the altar from the view of the people until the reading of the Passion on Wednesday of Holy Week at the words "the veil of the temple was rent in two." The veil in the temple of Jerusalem separated the Holy of Holies from the main body of the temple.

Some scholars say the custom was a remnant of the ancient practice of ritually expelling public penitents from the church at the beginning of Lent. After the custom of public penance fell into disuse and the entire congregation was symbolically incorporated into the order of penitents through the imposition of ashes on Ash Wednesday, it was no longer possible to expel them from the church and so instead the altar, or "Holy of Holies", was shielded from view until they were reconciled with God at Easter. Later on in the Middle Ages the images of crosses and saints were also covered at the beginning of Lent. The custom of limiting this veiling to the last two weeks of Lent, appears in the Ceremonial of Bishops in the seventeenth century.

The great nineteenth-century Benedictine liturgist Dom Prosper Gueranger gives a mystical interpretation of the veiling, based on the Gospel of St John, which was formerly read on Passion Sunday. Just as Jesus hid himself from the Jews who wanted to stone him (cf. *Jn* 8:59), so by the veils he is now hidden from the world in preparation for the mysteries of his passion. The statues of the saints are covered too since, if the Master himself is covered, so should be his servants. Dom Gueranger also explains that while on the two feasts of the Finding and the Exaltation of the Holy Cross the cross is honoured as the throne of Christ's victory, with its veiling in Lent it speaks to us of his suffering and humiliation.

Another spiritual interpretation of the veiling is based on the fact that in Christ's passion not only was his divinity obscured but so was, in a certain sense, his humanity. He was so disfigured by the blows and scourges that he was hardly recognisable as a human being. We read in the prophet Isaiah's depiction of the Suffering Servant, which has always been taken to refer to Christ: "As many were astonished at him – his appearance was so marred, beyond human semblance, and his form beyond that of the sons of men – so shall he startle many nations" (*Is* 52:14). Likewise, we read in the psalm Jesus quoted while he hung on the cross: "But I am a worm, and no man; scorned by men, and despised by the people" (*Ps* 22:6). So, in a sense, the veil hides Our Lord's divinity and humanity, as did the wounds suffered in his passion.

Regardless of the original meaning of the veiling of the crucifix and statues, it has much to commend it as a way of helping us prepare for Our Lord's Passover in the last two weeks of Lent.

574 Why do we call it Easter?

I remember reading somewhere that the name Easter is of pagan origin. Could this be true?

Before we enter into the origin of the word Easter we should remind ourselves that when we celebrate Easter, by whatever name we call it, we are celebrating the Resurrection of Christ and with it our Redemption. It is the most important feast day of the year for Christians and it is truly a happy day: "This is the day which the Lord has made, let us rejoice and be glad in it" (*Ps* 118:24). What really matters is not what we call it, or where the name comes from, but what we are celebrating.

Turning to the name for the feast, in most western languages and in some eastern ones the name is derived from the word for Passover, which we often render Pasch. We recall that at the time of the exodus from slavery in Egypt, the Israelites were told to slaughter a lamb and put some of the blood on the doorposts and the lintel of their house. That night the angel of death passed over the homes of the Israelites and killed the first-born males of the Egyptians. Since then the Jews have celebrated the Passover each year to commemorate this event. We use the word Pasch to refer to Christ, the true paschal lamb, by whose death and resurrection we are freed from slavery to sin, death and the devil. St Paul says this in his first letter to the Corinthians: "For Christ, our Paschal Lamb, has been sacrificed" (*1 Cor* 5:7).

So Easter is called Pasch in many languages. In French one wishes someone happy Easter with "Joyeuses Pâques", in Spanish "Felices Pascuas", in Italian "Buona Pasqua", and even in Indonesian "Selamat Paskah". The northern European languages also use that term so that in Dutch one says "Vroliik Pasen", in Norwegian "God påske" and in Swedish "Glad Påsk".

But in German and other languages derived from German, like English, we call it Easter. In German we wish someone "Frohe Ostern", in Luxembourgish "Schéin Ouschteren", in Swiss German "Schöni Oschtere" and in English "Happy Easter". We are clearly the odd ones out!

So where does the name Easter come from? The English monk St

Bede (672-735) wrote about the month of Eostre, corresponding to April, which he says was named after the goddess Eostre, because feasts were celebrated in her honour in that month (*De temporum ratione*, ch. 13). The Germans too, going back at least to around the year 300, called the month of April after their corresponding goddess Ostra.

The name Easter, Eostre or Ostra, is related to the word for east, or ost in German, since Ostra was the goddess of the dawn, of the rising sun and the new day. She was worshipped in the Spring, when the darkness of the long winter days gives way to increasing sunlight, bringing with it new life and growth. It is understandable that Christians would have associated the name with the feast of the Resurrection, when we celebrate the rising from the dead of Jesus Christ, the light of the world. Christ is often referred to as the sun of justice and he is associated with the east.

For example, Origen in the third century writes: "Atonement comes to you from the east. From the east comes the one whose name is Dayspring, he who is mediator between God and men. You are invited then to look always to the east: it is there that the sun of righteousness rises for you, it is there that the light is always being born for you... So that you may always enjoy the light of knowledge, keep always in the daylight of faith, hold fast always to the light of love and peace" (*Ex hom. in Leviticum* 9, 5.10).

Also, in the ceremony of baptism in the early centuries the catechumens would first face west, the direction of darkness and Satan, to answer the questions we still use in the ceremony: "Do you reject Satan ... and all his works? Then they would turn to the east, the direction of Christ, to answer the three questions of the profession of faith: "Do you believe in God the Father Almighty... in Jesus Christ... in the Holy Spirit?

In the Easter Vigil ceremony we express this in the lighting of the Easter candle, Christ our light, who takes us from the darkness of sin into the light of God's grace.

So while Eostre may have been a pagan goddess, the name Easter is rich in meaning for us. Let us not worry about the name but rather celebrate the joy of Christ's resurrection.

575 Why Easter eggs?

My ten year-old daughter recently asked me why we eat chocolate Easter eggs and bunnies, and sometimes chocolate lambs, at Easter and I wasn't sure of the answer. Is this a secular custom or a Christian one?

Let us start with Easter eggs, which are probably the most common popular symbol of Easter. They can be chocolate, as your daughter mentions and which are so common in this country, or more commonly hard boiled and brightly coloured, as in some European and other countries.

What do eggs have to do with Easter? The egg can be seen as a symbol of the sealed tomb from which Christ emerged after his resurrection, just as the chick emerges from the closed egg. From ancient times it was also seen as a symbol of new life. And since eggs were one of the foods from which people fasted in Lent in the early Church as they still do in the Orthodox tradition, people looked forward to eating them again and associated different customs with them.

It seems that as far back as the fourth century in the East eggs were blessed at Easter time. The *Benedictio Ovorum*, blessing of eggs, came to the West in the twelfth century, perhaps brought from the East by the Crusaders. In the East the eggs were stained red in memory of the blood Christ shed on the Cross. Red eggs, sometimes emblazoned with a cross, are still the custom in the Orthodox and Eastern Catholic traditions. They are blessed by the priest at the end of the Easter Vigil and distributed to the faithful.

In medieval times it was the custom to give eggs at Easter to one's servants. It is reported that in 1290 King Edward I of England had 450 eggs boiled, dyed or covered with gold leaf before Easter to be distributed to the members of the royal household on Easter Day. Later the famous Fabergé workshops were well known for creating beautiful jewelled Easter eggs for the Russian Imperial Court.

In northern Europe the custom of painting eggs in bright colours at Easter, having them blessed and giving them as gifts goes back many centuries. The old Roman Ritual, the first edition of which dates to 1610, had a special blessing for Easter eggs. In countries like Poland, Lithuania, the Ukraine and the Czech Republic eggs are decorated with magnificent intricate designs which are true works of art. They are often given as gifts to relatives and friends, with the design on the egg chosen to match the character of the person to whom it is given.

In Poland the so-called *swieconka* involves the blessing of baskets of Easter eggs and other symbolic foods in the Easter Vigil. A similar custom is lived in the Ukraine. Upon returning home after the Vigil the family breaks the Lenten fast by eating the eggs and other foods.

In Germany thousands of brightly coloured emptied-out eggs are hung on the barren branches of outdoor trees known as Easter egg trees to give a festive appearance to them. They are also hung on tree branches in flower pots and used as table decorations.

In some traditions Easter eggs are even offered to the deceased. After a memorial service the people go on the second Monday or Tuesday after Easter to take blessed eggs to the cemetery where they say the traditional Easter greeting "Christ is risen" in honour of those buried there.

As for Easter lambs, these too go back a long way. They are usually represented with the cross and the flag of victory, symbolizing the resurrection of Christ. Just as the Jews ate a lamb in the annual celebration of the Passover, Christians took up the lamb as a symbol of

Christ, the lamb of God who by his death and resurrection takes away the sins of the world.

The oldest prayer for the blessing of lambs is in the seventh-century sacramentary of the Benedictine monastery in Bobbio, Italy. Rome adopted it two hundred years later and for many centuries afterwards lamb was served in the Pope's Easter dinner. In more recent times figures of a lamb made of butter, pastry or sugar – and yes, chocolate – have become popular.

And as for Easter bunnies, rabbits have always been seen as a figure of fertility and new life, and so they are associated with Easter. It seems that Germany was the origin of the legend that the Easter bunny brought eggs and hid them in the garden. Naturally, there is no scriptural basis for Easter bunnies.

576 The feast of the Blessed Trinity

Can you tell me something about the feast of the Blessed Trinity? Has it been celebrated for a long time or is it relatively new?

We should say at the outset that it is fitting that there be a special feast in honour of the Blessed Trinity. As the *Catechism of the Catholic Church* explains, "The mystery of the Most Holy Trinity is the central mystery of Christian faith and life. It is the mystery of God in himself. It is therefore the source of all the other mysteries of faith, the light that enlightens them. It is the most fundamental and essential teaching in the hierarchy of the truths of faith" (*CCC* 234).

When we ask how old the feast is we should remember that the Church formulated her teaching on this mystery gradually. There was never any question that there was one God, nor that the Father revealed by Jesus Christ was God. Neither in the first centuries was there any question about the divinity of Jesus, the second Person of the Trinity, as the angel had announced to Mary: "... therefore the child to be born will be called holy, the Son of God" (*Lk* 1:35). Nonetheless, in the fourth century Arius taught that Jesus was a created being, leading to his divinity being proclaimed in the Council of Nicaea in the year 325. The divinity of the third Person of the Trinity, the Holy Spirit, was proclaimed in the First Council of Constantinople in 381, from which we have the Nicene-Constantinopolitan Creed. Thus, what Jesus himself had announced in sending the apostles out to baptise "in the name of the Father and of the Son and of the Holy Spirit" (*Mt* 28:19) was now firmly established in the teaching of the Church.

The Mass in honour of the Blessed Trinity gradually took shape over the following centuries, as Fr Francis X. Weiser, S.J. explains in his *Handbook of Christian Feasts and Customs* (Harcourt, Brace and Company, New York 1958). Already at the time of the Arian heresy in the fourth century a special Mass in honour of the Blessed Trinity was introduced and celebrated in Rome. It was not assigned to any particular day but could be used on certain Sundays, at the discretion of the priest.

A special feast day in honour of the Trinity came to be celebrated in the ninth century in France, where various bishops promoted it in their own dioceses. It was usually celebrated on the Sunday after Pentecost, as it is today. The Mass text was said to have been composed by St Alcuin, Abbot of Tours, who died in 804. Thereafter, a special feast in honour of the Blessed Trinity gradually spread to other countries of northern Europe, with several synods prescribing it for their respective territories in France, Germany, England and the Netherlands. It was celebrated on different Sundays in different places until 1334, when Pope John XXII approved it for the official calendar of the Western Church to be celebrated on the Sunday after Pentecost.

A new Mass text was written and published for the feast. It is interesting to note that the Preface we use today first appeared in the Sacramentary of Pope St Gregory the Great at the end of the sixth century. Most of the other prayers are of later origin. The Divine Office was arranged under Pope St Pius V (1572).

The Trinitarian prayer "Glory be to the Father and to the Son and to the Holy Spirit..." appeared very early on in the East, with the second part of the prayer, "as it was in the beginning, is now and ever shall be..." apparently added at the time of the Emperor Constantine in the fourth century. The prayer came to be used in the West in the fifth century. Since then it has been in constant use in both liturgical and private prayers. As early as the sixth century, the Council of Narbonne (589) prescribed its use after every psalm and hymn in the Divine Office, a custom that obtains to this day.

From the fourteenth century on the Blessed Trinity was often invoked during epidemics of the plague. There are hundreds of churches in Europe dedicated to the Blessed Trinity that owe their existence to public vows made at the time of the plague. Later, in the seventeenth and eighteenth centuries, marble or granite columns in honour of the Blessed Trinity were placed in the main squares of cities and towns in central Europe for the same purpose. For example, Vienna has eleven such columns erected during the epidemics of 1679 and 1713.

577 The feast of Corpus Christi

I have always liked the feast of Corpus Christi, especially the procession with the Blessed Sacrament. Is this feast celebrated around the world or only in some countries, and is it a recent or an old feast?

The feast of Corpus Christi, the Body and Blood of Christ, dates back to the thirteenth century and so it can be called an old feast, although there are many feasts which go back much farther than that in the two thousand year history of the Church. And it is celebrated the world over.

I have written about the origin of the feast in previous columns (cf. *Question Time 1*, q. 150, *Question Time 2*, qq. 270-271) so here I will limit myself to recalling some of the principal events and then go on to explain how it came to be celebrated as a universal feast.

It was Our Lord himself who asked for a special feast in honour of the Blessed Sacrament. He did it in apparitions to St Juliana, a nun in a convent in Liège, Belgium, over a period of twenty years beginning in 1208. He told her that he wanted the feast for three reasons: to confirm people's faith in the Real Presence, to strengthen them in virtue by their love and adoration for the Eucharist, and to make reparation for the lack of respect shown to the Blessed Sacrament.

When St Juliana became Mother Superior, she confided the apparitions to her confessor and to several others, including the Archdeacon of Liège, Jacques Pantaleon, who would later become Pope Urban IV. The idea was warmly received and it led to the introduction of the feast in Liège in 1246, to be celebrated on the Thursday after Trinity Sunday. Soon it spread to neighbouring dioceses.

Then in 1263 a Eucharistic miracle took place in Bolsena, Italy, which hastened the introduction of the feast in the universal Church. A German priest on a pilgrimage to Rome was celebrating Mass in Bolsena and he found it difficult to believe that Christ was truly present in the consecrated host. He had barely spoken the words of Consecration when blood started to seep from the host and trickle down over his hands onto the altar and the corporal. The priest, filled with consternation, interrupted the Mass and asked to be taken to the nearby city of Orvieto, where Pope Urban IV, the former Archdeacon of Liège was residing. The Pope ordered an investigation and when he was satisfied that this was indeed a miracle asked the bishop of the diocese to bring the host and the blood-stained linens to Orvieto in procession.

The following year, in August of 1264, Pope Urban by the Bull *Transiturus* instituted the feast of Corpus Christi for the whole Church and asked St Thomas Aquinas, who was residing in Orvieto at the time, to write the texts for the Mass and the Divine Office. These texts are still in use today. The actual introduction of the feast around the world was only gradual, with some German dioceses taking it up early on, as did the Cistercians and the diocese of Venice. It became truly universal after the Bull of Pope Urban IV was included in the collection of laws known as the "Clementines", compiled under Pope Clement V and promulgated by his successor Pope John XXII in 1317.

The hymn Pange lingua, "Sing my tongue", which St Thomas Aquinas composed for Vespers in the Divine Office on the feast of Corpus Christi, is also used on Holy Thursday during the procession of the Blessed Sacrament to the altar of repose after the Mass of the Lord's Supper. The last two verses of the hymn, beginning with Tantum ergo, "Down in adoration falling", are used as a separate hymn for Benediction with the Blessed Sacrament to this day. *O salutaris hostia*, "O Saving Victim", another hymn sung at Benediction, is the last two verses of *Verbum Supernum Prodiens*, Aquinas' hymn for Morning Prayer on the feast of Corpus Christi.

So, as you can see, this much beloved feast is celebrated the world over, much to the benefit of those who participate in it.

578 The feast of the Sacred Heart of Jesus

Some of your readers have asked about the origin of feast days and I would like to ask about the feast of the Sacred Heart. Can you tell me something about the history of the devotion and the feast, which I like very much?

The beginnings of devotion to the love of God as represented by the heart of Jesus can be traced back as far as some of the Fathers of the Church, including Saints Justin, Irenaeus, Cyprian, Ambrose, Jerome and Augustine. Later St Anselm of Canterbury in the eleventh century and St Bernard of Clairvaux in the twelfth spoke about the heart of Christ as the object of particular devotion, as did St Bonaventure in the thirteenth.

Important in this history is St Gertrude of Helfta, a German Benedictine nun who died in 1302. On the feast of St John the Evangelist she had a vision in which she laid her head near the wound in Christ's side and heard the beating of his heart. She asked St John if he had felt this same beating on the night of the Last Supper and why he had never spoken of the experience. St John replied that this revelation had been reserved for subsequent ages when the world, having grown cold, would need it to rekindle its love.

In the sixteenth century St Francis de Sales encouraged the devotion in the Visitation order he had founded and several Jesuits, among them St Francis Borgia, St Peter Canisius and St Aloysius Gonzaga had personal devotion to the Sacred Heart. In the following century St John Eudes, founder of the Congregation of Jesus and Mary and the Order of Our Lady of Charity, did much to promote devotion to the heart of Jesus. He wrote the proper texts for a Mass and Divine Office of the Sacred Hearts of Jesus and Mary which were used with the approval of the bishop in the first liturgical celebration of the feast on 31 August 1670 in the seminary of Rennes, in France.

Especially important in promoting the devotion was the Visitation nun St Margaret Mary Alacoque, who had private revelations from Our Lord at Paray-le-Monial in France between 1673 and 1675. Our Lord asked her to spread awareness and gratitude for his great love for humankind, and to make reparation for the ingratitude shown especially by those consecrated to him. He asked that the Friday after the octave of Corpus Christi be set aside as a feast in honour of his Sacred Heart, and that people should receive Holy Communion in reparation.

It was to St Margaret Mary that Jesus revealed the devotion of the nine First Fridays. He told her: "I promise you, in the excess of the mercy of my Heart, that its all-powerful love will grant to all those who shall receive Communion on the first Friday of nine consecutive months the grace of final repentance; they shall not die under my displeasure nor without receiving the Sacraments, my Divine Heart becoming their assured refuge at that last hour."

A further development in the liturgical celebration of the Mass of the Sacred Heart came when papal approval was given for its use in Poland and Portugal in 1765 and in Venice, Austria and Spain in 1788. In 1856 Pope Pius IX established the feast of the Sacred Heart as obligatory for the universal Church, to be celebrated on the Friday after the Octave of Corpus Christi. Pope Pius XI raised the feast to the highest liturgical rank in 1928 and added an Octave. The Octave was suppressed in the 1955 reform of the general calendar along with the Octaves of most other feasts.

In 1899 Pope Leo XIII, in his Encyclical *Annum sacrum*, decreed the consecration of the whole world to the Sacred Heart and in 1956, on the centenary of the extension of the feast to the universal Church, Pope Pius XII wrote the Encyclical *Haurietis aquas*, outlining the theological basis for the devotion in Scripture and tradition. Since 2002 the Solemnity of the Sacred Heart is also to be a special Day of Prayer for the Sanctification of Priests, as declared by Pope St John Paul II.

This feast is much to be encouraged in order to rekindle love for Our Lord at a time when it has grown cold in the hearts of many.

579 The feast of the Immaculate Conception

Recently a friend showed me a prayer book printed in 1688 that has a calendar of feast days, and I happened to notice that December 8 was the feast of the Conception of the Blessed Virgin Mary, even though the dogma was proclaimed much later, in 1854. How did this come about?

The question you ask raises the further question of how matters of belief come to be defined as dogmas by the Church. Usually, as is the case with the Immaculate Conception of Our Lady, the whole Church comes to accept and believe a truth long before it is proclaimed a dogma. During this time it is not uncommon for the Church to include in its calendar the liturgical celebration of the feast. Such is the case here, as it was also with the Assumption of Our Lady into heaven. This latter feast had been celebrated for centuries before the proclamation of the dogma in 1950.

Returning to your question, belief in the Immaculate Conception of Our Lady and the liturgical celebration of the feast go back a long way. For example, in the fourth century St Ephrem, a Doctor of the Church, writes: "You and your mother are the only ones who are totally beautiful in every respect; for in you, O Lord, there is no spot, and in your mother no stain" (*Carm. Nisib.* 27).

By the seventh century a feast of the conception of Mary was being celebrated in the monasteries of Palestine. This celebration, however, did not imply belief in Mary's Immaculate Conception, but only her conception in the womb of her mother St Anne. In fact the feast was more commonly known at that time as the "Conception of St Anne, the ancestress of God".

The *Catholic Encyclopedia* says there is strong evidence that the feast goes back even further, to the Patriarchate of Jerusalem in the fifth century. In any case, the oldest genuine extant document is a canon of the feast composed by St Andrew of Crete at the monastery of St Sabas near Jerusalem in the second half of the seventh century. The monks arranged the psalms to be recited and the hymns and other texts of the Divine Office. They also selected the date, which was originally 9 December, a date retained in other Eastern calendars. Gradually the feast passed from the monasteries to the cathedrals and other churches, and finally it was approved officially by the Popes.

The feast did not reach the West until probably early in the eleventh century. In 1030 it appeared in a calendar in Winchester, England, and around the same time a "Blessing for the Conception of Holy Mary" appeared in a pontifical, or liturgical book used by the bishop, in Exeter. In Normandy in the second half of the twelfth century the feast was celebrated as a holyday of obligation, equal in dignity to the Annunciation. From there it spread to the rest of Europe. The Western date was December 8, as it is today.

The feast was also listed in the calendar of the Byzantine Emperor Basil II (976-1025). Since southern Italy, Sicily and Sardinia still belonged to the Byzantine Empire at that time, it is probable that the feast was kept in those regions as early as the ninth century.

After a controversy involving the best theologians of the day, including St Thomas Aquinas, St Bonaventure and others as to whether Mary was conceived free from original sin (cf. J. Flader, *Question Time 1*, q. 32) the matter was finally resolved in the affirmative by the Franciscan Duns Scotus. After that the Council of Basle in 1439 declared that the Immaculate Conception of Mary was a doctrine which was pious and consistent with Catholic worship, Catholic faith, right reason and Holy Scripture.

In 1476 Pope Sixtus IV instituted the feast of the Immaculate Conception for the entire Latin Church, and in 1483 he condemned those who said it was sinful to preach and believe the Immaculate Conception. The Council of Trent upheld the constitutions of Pope Sixtus IV. In 1708 Pope Clement XI declared the feast to be a holyday of obligation in the universal Church. And in 1854 Pope Pius IX finally defined the dogma of the Immaculate Conception.

So it is clear that belief in the Immaculate Conception of Mary and the celebration of the feast predated the proclamation of the dogma by many centuries.

580 The feast of St Stephen

I have always wondered why the Mass on the day after Christmas is that of the martyr St Stephen. Is there some special reason for this?

It is a question many have asked. In this time of joy when we celebrate other feasts closely associated with the birth of Christ like those of the Holy Family, the Holy Innocents, the Divine Maternity of Mary and the Epiphany, it seems strange that the very day after Christmas we should commemorate the death of an early martyr.

A consideration of who St Stephen was can shed light on the question. He was one of the seven deacons chosen by the apostles to help them in the service of those in need. Stephen is the first one mentioned in the list of seven, and he is described as "a man full of faith and of the Holy Spirit" (*Acts* 6:5). The account goes on to say that the seven were "set before the apostles, and they prayed and laid their hands upon them" (*Acts* 6:6), indicating that by the rite of the laying on of hands by the apostles these men received the sacrament of Holy Orders.

A few lines later the Acts tell us that "Stephen, full of grace and power, did great wonders and signs among the people" (*Acts* 6:8). Then some of the Jews rose up and disputed with Stephen, but "they could not withstand the wisdom and the Spirit with which he spoke" (*Acts* 6:10). They brought Stephen before the council and found false witnesses to accuse him of blasphemy against Moses and God.

In his defence Stephen gave a long discourse in which he traced the history of God's mercy on the Jewish people from Abraham through Moses and David to the present. He called his accusers "stiff-necked people, uncircumcised in heart and ears" who "always resist the Holy Spirit" (*Acts* 7:51) and he reminded them that their fathers had persecuted the prophets who announced the coming of the Messiah, and now they themselves had put the Messiah to death. This infuriated them. Stephen then "gazed into heaven and saw the glory of God, and Jesus standing at the right hand of God" and said, "Behold, I see the heavens opened, and the Son of man standing at the right hand of God" (*Acts* 7:55-56). At this they took him outside the city and stoned him to death. Stephen prayed, "Lord Jesus, receive my spirit" and cried out with a loud voice, "Lord, do not hold this sin against them" (*Acts* 7:59-60).

Stephen thus became the first martyr to witness to Christ. He was united with Christ in his life and in his death. Like Christ he did signs and wonders, he was falsely accused of blasphemy, he was put to death outside the city, he commended his soul to God and he forgave those who were putting him to death. Thus the Church, in putting this feast on the day after Christmas, is calling to our mind the example of this first witness to Christ and reminding us that we are all called to imitate and witness to the One who was born in Bethlehem and later died for us.

In his Angelus message on the feast of St Stephen in 2006, Pope Benedict XVI said that even the circumstances of Christ's birth remind us of his death. The swaddling cloths in which he was wrapped and laid in the manger foretold the linen cloths in which his body was wrapped when he was laid in the tomb after his death. Indeed, Christmas iconography sometimes represents the newborn Jesus lying in a small sarcophagus, or coffin, indicating that he came into the world to die for us.

Pope Benedict also pointed out that the day of death of a saint is often referred to as the *dies natalis*, the birth day on which they were born to eternal life. So it is not surprising that the Church associates the birth of Christ with the spiritual birth of St Stephen. Because Christ was born in Bethlehem in order to die for our redemption, all mankind is able to be born to eternal life.

The feast of St Stephen has been celebrated on 26 December for many centuries. Already at the end of the fifth century or beginning of the sixth St Fulgentius of Ruspe in North Africa preached a sermon on the feast of St Stephen, relating it to the feast of Christmas celebrated the day before. The beautiful English Christmas carol "Good King Wenceslas", written by John Mason Neale in 1853, tells the story of the tenth-century Bohemian martyr St Wenceslas looking out "on the feast of Stephen, when the snow lay round about". In the Eastern Orthodox and the Eastern Catholic Churches which follow the Byzantine rite, St Stephen's feast is celebrated on 27 December. St Stephen is also honoured by Anglicans and Lutherans.

581 The feast of the Assumption of Our Lady

I know that the dogma of the Assumption of Our Lady was defined in 1950 but was wondering whether belief in Our Lady's Assumption and the celebration of the feast might be much older. Can you enlighten me?

As you say, the dogma of Our Lady's bodily Assumption into heaven was proclaimed as recently as 1950 by Pope Pius XII. In the Apostolic Constitution *Munificentissimus Deus* on 1 November 1950, he defined it in the following terms: "The Immaculate Mother of God, the ever-virgin Mary, having completed the course of her earthly life, was assumed body and soul into heaven."

While the dogma was defined recently, belief in the bodily Assumption of Our Lady goes back to the early centuries. The first accounts of it are actually in apocryphal writings from the fourth century. The earliest known one is the *Liber Requiei Mariae* (Book of Mary's Repose), probably composed in the fourth but possibly as early as the third century. By apocryphal in this sense we mean writings which were not officially approved by the Church. But the very fact that they speak of Mary's Assumption is evidence of the belief of some people at the time. Other apocryphal works which attest to the belief are the *Six Books Dormition Narratives* of the fifth and sixth centuries and the *De Obitu S. Dominae* (On the death of the Holy Lady), from around the sixth century, which is a summary of the Six Books narrative.

Some of the Fathers of the Church mention Mary's death and subsequent Assumption, among them St Andrew of Crete, St John Damascene and St Modestus of Jerusalem. The first Father in the West to do so was St Gregory of Tours, who died in 594 AD. He writes: "Finally, when blessed Mary, having completed the course of her earthly life, was about to be called from this world, all the apostles, coming from their different regions, gathered together in her house. When they heard that she was about to be taken up out of the world, they kept watch together with her. And behold, the Lord Jesus came with his angels and, taking her soul, handed it over to the archangel Michael and withdrew. At dawn, the apostles lifted up her body on a pallet, laid it in a tomb, and again the Lord presented himself to them and ordered that her holy body be taken and carried up to heaven. There she is now, joined once more to her soul; she exults with the elect, rejoicing in the eternal blessings that will have no end" (L. Gambero, *Mary and the Fathers of the Church*, Ignatius 1999, p. 353).

Two centuries later in the East St John Damascene wrote in a prayer to Mary: "The assembly of apostles carried you, the Lord God's true Ark, as once the priests carried the symbolic ark, on their shoulders. They laid you in the tomb, through which, as if through the Jordan, they will conduct you to the promised land, that is to say, the Jerusalem above, mother of all the faithful, whose architect and builder is God. Your soul did not descend to Hades, neither did your flesh see corruption. Your virginal and uncontaminated body was not abandoned in the earth, but you are transferred into the royal dwelling of heaven, you, the Queen, the sovereign, the Lady, God's Mother, the true God-bearer..." (*Homily 1 on the Dormition* 12-13).

So belief in the Assumption goes back to the early centuries. The place where Mary was supposed to have been assumed into heaven is ascribed variously to Jerusalem and Ephesus. The former is the earlier tradition, although nothing is known with certainty. There is a church of the Dormition on Mt Zion in Jerusalem, on the site where Our Lady was believed to have died and been assumed into heaven. It is now a Benedictine Abbey. Similarly, the year assigned to the Assumption varies between three and fifteen years after Our Lord's Ascension. What is clear is that nowhere in the world are the relics of Mary venerated.

As regards the celebration of the feast, from at least the sixth century the Church has celebrated the feast of the "Dormition"; that is, the falling asleep, or death, of Mary. The monks in Egypt celebrated it in January and from there the custom passed to Gaul, whereas in Jerusalem and elsewhere in the Greek Empire it was celebrated on 15 August, as it is today. It seems to have been celebrated in Rome on 15 August as early as the sixth century. It should be understood that this early feast was not properly of the bodily assumption of Our Lady but more of her death. The Orthodox too celebrate the feast on 15 August, preceded by two weeks of fasting.

582 The feast of the Queenship of Mary

I have always been intrigued by the feast of the Queenship of Mary on 22 August each year. In what sense is Mary a queen? Also, if possible, can you tell me when and why the feast was instituted?

To answer your second question first, the feast of the Queenship of Mary was instituted by Pope Pius XII in 1954 on 11 October, which at that time was the feast of the Divine Maternity of Mary. The Pope instituted the feast and explained the reason for it in an Encyclical entitled *Ad Caeli Reginam*, "To the Queen of Heaven".

At the beginning of the Encyclical Pope Pius explains, referring no doubt to the recently concluded Second World War and the communist regimes in Eastern Europe, the circumstances that led him to institute the feast: the "frightful calamities which before our very eyes have reduced flourishing cities, towns and villages to ruins", the "many great moral evils being spread abroad in what may be described as a violent flood" and "the victory of the powers of corruption". In view of this situation, he says that "with confidence we have recourse to Mary our Queen, making known to her those sentiments of filial reverence which are not ours alone, but which belong to all those who glory in the name of Christian" (n. 2).

Toward the end of the Encyclical he gives another reason for recourse to Our Lady as Queen, one which is exceptionally relevant to our own time: "In some countries of the world there are people who are unjustly persecuted for professing their Christian faith and who are deprived of their divine and human rights to freedom... May the powerful Queen of creation, whose radiant glance banishes storms and tempests and brings back cloudless skies, look upon these her innocent and tormented children with eyes of mercy" (n. 50).

Pope Pius XII dedicates a good part of the Encyclical to showing how appropriate it is to refer to Mary as queen: "From early times Christians have believed, and not without reason, that she of whom was born the Son of the Most High received privileges of grace above all other beings created by God. He 'will reign in the house of Jacob forever' (*Lk* 1:32), 'the Prince of Peace' (*Is* 9:6), the 'King of Kings and Lord of Lords' (*Rev* 19:16). And when Christians reflected upon the intimate connection that obtains between a mother and a son, they readily acknowledged the supreme royal dignity of the Mother of God" (n. 8). For this reason, early writers of the Church called Our Lady "Mother of the King" and "Mother of the Lord", signifying that she derived a certain eminence from the royal dignity of her Son (cf. n. 9).

He goes on to consider numerous testimonies of Fathers of the

Church who call Mary queen. For example, St Andrew of Crete relates Mary's queenship to her assumption into heaven: "Today he transports from her earthly dwelling, as Queen of the human race, his ever-Virgin Mother" (*Homilia II in Dormitionem Ssmae Deiparae*; n. 17). St Ephrem prays to Mary: "Majestic and Heavenly Maid, Lady, Queen, protect and keep me under your wing lest Satan the sower of destruction glory over me, lest my wicked foe be victorious against me" (*Oratio ad Ss.mam Dei Matrem*). Similarly, St Germanus speaks to Our Lady in these words: "Be enthroned, Lady, for it is fitting that you should sit in an exalted place since you are a Queen and glorious above all kings" (*In Praesentationem Ss.mae Deiparae*). He likewise calls her the "Queen of all of those who dwell on earth" (idem).

In view of this, theologians down the ages have called the Blessed Virgin "the Queen of all creatures, the Queen of the world, and the Ruler of all" (n. 22). Similarly the Popes have called Mary Queen. As early as the eighth century Pope Gregory II wrote a letter to St Germanus, which was read out and accepted in the Second Council of Nicaea in 787, in which he called Our Lady "the Queen of all, the true Mother of God," and also "the Queen of all Christians" (Hardouin, *Acta Conciliorum*, IV, 234).

St Alphonsus Liguori sums up this teaching: "Because the Virgin Mary was raised to such a lofty dignity as to be the mother of the King of Kings, it is deservedly and by every right that the Church has honoured her with the title of 'Queen'" (*The Glories of Mary*, p. I, c. I, §1; n. 25).

Mary's queenship has been expressed in such ancient and modern hymns as the "Hail, Holy Queen" and "Hail, Queen of Heaven"; in the *Regina Caeli*, which begins "Queen of Heaven, rejoice"; and in the medieval Litany of Loreto, which invokes Mary as Queen thirteen times. In short, it is a solidly based tradition and we do well to have recourse to Mary's powerful intercession as queen for all our needs.

Pope Pius asked that on the feast of the Queenship of Mary each year "the consecration of the human race to the Immaculate Heart of the Blessed Virgin Mary be renewed, cherishing the hope that through such consecration a new era may begin, joyous in Christian peace and in the triumph of religion" (n. 47). While Pope Pius established that the feast was to be celebrated on 31 May each year, it is now celebrated on 22 August, the octave of the feast of the Assumption of Our Lady into heaven. This day is particularly fitting, since on her entry into heaven Mary was crowned Queen of Heaven, a truth we commemorate in the fifth glorious mystery of the rosary.

So there is every reason to call Mary our Queen. We should honour her and put into practice what Pope Pius recommended at the end of his Encyclical: "Let all, therefore, try to approach with greater trust the throne of grace and mercy of our Queen and Mother, and beg for strength in adversity, light in darkness, consolation in sorrow; above all let them strive to free themselves from the slavery of sin and offer an unceasing homage, filled with filial loyalty, to their Queenly Mother" (n. 48).

583 The feast of the nativity of Mary

In our family we celebrate the birthday of Our Lady in a special way to teach the children love for their heavenly mother. Sometimes they ask me about her birth and how we come to celebrate the feast, but I don't know the answers. Can you help me?

There is of course nothing in the Scriptures about Our Lady's birth, so what we know comes from pious traditions. One of the sources is the second century apocryphal writing, the *Protoevangelium of James*, a work whose historical accuracy is not the least bit certain. Nonetheless it is from that work that we obtain the names of Mary's parents, Joachim and Anne, whose feast we celebrate on 26 July.

Another source is the visions of Blessed Anne Catherine Emmerich

(1774-1824), related in her work *The Life of Jesus Christ* (TAN, Rockford Illinois 1986). It gives the same names for Mary's parents. According to this work, St Anne was the second child of Eliud and Ismeria. The first child, also a girl, was named Sobe. Sobe gave birth to a daughter named Mary Salome, who married Zebedee, and from this couple were born the apostles James and John. Thus St Anne would have been the great aunt of the apostles and Jesus their second cousin.

According to the visions of Blessed Anne Catherine, eighteen years after the birth of Sobe St Anne was born. At the age of eighteen she married Joachim, who was of the house of David and a relative of St Joseph. Sometime later they had a daughter whom they named Mary, although this was not the Blessed Virgin. Mary Heli, as she was known, later married Cleophas, or Clopas, and she was at the foot of the cross when Jesus died. Thus St John records in his gospel that "standing by the cross of Jesus were his mother, and his mother's sister, Mary the wife of Clopas" (*Jn* 19:25).

After the birth of Mary Heli nineteen years passed without Joachim and Anne having any more children. During this time they endured the taunts of their servants and other acquaintances for their sterility. Finally, after much prayer and penance, an angel appeared separately to both Joachim and Anne to announce that their prayers had been answered and they would have another child. This was Mary, the Blessed Virgin.

When the time came for Anne to give birth, she asked three women to be with her, among whom were another sister Maraha and her niece Salome, the wife of Zebedee. The apostles James and John had not yet been born. While awaiting the birth these women accompanied Anne in prayer, using some of the psalms. Just before Mary was born a great light surrounded Anne in the form of the burning bush on Mt Horeb. The burning bush is often seen as a figure of Mary, who gave birth without loss of her virginity, just as the bush gave off fire without being consumed. When Mary finally came into the world, St

Anne and the other women gave praise to God. Angels also appeared, announcing that the baby girl was to be called Mary.

Since these details come from the visions of Blessed Anne Catherine Emmerich, we cannot be certain of their historical accuracy but they are at least plausible and consistent with the Scriptures.

When did the Church begin to celebrate this feast? It appears to have originated in Jerusalem in the fifth century in association with the dedication of the *Basilica Sanctae Mariae ubi nata est*, the basilica of Holy Mary where she was born. The basilica, now known as the Basilica of St Anne, is believed to be on the spot where Saints Joachim and Anne lived. In the seventh century the feast was celebrated in the East as the Nativity of the Blessed Virgin Mary.

In Rome the feast came to be celebrated toward the end of the seventh century, brought there by monks from the East. Over the following centuries it gradually spread to other parts of the West. It has been celebrated on 8 September for many centuries in both East and West. That date led to the celebration of Mary's Immaculate Conception on 8 December, nine months earlier.

Our Lady and the Saints

584 Our Lady of Mercy

I read recently that Pope Francis had written to a bishop about some apparitions of Our Lady known as Our Lady of Mercy. What do we know about these apparitions?

Pope Francis placed the Extraordinary Jubilee Year of Mercy under the protection of Our Lady of Mercy, who is venerated under that title in Savona, Italy. On 10 May 2015 the Pope wrote to the bishop of Savona-Noli to this effect, speaking of "the cascade of grace from heaven" at the shrine of Our Lady of Mercy in Savona. "The Mother of Mercy is always close and helps all her children who are in danger", he wrote.

The devotion in Savona owes its origin to the apparitions there in 1536 to Blessed Antonio Botta, a farmer born in 1471. He was a pious man, who always prayed the rosary as he went to work. On Saturday, 18 March 1536, as he was on his knees washing his hands in a little stream, he saw a great light come down from heaven and he heard a voice say, "Rise up and do not doubt – I am the Virgin Mary." He described Our Lady as being dressed in white and surrounded by a dazzling light. She was standing on a large rock overlooking the stream in the valley of the river Letimbro.

Our Lady told him to ask his confessor to announce in the church that the people should fast on the next three Saturdays and make processions in honour of God and his Blessed Mother. She also asked Antonio to go to confession and Communion and to return to the same place on the fourth Saturday to receive another message.

Antonio went immediately to tell the parish priest, Monsignor Bartholomew Zabreri, who in turn passed the news on to the bishop.

Although they were receptive to what Antonio had told them because they knew his sincerity and humility, the mayor, Genoese Doria, was not. Doria asked Antonio to go to him that night, where he questioned him about what he had seen. Soon the whole town learned what had happened and they took the message to heart.

On Saturday, 8 April, the day before Palm Sunday, Antonio returned to the place of the apparition and got down on his knees to pray. Again he saw a bright light, even brighter than the first time, which came down and rested on a rock in the river. He saw in the light the figure of a lady dressed in white with a gold crown on her head. This time Antonio said she stood with her arms extending downwards in a gesture of mercy. Again she asked him for the three Saturdays of fasting and the processions and for the people to give up their evil ways, or their life would be shortened.

When Antonio asked Our Lady for a sign so that the people would believe him she answered that he didn't need one and that she would inspire the people as to what they should do. Then she raised her hands and eyes to heaven, as if in prayer to God, saying "Mercy and not justice", and disappeared. A strong fragrance remained in the place for some time afterwards. Antonio went immediately to tell the people of Savona this second and last message from the Blessed Virgin. Since then Our Lady has been venerated in Savona as Mother of Mercy.

News of the apparitions spread quickly and soon large numbers of people were making pilgrimages to the site. A committee was organised to coordinate the influx of pilgrims, and the large sums of money they gave were used to build a shrine. On 21 April the bishop, Bartholomew a Chiabrera, authorised the building of a chapel. The project was also approved by the municipal council and by Cardinal Augustine Spinola on 24 July. The construction of a new church began on 11 August that year. Four years later the local community declared that 18 March was to be observed each year as a festival with a procession to the shrine.

From 1809 to 1812 Pope Pius VII was imprisoned in Savona by order of Napoleon, and he declared that if he were freed he would place a crown on the statue of Our Lady of Mercy. This he did on 10 May 1815. Now, exactly two hundred years later, Pope Francis has written to the bishop of Savona entrusting the Jubilee Year to Our Lady of Mercy.

We do well, as Pope Francis has done, to entrust ourselves to Our Lady, Mother of Mercy, knowing that she will always hear and answer us.

585 Mary, Undoer of Knots

I understand Pope Francis has devotion to Our Lady under the unusual title "Undoer of Knots". I hadn't heard of this devotion before and found it intriguing. What is its origin?

The devotion is depicted in a Baroque painting by German artist Johann Georg Schmidtner, painted around 1700 and presently kept in the church of St Peter in Perlach, Augsburg. It shows Our Lady surrounded by angels, untying a knot in a long band of cloth, with the band extending from her right hand free of knots and that in the left full of them. She is standing on a crescent moon with her foot on a serpent with a knot in it.

The painting is believed to be connected with an event in the family of the donor, Hieronymus Ambrosius Langenmantel (1641-1718), a canon in the monastery of St Peter in Augsburg. His grandfather was considering separating from his wife and sought help from a Jesuit priest, Jakob Rem. Fr Rem prayed to the Blessed Virgin, begging her, "In this religious act I raise the bond of matrimony: untie all the knots and smooth it out." Immediately peace was restored and the spouses did not separate. In gratitude, the grandson commissioned the painting.

The idea of Our Lady untying knots goes back to St Irenaeus of

Lyons. Comparing the Blessed Virgin with Eve he wrote: "The knot of Eve's disobedience was untied by the obedience of Mary; what the virgin Eve bound by her unbelief, the virgin Mary loosened by her faith" (*Adv. Haer.*, III, 22, 4).

Fr Jorge Mario Bergoglio, the future Pope Francis, saw the painting while studying in Germany and promoted the devotion when he returned to Argentina in the 1980s. In Buenos Aires a copy of the painting has been venerated in the church of San José del Talar since the feast of the Immaculate Conception, 8 December 1996, and on the eighth day of each month large crowds go there to venerate it. Cardinal Bergoglio later had this image of Our Lady engraved on a chalice which he presented to Pope Benedict XVI.

What sort of knots does Our Lady untie? The most important one is the knot of sin, which holds us in some way bound by Satan. The Blessed Virgin, through her obedience, received the Son of God into her womb and it was he who crushed the head of the serpent to untie the knot of original sin (cf. *Gen* 3:15). But Mary can untie all the knots and difficulties that crop in our life: strained and broken relationships, addictions, mental and bodily illnesses, financial problems...

Pope Francis, in an address in St Peter's Square on 12 October 2013, reflected on this role of Mary: "When children disobey their parents, we can say that a little 'knot' is created. This happens if the child acts with an awareness of what he or she is doing, especially if there is a lie involved. At that moment, they break trust with their parents. You know how frequently this happens! Then the relationship with their parents needs to be purified of this fault; the child has to ask forgiveness so that harmony and trust can be restored.

"Something of the same sort happens in our relationship with God. When we do not listen to him, when we do not follow his will, we do concrete things that demonstrate our lack of trust in him – for that is what sin is – and a kind of knot is created deep within us. These knots take away our peace and serenity. They are dangerous, since many knots can form a tangle which gets more and more painful and difficult to undo.

"But we know one thing: nothing is impossible for God's mercy! Even the most tangled knots are loosened by his grace. And Mary, whose 'yes' opened the door for God to undo the knot of the ancient disobedience, is the Mother who patiently and lovingly brings us to God, so that he can untangle the knots of our soul by his fatherly mercy. We all have some of these knots and we can ask in our heart of hearts: What are the knots in my life? 'Father, my knots cannot be undone!' It is a mistake to say anything of the sort! All the knots of our heart, every knot of our conscience, can be undone. Do I ask Mary to help me trust in God's mercy, to undo those knots, to change? She, as a woman of faith, will surely tell you: 'Get up, go to the Lord: he understands you'. And she leads us by the hand as a Mother, our Mother, to the embrace of our Father, the Father of mercies." Truly, there is no knot that cannot be untied through Mary, "Untier of knots".

586 Our Lady of Ransom

I know that in Barcelona and England they celebrate the feast of Our Lady of Ransom on 24 September. I have always been intrigued by the name of this feast. What is the background to it?

The feast goes back to the thirteenth century, when the Moors dominated much of Spain and ruled the Mediterranean. They were taking many Christians captive and selling them as slaves, where they were always in danger of giving up their faith. In order to free some of these captives Our Lady asked St Peter Nolasco to found a new religious Order.

St Peter was born into a wealthy noble family in Languedoc, France, around 1189. From his youth he was noted for his piety, almsgiving and charity. In 1214 at the age of 25 he took a vow of virginity and gave all his possessions to the Church. In order to flee the Albigensians, a heretical sect that was predominant in his area at that time, he moved to Barcelona, Spain, where he became the tutor of the young King James I of Aragon.

On 1 August 1218 Our Lady appeared to him as well as to his confessor St Raymund of Peñafort and to King James, asking them to establish a religious Order dedicated to ransoming captives from the Moors. The members of the Order were to undertake to free captives and to offer themselves, if necessary, as ransom. Word of the apparitions soon spread all over Spain.

On 10 August of that year, during Mass in the cathedral of Barcelona celebrated by the bishop and attended by the king, St Raymund told the congregation about his vision. The king asked the bishop to bless this obviously heaven-sent initiative and the bishop bestowed the habit on St Peter, who took a solemn vow to give himself as a hostage if necessary.

On 10 August 1223 the Order was legally established by King James. Its official name was the Royal and Military Order of Our Lady of Mercy for the Redemption of Captives but it was more popularly known as the Mercedarians, from the Spanish name for mercy, *merced*. The Order was approved by Pope Gregory IX in 1235. It originally attracted both young noblemen, who could use their wealth to ransom captives, and friars in Holy Orders, whose role was to pray for the success of the work of the knights. St Peter Nolasco was the first Superior but was never ordained a priest. In addition to the three traditional vows, the knights took a fourth vow to devote their wealth and their liberty if necessary for the ransom of captives. They wore a white habit, signifying innocence on which was emblazoned the coat of arms of King James. St Peter died in Barcelona in 1256 and was canonised in 1628.

In 1615 a feast of Our Lady of Mercy was instituted to be celebrated on September 24. At first it was observed only in the Order itself but it soon spread to Spain and France. In 1696 Pope Innocent XII extended the feast to the whole Church. Its official title in Latin is *Solemnitas Descensionis Beatae Mariæ Virginis de Mercede*, the Solemnity of the Descent of the Blessed Virgin Mary of Mercy. The feast is no longer celebrated in the universal calendar.

Our Lady of Ransom, or of Mercy, is the principal patroness of Barcelona. In England devotion to Our Lady of Ransom was revived in modern times to pray for the rescue of England as Our Lady's dowry. There is also great devotion to Our Lady under that title in Peru as well as in Sicily, which suffered much at the hands of the Moors. After the Second Vatican Council the name of the feast was changed to Our Lady of Mercy.

In 1891 Pope Leo XIII, in his Encyclical *Octobri Mense*, looking at the needs of the Church and the world at that time, wrote powerfully of the role of Our Lady as Mother of Mercy: "The design of this most dear mercy, realised by God in Mary and confirmed by the testament of Christ, was comprehended at the beginning, and accepted with the utmost joy by the Holy Apostles and the earliest believers… No other reason is needed than that of a divine faith which, by a powerful and most pleasant impulse, persuades us towards Mary" (n. 5).

Today too, as we look around us and see so many people held captive by sin and disbelief, we do well to have recourse to Our Lady of Mercy, begging her to free them from this bondage and restore them to the freedom of the children of God.

587 St Michael, St Gabriel and St Raphael

Why do we call St Michael, St Gabriel and St Raphael saints, and why does the Church celebrate their feast day each year?

As you imply in your question, we normally reserve the term saint for human beings who led exemplary, holy lives and who have been recognised as saints by the Church. Why would we include angels, or in this case archangels, among the saints? The answer can only be that the tradition of the Church has for many centuries included these archangels among the saints and has given them that title. If a saint is someone who led a holy life then surely the angels deserve this title. This does not mean that we are meant to imitate angels, for as purely spiritual beings they are able to do things we humans cannot do, but we can certainly invoke their intercession for our many needs.

Why do we celebrate their feast day each year? Each of these archangels is mentioned in the Bible and so it was natural that devotion to them would have taken root and grown over the years. Let us look at each one in particular.

We can begin with St Michael, whose name means "Who is like God", alluding to his special place among the angels and his power over Satan. St Michael appears four times in the Bible, two of them in the book of Daniel. In the first, Daniel has a vision of a powerful man or angel who tells him, "The prince of the kingdom of Persia withstood me twenty-one days; but Michael, one of the chief princes, came to help me... There is none who contends by my side against these except Michael, your prince" (*Dan* 10:13, 21). The second is more succinct: "At that time shall arise Michael, the great prince who has charge of your people" (*Dan* 12:1).

In the New Testament, in the letter of St Jude, we again find St Michael, now called an archangel, battling against the devil: "But when the archangel Michael, contending with the devil, disputed about the body of Moses, he did not presume to pronounce a reviling judgment upon him, but said, 'the Lord rebuke you'" (*Jude* 9). The most well known biblical reference to St Michael is in the book of Revelation: "Now war arose in heaven, Michael and his angels fighting against the dragon; and the dragon and his angels fought, but they were defeated and there was no longer any place for them in heaven. And the great dragon was thrown down, that ancient serpent, who is called the Devil and Satan, the deceiver of the whole world – he was thrown down to the earth, and his angels were thrown down with him" (*Rev* 12:7-9). It is especially on account of this text that St Michael is often depicted as a warrior, with a helmet and shield, standing over the dragon and striking him with a lance.

In Rome the feast of St Michael has been celebrated since at least the fifth century and it was celebrated on 29 September, as it is today, from at least the seventh century.

St Gabriel, whose name means "power, or strength, of God", is also mentioned in both Testaments. In the Old Testament he interprets the prophet Daniel's visions (*Dan* 8:15-26, 9:20-27), and in the New Testament he appears first to Zachary to announce the birth of John the Baptist, and then to Our Lady to announce the birth of Jesus (cf. *Lk* 1:11-38). St Gabriel is not called an archangel in the Bible. The feast of St Gabriel, which was celebrated in the East from the ninth century, was included in the liturgical calendar of the Roman Rite for the first time in 1921, to be celebrated on 24 March, the day before the feast of the Annunciation. In 1969 it was transferred to 29 September and joined to the celebration of St Michael and St Raphael.

The name Raphael means "God heals" or "Medicine of God". St Raphael appears in the Book of Tobit in the Old Testament, where he comes as a young man and accompanies the young Tobias on a long journey to recover money owed to his father, bringing back medicine to cure his father's blindness and finding a good wife. At the end of the journey he identifies himself: "I am Raphael, one of the seven holy angels who present the prayers of the saints and enter into the presence of the glory of the Lord" (*Tob* 12:15).

His feast has been celebrated since the sixteenth century in various locations where he is said to have appeared, and it was added to the general Roman calendar in 1921, to be celebrated on 24 October. In 1969 it was transferred to 29 September, where it is today.

588 St George

I recently came across the feast of St George, on 23 April, and noticed that he is patron saint of England. I don't know anything about him. Can you tell me who he was and why he is often depicted doing battle with a dragon?

It is likely that St George was born into a noble Greek Christian family in Lydda, in Palestine, sometime between 275 and 285 AD. His father, Gerontios, was a Greek from Cappadocia and an officer in the Roman army and his mother, Polychronia, was a Greek native of Lydda. When George was fourteen his father died, followed by his mother a few years later.

After his mother's death George went to Nicomedia, the imperial city of the time, and presented himself to the Emperor Diocletian to become a solider. Diocletian welcomed him with open arms since he had known his father Gerontios and regarded him as one of his finest soldiers. By his late twenties George had risen through the ranks to become a tribune and was stationed as a guard of the Emperor at Nicomedia.

In 302 Diocletian issued an order that every Christian soldier should be arrested and all should offer a sacrifice to the Roman gods. George objected and went to see Diocletian, who was upset, not wanting to lose his best tribune and the son of Gerontios. The Emperor tried to convert him, offering him gifts of land, money and slaves, but to no avail. George refused to accept the gifts and held steadfastly to his faith.

What is more, George publicly denounced the Emperor's edict and declared himself a Christian in front of his fellow soldiers and tribunes. This left the Emperor with no choice but to have him executed. Before his execution George gave his wealth to the poor and prepared himself for the ordeal. After several torture sessions including being lacerated on a wheel of swords, from which he was resuscitated three times, he was finally decapitated on 23 April 303. According to one account, a witness to his death convinced the Empress Alexandra and a pagan priest, Athanasius, to become Christians and so they joined George in martyrdom. His body was returned to Lydda for burial, where Christians soon began to venerate him as a martyr.

A church built in Lydda during the reign of the Emperor Constantine I (306-337), was consecrated to "a man of the highest distinction", according to the historian Eusebius. Later this was asserted to be St George. In any case by the time of the Muslim conquest in the seventh century, there was a basilica dedicated to St George in Lydda. It was destroyed in 1010 but was later rebuilt and dedicated to St George by the Crusaders.

During the fourth century veneration of St George spread from Palestine through Lebanon to the rest of the Eastern Roman Empire and to Georgia. It reached the Western Roman Empire in the fifth century. In 494 Pope Gelasius included St George in a canon of those "whose names are justly reverenced among men, but whose acts are known only to God".

As for the matter of the dragon, this can only be called a legend, with no historical authenticity. Apparently the legend was brought back by the Crusaders. According to the story, a dragon made its nest at the spring that provided water for the city of Silene, which might be Cyrene in Libya or Lydda in Palestine. In order to distract the dragon so that the people could collect water, they offered the animal a sheep or, if no sheep was available, a maiden, determining who it was to be by drawing lots. One day the lot fell to the princess. As she was being offered to the dragon St George appeared and, after making the sign of the Cross, killed the dragon and rescued the princess. The citizens of the place then abandoned their ancestral paganism and converted to Christianity.

Following the legend, St George is often depicted with a red cross on a white background on his armour, riding on a white horse and killing a dragon with a spear, with a woman standing in the background. The flag of England features the red cross of St George on a white background, and the flag of the United Kingdom also incorporates the St George cross. Other places which have St George as a patron, including Georgia, Genoa and Barcelona, also have the cross on their flag.

589 St Thomas à Becket

I have always liked the play "Murder in the Cathedral" about St Thomas à Becket, but I don't really know much about the saint. What can you tell me about him and why do we celebrate his feast after Christmas?

Starting with your second question, the reason we celebrate his feast in the octave of Christmas, on 29 December, is simply that he died on that day in 1170. He is often known as St Thomas of Canterbury because he was Archbishop of Canterbury. He has an interesting story which, in some ways, parallels that of his namesake, St Thomas More, four centuries later.

St Thomas was born in 1118 or 1120 of parents from Normandy who had settled in England some years previously. At the age of ten he was sent as a student to Merton Priory and later to a grammar school in London. Around the age of twenty he also studied in Paris. On his return Thomas began to work as a clerk and found his way into the service of Theobald of Bec, the Archbishop of Canterbury. Theobald sent him to Bologna and Auxerre to study canon law and in 1154 he ordained him a deacon, giving him several offices, including Archdeacon of Canterbury.

After the reigning King Stephen died, Theobald recommended

Thomas to the young King Henry II as his Lord Chancellor, and he was appointed to that important post at the age of thirty-six in 1155. Even though Henry was twelve years his junior, the two became very good friends and they hunted and went to war together, Thomas distinguishing himself by his bravery. Nothing was ever alleged against him in the area of chastity, and he severely punished bad language, lying and unchastity. King Henry even sent his son Henry to live in the Becket household, where he said he received more fatherly love in one day than he did from his father in a lifetime.

Several months after Theobald's death, Henry proposed that Thomas be made Archbishop of Canterbury, something he resisted. But at the insistence of Cardinal Henry of Pisa he accepted and was ordained priest on the Saturday after Pentecost, 2 June 1162, and bishop the following day. It seems it was Thomas who obtained for England the privilege of celebrating the feast of the Blessed Trinity on the Sunday after Pentecost, the anniversary of his consecration. The feast was adopted by the Pope a century later and afterwards it was extended to the whole Church.

After his consecration as Archbishop, Thomas began to live a very austere life, practising fasting, using a hair shirt, keeping long vigils and constant prayers, and giving up all signs of the worldliness he had previously lived. He went barefoot to receive the papal envoy bringing him the pallium, the insignia of his office as Archbishop of Canterbury. Then, contrary to the King's wish, he resigned his role as Chancellor. When Thomas began to reclaim estates that belonged to the Church, he incurred the displeasure of King Henry, as he did when he refused to pay a tax to the sheriff for the royal treasury. Little by little the relations with Henry became progressively strained. When Henry tried to get the bishops to accept the Constitutions of Clarendon, a statement of rights of the crown over the Church, Thomas steadfastly refused.

Finally, in 1164 Thomas was convicted by a state council of contempt of royal authority and mismanagement in his role as Chancellor. He fled to the continent, where he was welcomed by Pope Alexander III. Meanwhile Henry confiscated all Thomas' property and banished his family. In 1170, Pope Alexander sent delegates to the King to mediate a solution and Henry offered a compromise that allowed Thomas to return to England. There Thomas excommunicated the bishops of York, London and Salisbury, who had crowned Henry's heir apparent, "young Henry", as the Young King, contrary to the convention that coronations were reserved to the Archbishop of Canterbury. At this Henry II expressed his extreme anger, and on 29 December 1170 four knights confronted Thomas in the cathedral at Canterbury and killed him with swords. He died saying, "For the name of Jesus and the protection of the Church, I am ready to embrace death." He was found with a hairshirt under his vestments.

Soon he was being venerated as a martyr all over Europe and in 1173, a little over two years after his death, he was canonised by Pope Alexander III. The following year Henry humbled himself with public penance at Becket's tomb.

590 St Dymphna

A friend recently told me she was praying to St Dymphna for her mother, who is suffering from a mental illness, since there is a tradition of praying to that saint for the mentally ill. Who is St Dymphna?

The first thing to say is that the story of St Dymphna, also spelled Dympna and Dimpna, is shrouded in mystery, but there is no question of a tradition of invoking her for the mentally ill.

The earliest historical account of veneration of the saint dates from the middle of the thirteenth century in Belgium, where the Irish saint Dymphna died and was buried in the seventh century. The author of the account, a canon of the church of St Aubert at Cambrai, wrote a life of the saint commissioned by the Bishop of Cambrai, Guy I (1238–1247). He states expressly that the basis for his biography was oral tradition. In any case, he acknowledges that St Dymphna had been venerated for many years in a church in Gheel, in the province of Antwerp in Belgium.

According to the account, Dymphna was born in Ireland in the seventh century, the daughter of a pagan Irish king named Damon and a devout, very beautiful Catholic mother. When Dymphna was only fourteen, her mother died. Damon loved his wife dearly and after her death his mental health declined greatly. When at length he decided to remarry he looked for a woman who resembled his deceased wife, but none could be found. He then began to desire his daughter who bore a strong resemblance to her mother.

When Dymphna learned of her father's intentions she fled Ireland along with her elderly confessor Fr Gerebernus and two servants. They sailed to the continent and landed in Belgium, where they took up residence near the chapel of St Martin in the town of Gheel. According to one tradition, St Dymphna built a hospice there for the poor and sick of the region.

After some time her father sent some of his men to try to find her, and since she had used coins from Ireland this allowed them to trace her to Gheel. They reported this to Damon, who then went to Belgium to try to take Dymphna back to Ireland. When she resisted, Damon had his soldiers kill Fr Gerebernus and then, in a fit of rage, he drew his sword and cut off Dymphna's head. She was only fifteen at the time.

The people of the town buried the two bodies in a cave near Gheel. Years later, when it was planned to transfer the remains to a more suitable place, workmen found the bones in two sarcophagi, one of which had a red tile with the inscription "Dympna". According to the tradition, immediately after the discovery of the bodies a number of people who had visited the tomb and were suffering from epilepsy and various mental illnesses were cured. This is apparently the origin of the custom of praying to her for those with mental illness.

The remains of St Dymphna were put in a silver reliquary in a church named after her in Gheel, while those of St Gerebernus were transferred to Xanten, an historic town in North Rhine-Westphalia in Germany. In 1489 the church of St Dymphna in Gheel was destroyed by fire. It was replaced by a magnificent structure, built on the site where her body was first buried. It was consecrated in 1532 and still stands today.

St Dymphna's feast is celebrated on 15 May, where it appears in the Roman martyrology. She is venerated not only by Catholics but also by the Eastern Orthodox. She is invoked as the patron saint of the nervous, emotionally disturbed, mentally ill and those suffering from neurological disorders. She is also the patron saint of victims of incest. St Dymphna is often depicted in artworks with a sword in her hand and a devil in chains at her feet.

591 St Catherine of Siena

I have often heard people talk about St Catherine of Siena but I know practically nothing about her. When did she live and what was she famous for?

St Catherine was one of the most influential figures of the fourteenth century. She was born in Siena, Italy, in 1347 to Giacomo and Lapa di Benincasa along with her twin sister Giovanna, the twenty-third and twenty-fourth of twenty-five children. Half of the children had already died and Giovanna too died shortly after birth. Catherine was so cheerful that her parents gave her the nickname Euphrosyne, the Greek word for joy.

When she was only six Catherine had her first vision of Christ and at the age of seven she promised to give her whole life to God. At the age of sixteen she refused the request of her parents to marry her deceased sister's husband and instead entered the Third Order of St Dominic, living a life of prayer and arduous penance in a small room in the family home.

In 1366 she experienced what she later described in her letters as a "mystical marriage" with Jesus and two years later she received special revelations of divine mysteries, which brought her to a sort of mystical death in which she had a vision of hell, purgatory and heaven, and she heard a divine command to become involved in the affairs of the world. In 1375 while in Pisa she received the stigmata, which were visible only to her during her lifetime but clearly seen after her death. Her holiness and charitable activities, along with her great personal charm and wisdom, soon led a group of men and women, including priests, to gather around her.

From the age of twenty-four she became more and more involved in public life, travelling around northern and central Italy advocating the reform of the clergy and calling people to repentance and renewal through total love for God. In Pisa in 1375 she used her influence to sway that city away from an alliance with several Italian cities which were forming a league to free themselves from the Pope's civil authority. She began dictating numerous letters through her scribes to people in authority, calling for peace between the republics and principalities of Italy. Almost four hundred of her letters have survived.

Moved by her great love for the Church, she carried on a long correspondence with Pope Gregory XI, begging him to return to Rome from Avignon in France, where the Popes had resided for over 70 years. In 1376 Catherine went to Avignon herself as ambassador of the Republic of Florence, which had been placed under interdict, to try to broker peace with the Papal States, a peace which came two years later. While in Avignon Catherine urged the Pope to return to Rome to fulfil a promise he had made to return, a promise he had not divulged to anyone. Seeing Catherine's knowledge of his promise as a sign from God, the Pope returned in January 1377.

After Pope Gregory died in 1378, Urban VI was elected to succeed him but some of the Cardinals, especially the French, were unhappy with him and declared his election invalid, choosing Clement VII instead. The Western Schism, which would last for forty years, had begun. Catherine exhausted herself trying to heal this division, writing letters to the princes and leaders of Europe. Such was her stature that Pope Urban summoned her to Rome to advise him.

For many years Catherine ate very little, surviving with the help of the Eucharist, which she received almost daily. From the beginning of 1380 she could neither eat food nor swallow water and on 21 April she suffered a stroke which paralysed her from the waist down. She died in Rome on 29 April 1380 at the age of thirty-three. She was canonised by Pope Pius II in 1461 and was named a Doctor of the Church by Pope Paul VI in 1970. In 1999 Pope St John Paul II made her a patron saint of Europe along with Saints Edith Stein, Bridget of Sweden, Benedict, Cyril and Methodius.

St Catherine's most important writing, apart from her letters, is her *Dialogue*, a dialogue between God the Father and Catherine. Some of her contemporaries said that much of the book was dictated while she was in ecstasy. St Catherine was an early Christian feminist in the truest sense: a woman in love with God and at the same time a woman involved in the affairs of the world.

592 St Francis de Paola

I have heard that St Francis de Paola, a little known saint, performed some amazing miracles. Could you shed some light on his life and miracles?

St Francis was born in Paola, in Calabria, Italy in 1416 of very holy parents. They had not been able to have children for some years after their marriage but after much prayer, especially through the intercession of St Francis of Assisi, they were finally able to have three children, the first of whom was Francis. While still an infant he developed a swelling which endangered his sight in one eye. Again his parents had recourse to St Francis, promising that if Francis was cured he would spend a year in the "little habit" of St Francis in one of his monasteries. He was cured immediately.

Even in his childhood he showed signs of great holiness and at the age of thirteen he entered a monastery of the Franciscans in order to fulfil the promise of his parents. There he was distinguished by his love of prayer and penance, his humility and obedience. At the end of the year he went with his parents on a pilgrimage to Assisi, Rome and other holy places. On returning he began to live a life of solitude in an isolated place on his father's estate. Later he moved to a cave on the coast, where he remained alone for six years in prayer and penance.

In 1435, at the age of nineteen, he was joined by two young men. They built three cells and a chapel and so a new religious community began. The number of followers gradually increased and, around 1454, with the permission of the Archbishop of Cosenza, Francis built a large monastery and a church. The local people, including the nobles, were delighted with this new development and they helped build the monastery, carrying stones and joining in the work.

The rule of life of the new community was one of great severity. They observed perpetual abstinence from meat and meat products including eggs, butter, cheese and milk, and they also abstained from fish. Francis believed that heroic penance was necessary as a means of spiritual growth. The brothers lived in great poverty but their distinguishing mark was humility, as they sought to remain unknown and hidden from the world. The community was originally called the Hermits of St Francis of Assisi but later they obtained permission from the Holy See to be called the Minims, meaning the least of all. After the order was approved by the Pope, Francis founded new monasteries in Calabria and Sicily, plus convents of nuns and a third order for lay people, following the example of St Francis of Assisi.

Among St Francis' miracles were prophecies that later came true. Beginning in 1447 he told various people that Constantinople would fall to the Turks, as happened in 1453. Later he foretold the capture of Otranto, which was taken by the Turks in 1480, and its subsequent liberation by the King of Naples.

Among the more extraordinary miracles was the raising of a young boy from the dead. Francis' own nephew, Nicholas Alesso, had died and the Mass and Divine Office were said for the repose of his soul. St Francis asked that the body be carried from the church into his cell, where he prayed over it and the boy was restored to life and given back to his mother, St Francis' sister. The young man later entered the Minims and became famous for his sanctity.

There are also accounts of St Francis raising animals from the dead. According to one tradition, some workmen killed St Francis' pet lamb Martinello, roasted it and were eating it when the saint came looking for it. They said they had eaten it since they had no other food. He asked what they had done with the fleece and bones and they said they had thrown them into the furnace. St Francis went over to the furnace, looked into the fire and said "Martinello, come out!" The lamb jumped out, completely unharmed, bleating happily on being reunited with its master.

St Francis later went to France at the request of the dying King Louis XI, only after being ordered to do so by the Pope. On the way he cured many people in Provence who were stricken by the plague. After Louis' death, his successor Charles VIII kept the saint there and built a monastery for the Minims at Plessis. When Charles died, his successor Louis XII also kept St Francis there and it was in Plessis that he died at the age of 91 on good Friday in 1507. He was canonised in 1519. His feast day is April 2, the day of his death.

593 St Marie-Alphonsine

An Australian friend recently went to Rome for the canonisation of a relative, Sr Marie-Alphonsine, and although she told me something about her, I did not get a clear picture. Can you tell me more about her?

Sr Marie-Alphonsine Danil Ghattas was born Soultaneh Marie to a devout Palestinian family in Jerusalem on 4 October 1843. Her mother Catherine attended Mass everyday and her father Daniel hosted a group of neighbours and friends every evening to recite the rosary before a statue of the Blessed Virgin Mary. When she was fourteen she felt the call to religious life and in 1860 joined the Congregation of St Joseph of the Apparition, taking the name Marie-Alphonsine. She had a calm, thoughtful personality and was exceptionally humble.

In 1862 she was sent to teach catechism in Bethlehem, where she established religious associations promoting devotion to Our Lady through the rosary. At that time Our Lady began to appear to her, asking her to found a Palestinian congregation to be known as the Sisters of the Rosary. The apparitions went on for four years. Our Lady referred her to Fr Yussef Tannous, a Latin Patriarchate priest, who was to become her spiritual father and the apparent founder of the congregation, since Sr Marie-Alphonsine preferred to remain in the background. Out of humility she revealed the apparitions only to Fr Tannous. They remained a secret for fifty-three years, coming to light only because Fr Tannous asked her to write down what she had seen and heard.

While Our Lady had been very clear about making the new foundation, Sr Marie-Alphonsine found it very difficult to leave the Congregation of St Joseph, which she loved with all her heart. Finally, it was love for Our Lady and trust in her that moved her to leave and join the Sisters of Our Lady of the Rosary. The new foundation began in 1880, when seven girls prepared by Fr Tannous received the religious habit from the Patriarch. In 1883, with permission from the Holy See, Sr Marie-Alphonsine left the Sisters of St Joseph and entered the new congregation, receiving the habit on the feast of Our Lady of the Rosary, 7 October. It is the only Palestinian women's religious congregation.

Already during her lifetime Sr Marie-Alphonsine was credited with working a miracle. In July 1885 she was sent to Jaffa in Galilee with another nun. Sometime later a young girl named Nathira fell into a deep cistern filled with water. As there was no way to rescue her, Sr Marie-Alphonsine threw her large rosary to her and asked Our Lady to save her, meanwhile saying the rosary with some young people. Nathira emerged from the cistern alive and well. She later said she had seen a great light and a ladder in the form of a rosary to help her climb out.

In 1886 Sr Marie-Alphonsine founded a school for girls in Beit Sahour and in 1893 she established a workshop in Bethlehem to provide work for poor girls. She also worked in Salt, Nablus, Jerusalem, Zababdeh, and finally Ain Karem, where she established an orphanage. She died there in 1927 praying the rosary with her sister, Sr Hanneh Danil Ghattas, on the feast of the Annunciation, 25 March. She was the apostle of hope and trust in God and in the Blessed Virgin, and of the rosary. She firmly believed in Our Lady's words, "The rosary is your treasure."

On 15 October 1994 Pope John Paul II recognised her heroic virtues and on 22 November 2009 she was beatified by Cardinal Angelo Amato, Prefect of the Congregation for the Causes of Saints, in the Basilica of the Annunciation in Nazareth. On that occasion Pope Benedict XVI said: "Her merit is in having founded a Religious Congregation of women of the place with the aim of religious teaching, to overcome illiteracy and to improve the condition of women in the land where Jesus himself exalted their dignity. ... The beatification of this impressive woman is a comfort, especially for the Catholic community of the Holy Land and an invitation to rely, with firm hope, on Divine Providence and the maternal protection of Mary."

She was canonised in Rome by Pope Francis on 17 May 2015 along with another Palestinian nun, Sr Miriam Bawardy, who was born in Galilee in 1843 and died in 1878. We pray that through their intercession Our Lord will bring peace to that troubled land.

594 Venerable Montserrat Grases

A friend recently told me about a teenage girl who has cancer and whose family and friends are praying to the Venerable Montserrat Grases. I had never heard of her. Who was she?

Montse, as she was commonly known, was born in Barcelona, Spain, in 1941, the second of nine children of a close-knit, faith-filled Catholic family. Her older brother Henry became a priest for the Archdiocese of Barcelona. After finishing high school she began studies in domestic science, design, cooking and artistic techniques at the Women's Professional School in Barcelona.

Montse was a bright and cheerful girl, tall, strong and pretty, who loved life. She was good at basketball, tennis and skiing and she loved hiking in the mountains. She was also good at singing, playing the guitar and acting. She loved dancing the sardana, a traditional folk dance in Catalonia. She had a strong temper but little by little, with the help of prayer, she learned to dominate it.

At the age of thirteen she began to attend a centre of formation for girls run by members of Opus Dei and she came to have a strong life of piety, with great devotion to Our Lord and Our Lady. She was always concerned to help her friends come closer to God. On Christmas Eve, 1957 she asked to be admitted to Opus Dei in a life of celibacy. She was radiant with joy.

The following month, in January 1958, while skiing with a group of friends she had a fall which left her leg sore. She saw a doctor, who gave it little importance and recommended that she use a kneepad. Little by little the leg swelled and the pain increased. In June she was diagnosed with incurable Ewings Sarcoma, a cancer of the bone, but her parents thought it best not to tell her immediately. In July, after returning from a family holiday, Montse went into her parents' bedroom at one in the morning and asked to be told what she had. Her father told her and she reacted with such calmness that they were amazed. Her only question was, "What if they cut off my leg?" Her father told her it was not possible and the only solution was to leave everything in the hands of God. Montse went back to her room, did her examination of conscience and when her mother went in to check on her five minutes later she was sound asleep.

The following day she went to inform the directress of the Opus Dei centre, who already knew of the cancer. There they overheard her singing a Mexican song to God: "When I lived most happily without thinking of affection, you wanted me to love you, and I loved you with a passion. And I will continue to love you until after death. I love you with all my soul and the soul never dies." She chatted at length with the directress and told her: "I'm happy because I know everything now and I'm ready for everything."

After that she always acted with the greatest naturalness and cheerfulness, not wanting to talk about herself but turning the conversation to others. Even though the pain was considerable from September on, she was able to travel to Rome in November, where she met the founder of Opus Dei, Mgr. Josemaría Escrivá. He gave her a rosary, a prayer card and a medal and told her he would pray for her to get better but that he accepted God's will in everything. He was very moved.

From February on her leg became increasingly swollen and extremely painful, leaving her with sleepless nights. She accepted the pain with great fortitude and offered it for the Pope and the founder of Opus Dei. She was very anxious to go to heaven and spoke about it with great naturalness and joy. Finally, on Holy Thursday, 26 March 1959, she surrendered her soul to God after looking at an image of Our Lady beside her bed and whispering: "How much I love you. When are you coming to take me?" She was only seventeen.

Such was her fame of sanctity that only three years later her cause of beatification was opened in Barcelona. On 26 April 2016 Pope Francis signed a decree on her heroic virtues, making her the Venerable Montserrat Grases and paving the way for her beatification.

Many favours have been attributed to her intercession, among them that of a Barcelona doctor who in March 2003 suffered a cardiac arrest in the street. Two doctors who happened to pass by gave him cardio-pulmonary resuscitation and he was taken to hospital. His wife and friends prayed to Montse for his complete recovery. He said afterwards, "Nobody believed I would survive, or if I did, they all thought I would be left with heart disease or brain damage. I could have been left paralytic, blind, or simply in a vegetative state." In fact he is in good health and leads a normal life.

Apparitions

595 Our Lady of Mt Carmel

The Church celebrates the feast of Our Lady of Mt Carmel on July 16 each year but I don't know anything about its background, although I associate it with the scapular. Does it involve an apparition of Our Lady? I would appreciate your help.

Let me begin by saying something about Mt Carmel, which is located on the Mediterranean coast of Israel, overlooking the modern-day city of Haifa. Its name comes from the Hebrew word meaning "garden" or "garden land", undoubtedly because of its lush green plant life. The prophet Isaiah writes of it: "The wilderness and the dry land shall be glad, the desert shall rejoice and blossom; like the lily it shall blossom abundantly, and rejoice with joy and singing. The glory of Lebanon shall be given to it, the majesty of Carmel and Sharon" (*Is* 35:1-2). It was on Mt Carmel that the prophet Elijah defended the true faith and triumphed over the false prophets of Baal (cf. *1 Kings* 18:20-40). It was also there that he prayed for rain when Israel was in a prolonged drought and saw a small cloud rise out of the sea which brought heavy rain (cf. *1 Kings* 18:42-45).

The feast of Our Lady of Mt Carmel is associated with the Carmelite order, which had its beginnings on Mt Carmel in the twelfth century. Some penitential pilgrims who had gone there from Europe came to live together as hermits, following the example of Elijah. They built a chapel dedicated to Our Lady and became known as the Brothers of St Mary of Mt Carmel, or of Our Lady of Mt Carmel.

The Carmelites were approved as a religious order by Pope Innocent IV in 1247. Like the Dominicans and Franciscans, the Carmelites are a mendicant order. Their particular charism is to follow the prophet Elijah in loving the true God and making his Word known in the world, and to follow Our Lady in loving Our Lord and following in his footsteps.

Around 1235 the Carmelites were forced to abandon the Holy Land in the face of the incursions and persecution of the Saracens, who were reconquering the Holy Land from the crusaders. Most of them returned to their countries of origin in Europe, many of them to England, where there is documentary evidence of their presence around 1241-1242.

According to a pious tradition dating to the fourteenth century, Our Lady appeared to St Simon Stock, English Prior General of the Carmelites, on 16 July 1251. In answer to his appeal for help for his order, which was then misunderstood and attacked by the secular clergy and other religious orders, she offered him a scapular and said: "Take, beloved son, this scapular of your order as a badge of my confraternity and for you and all the Carmelites a special sign of grace. Whoever dies in this garment will not suffer everlasting fire. It is the sign of salvation, a safeguard in dangers, a pledge of peace and of the covenant" (cf. J. Flader, *Question Time 1*, q. 136).

So the date of July 16 for the feast of Our Lady of Mt Carmel goes back to that apparition of Our Lady to St Simon Stock. And the name Our Lady of Mt Carmel is the title given to the Blessed Virgin in her role of patroness of the Carmelite order. The feast of Our Lady of Mt Carmel is commonly associated with the scapular, for obvious reasons.

A "Doctrinal Statement on the Brown Scapular of Our Lady of Mount Carmel", approved by the Vatican's Congregation for Divine Worship on 29 November 1996 states: "Devotion to Our Lady of Mount Carmel is bound to the history and spiritual values of the Order of the Brothers of the Blessed Virgin Mary of Mount Carmel and is expressed through the scapular."

When was the feast first celebrated? It was instituted by the

Carmelites between 1376 and 1386 under the title "Commemoration of the Blessed Virgin Mary" to commemorate the victory of the order over its attackers through papal approval. The feast was to be celebrated on July 16 and was first approved by Pope Sixtus V in 1587. Little by little, with papal approval, it spread to more and more countries and in 1726 it was included in the universal calendar by Pope Benedict XIII. At present it is celebrated as an optional memorial, so it is not celebrated liturgically if it falls on a Sunday.

596 Our Lady of Guadalupe

A friend from Mexico often speaks of her devotion to Our Lady of Guadalupe and of the remarkable cloth image associated with it. What is so significant about this image?

There are a number of images of Our Lord and Our Lady around the world which are miraculous in themselves, independently of the devotion that has grown up around them. Two examples are the Shroud of Turin and the image of Our Lady of Guadalupe.

The image of Our Lady of Guadalupe dates back to the first half of the sixteenth century in Mexico. The Spanish at that time were having only limited success in converting the Aztecs, who held firmly to their traditional beliefs and practices. These included many tens of thousands of human sacrifices each year to appease their gods.

According to the tradition, on 9 December 1531 an early Aztec convert named Juan Diego was walking near Tepeyac Hill outside Mexico City when he saw a beautiful young woman whom he recognised as the Blessed Virgin Mary. Speaking in his native language, Our Lady asked Juan Diego to have a shrine built there in her honour. He approached the bishop, the Spanish Franciscan Fray Juan de Zumárraga, but the bishop was naturally sceptical and told Juan Diego to ask the woman for a sign.

Three days later, on 12 December, Juan Diego was hurrying past the hill to attend to his dying uncle when Our Lady once again appeared to him. He explained that he was in a hurry to look after his uncle but Our Lady put him at ease, saying that his uncle would be cured, as in fact he already was. Juan Diego then asked Our Lady for some sign that he could take to the bishop and Mary told him to go to the top of the hill where he would find some flowers growing. He did as he was told, even though December was not the season for flowers and normally nothing grew on the barren hilltop. To his surprise he found some beautiful flowers in full bloom. Our Lady helped him arrange the flowers in his cactus fibre cloak, or tilma, and he went off to give them to the bishop. When he arrived at the bishop's house and showed him the roses, an image of Our Lady suddenly appeared on his tilma.

The image now venerated in the Basilica of Our Lady of Guadalupe in Mexico City is the one that appeared miraculously on Juan Diego's tilma almost five hundred years ago. There are a number of extraordinary features of the image.

The first is the very preservation of the fabric itself. Normally a cactus fibre garment would disintegrate within some twenty to forty years, yet here the fabric is still intact after almost five centuries. Another is the brightness of the image, which has remained virtually unchanged over all these years. Various scientific studies have shown that the image was not painted, for it contains no pigment known to man. What is more, the image repaired itself after a nitric acid spill in 1791 that damaged it considerably. And an attempt to destroy the image completely by exploding a bomb on the altar immediately beneath it on 14 November 1921 left the image unharmed, even though a brass crucifix on the altar was bent double.

Perhaps the most extraordinary feature came to light when the image was photographed and then magnified 2500 times. In the partially closed eyes of Our Lady on the rough fabric there appeared the reflection of all those present in front of Juan Diego when the image first appeared. They include the bishop, his entourage and a family, a total of thirteen people.

Because of the miraculous origin of the image and the symbolism on it, eight million Aztecs were converted to the faith in the next seven years, at a time when millions were being lost to the faith in Protestant Europe. It is no wonder that Guadalupe is the most visited Marian shrine in the world. The feast of Our Lady of Guadalupe is celebrated on 12 December, and that of St Juan Diego, who was canonised by Pope St John Paul II in 2002, on 9 December.

Our Lady of Guadalupe has, among others, the titles Queen of Mexico, Patroness of the Americas and Protectress of Unborn Children.

597 Our Lady of Luján

A group of us were talking recently about large pilgrimages in different countries and someone mentioned the pilgrimage to Our Lady of Luján in Argentina. Can you tell me something about it?

When it comes to large pilgrimages the youth pilgrimage to Our Lady of Luján outside Buenos Aires might very well be the biggest in the world. Each year for the first Sunday of October some one million young people walk overnight the 68 kilometres from Buenos Aires to Luján to honour Our Lady there. The walk alone takes some fifteen hours.

Devotion to Our Lady of Luján goes back to 1630 when a farmer who had emigrated to Argentina from Portugal saw the lack of faith among the people of his village of Sumampa and the surrounding area and decided to build a chapel on his land. He wrote to a friend in Brazil asking him to send a small statue of Our Lady for it. Unsure of how he wanted Our Lady depicted, the friend sent two terra cotta statues, one of the Immaculate Virgin and the other of the Madonna with Child.

After the statues arrived by boat in Buenos Aires, they were placed on a horse-drawn cart and, because of the dangers from local Indians, the driver joined several other carts in a caravan. After three days' travel, the caravan stopped for the night at the isolated ranch of Don Rosendo de Oramus, some 68 kilometres northwest of Buenos Aires. Early the next morning the caravan prepared to leave and all the carts set off except the one carrying the images of Our Lady. The other drivers came to help but there was nothing they could do to get the horses to move. Finally they took the statue of the Immaculate Virgin off the cart and the horses readily set off. The statue was left behind at the ranch and the other was transported safely to Sumampa, near Córdoba, where it is still venerated under the title of Our Lady of Consolation.

The statue of the Immaculate Virgin was taken to the ranch house and entrusted to the care of a slave from Angola. He had great devotion to it and shortly afterwards a little chapel was built for it. The chapel soon became a popular shrine and was visited by many people. But one night the statue disappeared, even though the chapel was locked and guarded. The statue was later found at the spot where the horses had refused to move forward. This happened several times, moving the Church authorities to build a chapel there to house the statue.

Over the years several chapels were built and many miracles were attributed to Our Lady's intercession, increasing the devotion of the people, who came to pray in ever greater numbers. In 1677 a church was built and it was replaced by a larger one in 1763. In 1904 the statue was transferred to the magnificent neo-Gothic church then under construction. The church was completed and consecrated in 1910 and it was made a basilica in 1930.

The statue, which is some 35 centimetres tall, had for a long time been clothed in a beautiful blue and white cloak. The colours were in fact the inspiration for the Argentine flag, designed by Sergeant Major

Carlos Belgrano to reflect the "blue and white of the Immaculate Virgin of Luján."

In 1886 Pope Leo XIII decided to honour the statue with a canonical crowning and on 30 September of that year he blessed the crown, which was made of pure gold, set with 365 diamonds, rubies, emeralds and sapphires, 132 pearls, and enamels depicting the emblems of the Archbishop and the Argentine Republic. The papal coronation took place on 8 May 1887.

In 1930, on the three hundredth anniversary of the devotion, Pope Pius XI declared Our Lady of Luján the patroness of Paraguay, Uruguay and Argentina. In 1982, during the Falklands War, Pope St John Paul II became the first Pope to visit Our Lady of Luján, celebrating an outdoor Mass in front of the basilica and bestowing a Golden Rose on Our Lady. On 8 May 2013, during his Wednesday audience in Rome, Pope Francis commended the people of Argentina to their "heavenly Patroness".

The feast days of Our Lady of Luján are 8 May and 8 December, the feast of the Immaculate Conception. Some six million pilgrims visit the shrine each year.

598 Our Lady of Fatima

I have heard a lot over the years about the apparitions of Our Lady at Fatima but really don't know much about the details. Can you fill me in?

Our Lady first appeared in Fatima, Portugal, on 13 May 1917 to three young children: Lucia dos Santos, who was ten, and her cousins Francisco and Jacinta Marto, aged nine and seven respectively. At the time they were tending their sheep at Cova da Iria, over a kilometre from their homes. Our Lady was dressed in white and surrounded by light. She said she was from heaven and asked the children to come to that place on the thirteenth day of each month at the same time for six months. She asked if they were willing to offer themselves to God and to endure all the suffering he would send them in reparation for sins and for the conversion of sinners. They answered yes and Our Lady said they would have to suffer much but that the grace of God would be their comfort. She also asked them to recite the rosary every day to obtain peace for the world and the end of the war. It should be remembered that the First World War was then raging and it would end the following year on 11 November.

In the June apparition, with some fifty others present, Our Lady told the children that she would take Francisco and Jacinta to heaven but that Lucia would remain on earth for a long time to promote devotion to Mary's Immaculate Heart for the salvation of souls. In fact Francisco died in 1919 at the age of ten and Jacinta died the following year, aged nine. They were beatified by Pope John Paul II on 13 May 2000 and canonised by Pope Francis on 13 May 2017.

In the July apparition Our Lady repeated the plea to say the rosary every day and she said that in October she would reveal who she was and she would do a miracle that all would see. She also showed the children a vision of hell and said that to save souls God wanted to establish devotion to her Immaculate Heart. She said that if her requests were granted, Russia would be converted and there would be peace but, if not, that country would spread its errors throughout the world, provoking wars and persecution of the Church. She taught the children to say the prayer we now say at the end of each mystery of the rosary: "Oh my Jesus, forgive us our sins, save us from the fires of hell, and lead all souls to heaven, especially those in most need of your mercy."

The children could not go to Cova da Iria on 13 August because they were detained by the authorities, but Our Lady did appear to them on 19 August. She told them to pray very much and to offer sacrifices for sinners, adding, "You know that many souls go to hell because there is no one who prays for them."

On 13 September some 30,000 people accompanied the children to Cova da Iria, where they recited the rosary before Our Lady appeared. She reminded them to continue to recite the rosary and she said God was happy with their sacrifices but that they shouldn't sleep with the rough rope around their waists, which they had been doing for penance, but should use it only during the day.

Finally, 13 October came and some 70,000 people braved the torrential rain, mud and cold to go to Cova da Iria. When Our Lady appeared she identified herself as the Lady of the Rosary and asked that a chapel be built there in her honour. She asked the people to continue to recite the rosary everyday and said the war would end soon. Then she launched a ray of light towards the sun, which had suddenly broken through the clouds as the rain stopped. The sun began to revolve, sending out rays of light of different colours that lit up the surroundings. Then it went back to its place for a short time before seeming to fall from the sky towards the people, who fell to their knees and begged God for mercy. The sun then returned to its normal place. Meanwhile the children saw Our Lady dressed in white with a blue cope, St Joseph with the Child Jesus who blessed the crowd, and then Our Lord blessing the world standing next to Our Lady of Sorrows. At the end Our Lady appeared as Our Lady of Mt Carmel.

The people all saw the miracle of the sun. Even sceptics reported seeing it and anti-clerical newspapers in Lisbon wrote articles on it. The apparitions at Fatima were impressive indeed.

599 The legacy of Fatima

I like to tell my friends that Our Lady's apparitions at Fatima have had a great impact on the Church and the world, but they are not easily convinced. Do you agree with me?

I do agree and I think there is abundant evidence for it. One can start with how the three principal messages of Our Lady have been received, and then look at the fulfilment of some of the prophecies.

Perhaps the most important message is to pray for peace, especially through the rosary. In the last apparition Mary introduced herself as "The Lady of the Rosary" and in each of the apparitions she asked that the rosary be said daily, especially for peace and the end of the war. On one occasion when asked about the importance of the rosary, Sr Lucia answered: "My impression is that Our Lady wanted to give ordinary people, who might not know how to pray, this simple method of getting closer to God." There is no question but that the popularity of the rosary has grown much since then. It is being said by millions of people around the world, and daily by many of them.

A second message is the call to penance in reparation for the many sins committed against God. In the August apparition Our Lady told the children to "pray much and make sacrifices for sinners, for many souls go to hell because there is no one to make sacrifices for them." The reminder of hell is important, especially today when some people do not believe it exists or, if it does, no one goes there. In this regard Our Lady taught the children to say the prayer we now say at the end of each mystery of the rosary: "Oh my Jesus, forgive us our sins, save us from the fires of hell, and lead all souls to heaven, especially those in most need of your mercy." As regards what kinds of sacrifices to make, Sr Lucia said that Our Lord asked for the fulfilment of one's duties in life and the observance of his law, something within the reach of all.

A third message was the promotion of devotion to the Immaculate Heart of Mary. In the July apparition, after showing the children a vision of hell, Our Lady said that to save sinners God wished to establish devotion to her Immaculate Heart, and she asked for the consecration of Russia to her Immaculate Heart and for Communions of reparation on the first Saturdays of five months. Popes Pius XII and John Paul II consecrated the world to Mary's Immaculate Heart, and devotion to her Immaculate Heart and the devotion of the five first Saturdays are now very widespread, much to the good of those who practise them (cf. J. Flader, *Question Time 1*, q. 134).

The fulfilment of the prophecies made at Fatima has helped many people believe in God and change their lives. The miracle of the sun in the October apparition, which had been prophesied in July, was seen by some 70,000 people, with even sceptics coming to believe through it. Also, Our Lady said that Francisco and Jacinta would die soon but that Lucia would live for a long time. In fact Francisco died two years later at the age of ten and Jacinta the following year, aged nine. Lucia died in the Carmelite monastery of Coimbra, Portugal, in 2005 at the age of 97. Another prophecy was that the First World War would end soon. It ended just over a year later in November 1918.

In the July apparition Our Lady warned that if her call to prayer and penance was not heeded another more terrible war would begin and it would be preceded by a strange light. In fact on the night of 25 January 1938 an extraordinary red, green and blue shimmering light appeared all over western Europe and North America, leaving people thinking there was a great fire on earth or that the world was coming to an end. It was reported in newspapers all over the world. Sr Lucia knew it was the sign prophesied by Our Lady. A month later Hitler's troops marched into Austria and in September, with his invasion of Poland, the Second World War began with its terrible devastation.

Also in the July apparition, Our Lady said that if her requests were not heard, Russia would spread her errors throughout the world, bringing wars and persecution of the Church, the good would suffer martyrdom and the Holy Father would suffer much. All of this came to pass, with the spread of communism especially after the Second World War. It is significant that the attempt on Pope John Paul II's life in St Peter's Square came on the feast of Our Lady of Fatima, 13 May 1981, and the Pope attributed his survival to Our Lady. In 1989, following all the rosaries and prayers to Our Lady for peace, the communist regimes in Eastern Europe began to collapse almost bloodlessly. In short, the legacy of Fatima has been momentous indeed.

600 Our Lady of Akita

I have heard that Our Lady is supposed to have appeared some years ago in Japan and that the apparitions were approved by the Church. Is this true? Can you tell me more?

Our Lady spoke to Sr Agnes Sasagawa, of the Secular Institute of the Handmaids of the Sacred Heart of Jesus in the Holy Eucharist in Yuzawadai, near Akita in 1973.

The extraordinary events began on 12 June 1973 when Sr Agnes saw bright rays of light coming from the tabernacle in the chapel. This happened on the following two days as well. On 28 June a cross-shaped wound appeared on St Agnes' left palm. This bled profusely and caused her much pain.

On 6 July Sr Agnes received the first message from Our Lady. It seemed to come from a three-foot tall wooden statue of Mary in the chapel where she was praying. Even though Sr Agnes had been deaf, she was able to hear Our Lady, who told her that her deafness would be healed. She was to offer the pain in her hand and in her ears in reparation for the sins of mankind. And she was to pray very much for the Pope, the bishops and priests. Our Lady recited with Sr Agnes a prayer of consecration to the Sacred Heart of Jesus in the Eucharist that the sisters of the Institute said.

On that same day drops of a dark liquid, like blood, were seen flowing from what appeared to be a cross on the statue's right hand. This happened again on four separate occasions. The cross on the hand remained until 29 September, when it disappeared. On that same day a sweet smelling liquid appeared on the statue, especially on the forehead and neck. Two years later, on 4 January 1975 the statue began to shed tears from the eyes, and it did this at intervals until 15 September 1981, the feast of Our Lady of Sorrows. A scientific examination conducted by the faculty of medicine of the University of Akita revealed that the liquid was identical to human tears.

The second message came on 3 August. Again it asked for prayers to console Our Lord for all the offences committed against him. It spoke of a chastisement which would affect all mankind unless many people prayed and offered sacrifices and penances in reparation.

In the third message, on 13 October, Our Lady spoke again of the terrible punishment to be inflicted on all mankind, the good as well as the bad. The weapon to be used against it was the rosary, which was to be prayed everyday for the Pope, the bishops and priests. The devil would infiltrate the Church so that cardinals would oppose cardinals, bishops would oppose bishops, and priests who venerate Mary would be scorned by their confreres. The devil would lead many priests and consecrated souls to leave the service of the Lord.

It is no secret that what Our Lady predicted came to pass in the following years. There were deep divisions in the Church, tens of thousands of priests and religious left their vocation and those who venerated Our Lady or prayed the rosary were often ridiculed as old-fashioned. Pope Paul VI himself spoke of the smoke of Satan entering the Church of God.

Sr Agnes, who had been deaf in both ears, experienced a sudden improvement in her hearing in October 1974, but in March of the following year she began to have violent headaches and she lost her hearing again. Finally, on 30 May 1982, the feast of Pentecost, during Benediction of the Blessed Sacrament her hearing was completely restored.

Another extraordinary cure involved a South Korean woman, Teresa Chun Sun Ho. Suffering from brain cancer, she was reduced to a "vegetative" existence in July, 1981. Then the Virgin of Akita appeared to her and told her to get up. Almost at once she was able to get up, having entirely recovered her health.

On 22 April 1984 Bishop John Shojiro Ito, the bishop of the diocese, after a thorough examination of the events and after interviewing the persons concerned, declared that he did not find anything contrary to Catholic faith and morals in the messages or the extraordinary events. He acknowledged that Sr Agnes was sound in spirit, frank, without problems and very balanced. He recognised "the supernatural character of a series of mysterious events concerning the statue" and authorised veneration of the Holy Mother of Akita within his diocese, declaring that the events were a private revelation and not necessary for salvation, as would be public revelation.

INDEX

à Becket, St Thomas, 328-30

abortion, 51, 73, 101, 149-51, 187-8, 192, 194-5, 204, 240, 243, 253, 255, 260

Advent, 285-6

Alacoque, St Margaret Mary, 88, 96, 303

Alexander of Alexandria, St, 33

Alexander, Dr Eben, 72

Amoris laetitia, 134, 143-4, 161, 207

angels, 19-20, 23, 46, 60-1, 78, 114, 236, 271, 273, 276, 294, 298, 310, 315, 319, 324

    guardian, 14-18, 20, 98, 273

    Archangels Michael, Gabriel and Raphael, 17-18, 61, 273, 310, 323-5

Anthropic Principle, 6

Aquinas, St Thomas, 3, 22, 28, 44, 58, 74, 82-3, 233-4, 245, 251, 302, 306

Ash Wednesday, 287-91

    who can distribute ashes, 289-90

Assumption of Mary, feast of, 31, 277, 305, 309-11, 314

Athanasius, St, 33, 64, 327

Augustine, St, 5, 30, 40, 44, 82, 91, 93, 192, 207, 227, 236, 258-9, 283, 302

Baptism, 37, 42-5, 47, 51, 128-32, 136, 138, 147, 247

    and salvation, 128-30

    of children of non-practising parents, 130-2

Barron, Bishop Robert, 80

Basil, St, 82, 213

Benedict XVI, Pope, 36, 114-5, 156, 279, 308, 320, 338, 344

Bible, 22, 89, 132, 189, 197, 210-1, 275, 278, 280, 288, 324

    Sola Scriptura, 37-9, 41

blasphemy, 222, 244, 276, 307

Blessed Trinity, feast of, 298-300, 329

Bonaventure, St, 114-5, 303, 306

Burke, Cardinal Raymond, 189-90

Caesarius of Arles, St, 91, 157, 236, 259

canonisation, 28-9, 100, 337

capital punishment, 244-6

Casti connubii, 259

Catherine of Siena, St, 332-4

Chalcedon, Council of, 32-4

Clement I, Pope St, 38

Commandments (Ten), 43, 74, 219

    why God gave them, 195, 208

confession, 41, 73, 96, 142, 206, 209, 317

    Why go?, 147-9

conscience, 205, 237, 321, 340

    and moral absolutes, 191-3

erroneous, 167, 198-200, 205-7
following one's, 48, 53, 200-2, 225
freedom of, 203-5
formation of, 196-8
role of, 193-5
Constantinople, First Council of, 33, 82, 299
contraception, 194, 252
  Can the teaching on it change?, 257-60
  When it is allowed, 254-5
  Why the Church is opposed to it, 255-7
Coptic Orthodox, 32-4, 58, 107
Corpus Christi, feast of, 96, 300-4
creation, 10, 31, 99, 211, 226-7, 233, 255, 288
cremation, 246-9
Crossing the Threshold of Hope, 84
Cyprian, St, 66, 302
Cyril of Alexandria, St, 33, 135
Cyril of Jerusalem, St, 82, 92

Damascene, St John, 59, 271, 310
Davies, Paul, 13
death, 15, 24, 52, 67-71, 74-6, 79
  Christian meaning of, 65-7
  near-death experiences, 71-3
Denton, Michael, 8-9
devil (Satan), 17-20, 43, 46, 72, 78, 80, 85-6, 236, 294, 324, 332, 355

Didache, 38, 226, 275
Dies Domini, 226, 228
Directory on Popular Piety and the Liturgy, 285
Divine Mercy Chaplet, 88, 280-2
Divine Praises, 222, 275-7
dreams, morality of, 213-5
dubia, 189-91
Dulles, Cardinal Avery, 81-4
Dymphna, St, 330-2

Easter, 27, 45, 52, 122, 280, 285, 287, 291-2
  origin of the name, 293-6
  Easter eggs, 296-8
Ecclesia Dei, 132-3
Einstein, Albert, 12
Emmerich, Blessed Anne Catherine, 314, 316
Enneagram, 216-8
Escrivá, St Josemaría, 17, 72, 340
Eucharist (Communion), 73, 101, 109, 117, 119, 205, 303-4, 317, 353
  Communion and forgiveness of sins, 134-7
  Communion for divorced and remarried, 144-6, 166-7, 190, 206-7
  denying Communion, 141-3
  extraordinary ministers of Communion, 137-41, 170, 290
  Miracle of Bolsena, 301

INDEX

euthanasia, 51, 187-8, 192
Eutyches, 33
Evangelii gaudium, 54, 135
evangelisation, 53-5, 113
evolution, 11
Evolution, a Theory in Crisis, 8

faith,
   and works, 41-4, 103, 169, 230, 232, 235
   sola fide, 41-4
Familiaris consortio, 144, 169, 205, 256
Fatima, 67, 69, 77, 80, 100, 272, 348-53
Faustina Kowalska, St, 88, 96, 280-1
Feeney, Fr Leonard, 47
Florence, Council of, 34, 82
Francis de Paola, St, 334-6
Francis, Pope, 15-16, 28, 30, 34, 36, 54, 134-5, 143-5, 147-9, 157, 161, 163, 165, 167, 170, 173-4, 207, 234-5, 237, 317, 319-20, 339, 341, 348-9
Fulgentius, St, 46, 309
General Instruction on the Roman Missal, 111, 118, 140-1, 222
George, St, 326-8
God's Undertaker – Has Science Buried God?, 13-14
gossip, 193, 264-6
grace,
   sola gratia, 44-6, 51-7

Gregory Nazianzen, St, 82
Gregory of Nyssa, St, 59, 80, 82
Gregory the Great, St, 110, 250, 286, 299
Gregory the Wonder Worker, St, 64

Hahn, Scott, 211
heaven, 14, 19, 26-7, 29, 35, 48, 60, 64, 68-9, 72, 75-6, 91, 94, 97, 103, 114-5, 128, 213, 221, 224, 228-9, 232, 236-7, 269, 273, 285-6, 308-9, 311, 314, 317, 341, 348-9
   Is it real?, 99-101
hell, 69-72, 83-7, 94, 101, 153, 209, 349, 351
   Is it real?, 76-8
   Is there anyone in hell?, 78-80
Holy Spirit, fruits of, 211-3
holy water, 121-5
   history of, 121-3
   use of, 123-5
Hoyle, Sir Frederick, 9
Humanae vitae, 30-1, 254, 256, 260-1
Humani generis, 11
Hungry Souls, 69, 77, 94, 96

Ignatius of Antioch, St, 66
Immaculate Conception of Mary, feast of, 304-6, 316, 320, 348
indulgence, plenary, 281
infallibility, 28-31, 46, 55

internal forum, 165-7
Irenaeus, St, 59, 82, 208, 302, 319
Isidore of Seville, St, 40, 93

Jerome, St, 14, 40, 58, 213, 302
Jesus Christ, 21-9, 41-4, 51, 53-5, 66, 91, 99, 114, 116, 121, 145, 152, 167, 176, 209, 222, 226-7, 234, 272, 276, 281, 295-6
   Resurrection, 24-7, 43, 65, 90, 92, 100, 147, 225-7, 287, 294-8
John Damascene, St (see under Damascene)
John Paul II, Pope St, 4-5, 24, 28, 54, 84, 113, 132, 144, 166, 169-70, 188, 191-2, 198, 205, 222, 226-8, 232, 246, 250, 255-6, 280-1, 304, 334, 338, 346, 348-9, 351-2
John XXIII, Pope St, 28, 110, 277
Jubilee Year, 125-7, 147, 149, 151, 170, 233-4, 317, 319
justification, 36, 42-6, 79, 84
Justin, St, 47, 117, 227, 302

Laudato si, 30-2
Lectio divina, 278-80
Lennox, John, 14
Lent, veiling statues in, 291-3
Leo I, Pope, 33
Lewis, C.S., 76
life, origin of, 7-9, 11

Litany of Loreto, 62-4
liturgy, 80, 119-20, 152, 272, 285-6
   beauty in, 114-6
   care in, 116-8
   Latin in, 107-9
   Tridentine Rite, 109-11
   Western Rites, 111-3
Lord's Day, 225-32
   day of rest, 226, 230-2
   keeping it holy, 225, 228-30
   when changed to Sunday, 225-8
Lumen gentium, 35, 48, 53, 128, 139, 223-4
lust, 249-51, 258
Luther, Martin, 41-2

Mariana de Jesus Torres, 55-7
Marie-Alphonsine, St, 337-9
marriage, 51-2, 56, 131, 143, 159-61, 206, 240, 249-53
   nullity of, 161-3
   procedures for nullity cases, 170-4
   same-sex unions, 174-83
   validity of, 163-7
Mary, Blessed Virgin, 98, 222, 318, 337-8
   Ark of the Covenant, 62-4
   Assumption, 31, 38, 277, 305, 309-11
   birth of, 314-6
   Immaculate Conception, 304-6
   Our Lady of Akita, 353-5

Our Lady of Fatima, 348-53
Our Lady of Guadalupe, 344-6
Our Lady of Luján, 346-8
Our Lady of Mercy, 280, 317-9
Our Lady of Mt Carmel, 342-4
Our Lady of Ransom, 321-3
Pain in giving birth to Jesus?, 58-60
Queenship of, 311-4
Undoer of Knots, 319-21
virginity of, 60-2
Menendez, Sr Josefa, 76, 80, 85-9
mercy, 88, 102-3, 287, 304, 307
  nature of, 233-5
  Jubilee Year of, 125-7, 147, 149, 151, 170
  obligation to show, 235-7
  corporal works of, 230, 232, 237-9
  spiritual works of, 103, 239-41
Misericordiae Vultus, 234, 237
Mitis iudex Dominus Iesus, 170
monophysitism, 33
Montserrat Grases, Venerable, 339-41
Müller, Cardinal Gerhard, 190
Muslims, 34-6, 46-7, 223-4

natural family planning, 257
  morality of, 260-2
  benefits of, 262-4
Nicaea, Council of, 32, 299, 313

Nostra aetate, 35, 224

Orange, Council of, 44
Origen, 80, 82, 275, 278, 295
Pacwa, S.J., Fr Mitch, 217
pallium, 156-8, 329
Pascal's Wager, 74-6
Paul VI, Pope, 30-1, 34, 112, 254, 256, 260-1, 277, 334, 354
Pauline privilege, 159-61
Petrine privilege, 159-61
Padre Pio, St, 96
Pius IX, Pope, 55, 277, 304, 306
Pius V, St, 110, 112-3, 300
Pius XII, Pope, 249, 277, 304, 311-2, 351
Polo, Gloria, 72
prayer, 92, 151-3, 211, 214, 221
  Does God always answer?, 269-71
  in the early Church, 273-5
  perseverance in, 282-4
  To whom can we pray?, 271-3
purgatory, 69-70, 101, 103, 129, 210, 273, 333
  Biblical texts on, 89-91
  belief in the early Church, 92-4
  Is it real?, 94-6
  What is it like?, 96-9

Rahner S.J., Karl, 80, 83
Ratzinger, Cardinal Joseph, 166

Redemptionis Sacramentum, 108, 117-9, 137, 139

Redemptoris missio, 54

Roman Catechism (Catechism of Trent), 59

Sacred Heart of Jesus, feast of, 88, 302-4

salvation, 4-5, 24, 35, 41-6, 53, 80, 82-5, 128-30, 151, 156, 169-70, 173, 201, 253, 282

   of non-Catholics, 46-8

   of former Catholics, 48-50

   final repentance and, 101-3, 304

Salvifici doloris, 4

Scapular of Our Lady of Mt Carmel, 342-3

Second Vatican Council, 30-1, 35, 48, 50, 53, 108, 110, 112, 127-8, 139, 175, 188, 192, 197, 203-4, 223, 252, 279, 291-2, 323

Simon Stock, St, 343

slander, 265-6

St Pius X, Society of, 132-4

Stein, St Edith, 84, 334

Stephen, feast of St, 307-9

suffering, 3-5, 24, 65, 72-3, 86-7, 96, 247, 269-70

Summa Theologiae, 3, 233

Teresa of Avila, St, 67, 80

Thérèse of Lisieux, St, 67

Thomas Aquinas, St (see under Aquinas)

Tradition, Sacred, 15, 22, 32, 37-41, 44, 47, 118, 123, 197, 240, 245, 279, 313, 324

Trent, Council of, 45, 59, 306

vaccination of children, 241-3

van den Aardweg, Gerard, 70, 77

Veritatis splendor, 114, 188, 191-2, 198

Vianney, St John, 220

von Balthasar, Hans Urs, 80, 83-4

Wickramasinghe, Chandra, 9

www.ingramcontent.com/pod-product-compliance
Lightning Source LLC
Chambersburg PA
CBHW050159240426
43671CB00013B/2181